Essentials

of **Psychological A**

Everything you need to know to administer, score, and interpret the major psychological tests.

I'd like to order the following *Essentials of Psychological Assessment:*

- ❏ WAIS®-IV Assessment (w/CD-ROM) / 978-0-471-73846-6 • $46.95
- ❏ WJ III™ Cognitive Abilities Assessment / 978-0-471-34466-7 • $36.95
- ❏ Cross-Battery Assessment, Second Edition
  (w/CD-ROM) / 978-0-471-75771-9 • $46.95
- ❏ Nonverbal Assessment / 978-0-471-38318-5 • $36.95
- ❏ PAI® Assessment / 978-0-471-08463-1 • $36.95
- ❏ CAS Assessment / 978-0-471-29015-5 • $36.95
- ❏ MMPI-2™ Assessment / 978-0-471-34533-6 • $36.95
- ❏ Myers-Briggs Type Indicator® Assessment, Second Edition
  978-0-470-34390-6 • $36.95
- ❏ Rorschach® Assessment / 978-0-471-33146-9 • $36.95
- ❏ Millon™ Inventories Assessment, Third Edition / 978-0-470-16862-2 • $36.95
- ❏ TAT and Other Storytelling Assessments, Second Edition
  978-0-470-28192-5 • $36.95
- ❏ MMPI-A™ Assessment / 978-0-471-39815-8 • $36.95
- ❏ NEPSY®-II Assessment / 978-0-470-43691-2 • $36.95
- ❏ Neuropsychological Assessment, Second Edition / 978-0-470-43747-6 • $36.95
- ❏ WJ III™ Tests of Achievement Assessment / 978-0-471-33059-2 • $36.95
- ❏ Evidence-Based Academic Interventions / 978-0-470-20632-4 • $36.95
- ❏ WRAML2 and TOMAL-2 Assessment / 978-0-470-17911-6 • $36.95
- ❏ WMS®-III Assessment / 978-0-471-38080-1 • $36.95
- ❏ Behavioral Assessment / 978-0-471-35367-6 • $36.95
- ❏ Forensic Psychological Assessment, Second Edition / 978-0-470-55168-4 • $36.95
- ❏ Bayley Scales of Infant Development II Assessment / 978-0-471-32651-9 • $36.95
- ❏ Career Interest Assessment / 978-0-471-35365-2 • $36.95
- ❏ WPPSI™-III Assessment / 978-0-471-28895-4 • $36.95
- ❏ 16PF® Assessment / 978-0-471-23424-1 • $36.95
- ❏ Assessment Report Writing / 978-0-471-39487-7 • $36.95
- ❏ Stanford-Binet Intelligence Scales (SB5) Assessment / 978-0-471-22404-4 • $36.95
- ❏ WISC®-IV Assessment, Second Edition (w/CD-ROM)
  978-0-470-18915-3 • $46.95
- ❏ KABC-II Assessment / 978-0-471-66733-9 • $36.95
- ❏ WIAT®-III and KTEA-II Assessment (w/CD-ROM) / 978-0-470-55169-1 • $46.95
- ❏ Processing Assessment / 978-0-471-71925-0 • $36.95
- ❏ School Neuropsychological Assessment / 978-0-471-78372-5 • $36.95
- ❏ Cognitive Assessment with KAIT
  & Other Kaufman Measures / 978-0-471-38317-8 • $36.95
- ❏ Assessment with Brief Intelligence Tests / 978-0-471-26412-5 • $36.95
- ❏ Creativity Assessment / 978-0-470-13742-0 • $36.95
- ❏ WNV™ Assessment / 978-0-470-28467-4 • $36.95
- ❏ DAS-II® Assessment (w/CD-ROM) / 978-0-470-22520-2 • $46.95
- ❏ Executive Function Assessment / 978-0-470-42202-1 • $36.95
- ❏ Conners Behavior Assessments™ / 978-0-470-34633-4 • $36.95
- ❏ Temperament Assessment / 978-0-470-44447-4 • $36.95
- ❏ Response to Intervention / 978-0-470-56663-3 • $36.95

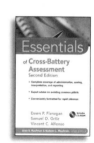

Please complete the order form on the back.
To order by phone, call toll free 1-877-762-2974
To order online: www.wiley.com/essentials
To order by mail: refer to order form on next page

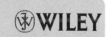

Essentials

of **Psychological Assessment** Series

ORDER FORM

Please send this order form with your payment (credit card or check) to:
John Wiley & Sons, Attn: J. Knott, 111 River Street, Hoboken, NJ 07030-5774

QUANTITY	TITLE	ISBN	PRICE
_____	_____	_____	_____
_____	_____	_____	_____
_____	_____	_____	_____
_____	_____	_____	_____
_____	_____	_____	_____

Shipping Charges:	Surface	2-Day	1-Day
First item	$5.00	$10.50	$17.50
Each additional item	$3.00	$3.00	$4.00

For orders greater than 15 items,
please contact Customer Care at 1-877-762-2974.

ORDER AMOUNT _____
SHIPPING CHARGES _____
SALES TAX _____
TOTAL ENCLOSED _____

NAME_____

AFFILIATION_____

ADDRESS_____

CITY/STATE/ZIP _____

TELEPHONE _____

EMAIL_____

❏ Please add me to your e-mailing list

PAYMENT METHOD:

❏ Check/Money Order   ❏ Visa   ❏ Mastercard   ❏ AmEx

Card Number _____ Exp. Date _____

Cardholder Name *(Please print)* _____

Signature _____

*Make checks payable to **John Wiley & Sons**. Credit card orders invalid if not signed.*
All orders subject to credit approval. • Prices subject to change.

To order by phone, call toll free 1-877-762-2974
To order online: www.wiley.com/essentials

Essentials of
Temperament Assessment

Essentials of Psychological Assessment Series
Series Editors, Alan S. Kaufman and Nadeen L. Kaufman

Essentials

of Temperament Assessment

Diana Joyce

 John Wiley & Sons, Inc.

Library of Congress Cataloging-in-Publication Data:
Joyce, Diana.
 Essentials of temperament assessment / Diana Joyce.
  p. cm. – (Essentials of psychological assessment series)
 Includes bibliographical references and index.
 ISBN 978-0-470-44447-4 (pbk.)
 1. Temperament. 2. Temperament–Testing. I. Title.
 BF798.J69 2010
 155.2'8–dc22
                          2009035134

Printed in the United States of America

10 9 8 7 6 5 4 3 2 1

To Dawn Sherie Grove, my daughter,
who provides boundless inspiration
through her visionary temperament qualities (ENTJ).

Table of Contents

Series Preface

In the *Essentials of Psychological Assessment* series, we have attempted to provide the reader with books that will deliver key practical information in the most efficient and accessible style. The series features instruments in a variety of domains, such as cognition, personality, education, and neuropsychology. For the experienced clinician, books in the series offer a concise, yet thorough way to master utilization of the continuously evolving supply of new and revised instruments, as well as a convenient method for keeping up to date on the tried-and-true measures. The novice will find here a prioritized assembly of all the information and techniques that must be at one's fingertips to begin the complicated process of individual psychological diagnosis.

Wherever feasible, visual shortcuts to highlight key points are utilized alongside systematic, step-by-step guidelines. Chapters are focused and succinct. Topics are targeted for an easy understanding of the essentials of, interpretation and clinical application. Theory and research are continually woven into the fabric of each book, but always to enhance clinical inference, never to sidetrack or overwhelm. We have long been advocates of "intelligent" testing—the notion that a profile of test scores is meaningless unless it is brought to life by the clinical observations and astute detective work of knowledgeable examiners. Test profiles must be used to make a difference in the child's or adult's life, or why bother to test? We want this series to help our readers become the best intelligent testers they can be.

In *Essentials of Temperament Assessment*, Dr. Diana Joyce reviews the theoretical foundations of temperament constructs as well as the assessment instruments designed to measure those qualities. Considerations in selecting evaluation methods and tests are reviewed. The book also highlights features and discusses interpretation strategies for a wide range of temperament measures from infancy through adulthood. Clinicians will find the sample reports to be of special value as they illustrate numerous practical applications for utilizing temperament data in pedagogy, counseling, and professional development.

Alan S. Kaufman, PhD, and Nadeen L. Kaufman, EdD, Series Editors
Yale University School of Medicine

Acknowledgments

The theoretical foundation and clinical expertise required for our profession are an invaluable gift from past and present visionaries who have dedicated their lives to understanding others. These brilliant minds, and their legacy of scholarship, make this text and line of inquiry possible. I am especially appreciative to Thomas Oakland, who first introduced me to the topic of temperament and has provided countless professional insights over the years. His quest to understand temperament across gender, ethnicity, and cultures beyond our national boundaries is admirable. It also has been my pleasure to work with Isabel Pratt, editor, Susan Moran, senior production editor, Kara Borbely, senior editorial assistant, and Stevie Belchak, editorial assistant, at John Wiley & Sons, as well as the Series Editors Alan and Nadeen Kaufman. Their comments, suggestions, positive regard, and expertise are greatly appreciated.

I am grateful to my family of extroverts who always understood and appreciated my introverted qualities and shared my judging characteristics that required organization. Thank you, Don & Carol Joyce, Buddy & Phyllis Joyce, Wanda & Dan Yadon, and Allen & Lisa Joyce.

One

OVERVIEW OF TEMPERAMENT THEORY

I nterest in temperament as an explanation for the nature of personal characteristics is long-standing, even pre-dating the formal discipline of psychology. Ancient scholars, philosophers, and historians first postulated temperament explanations for behavioral patterns they had observed across humanity. Classic Greek writings often linked their behavioral observations with intriguing and primitive speculations regarding internal functions of the human body (Galen, trans. 1916; trans. 1992). Temperament terminology included descriptions of dispositions, humors, moods, and tempers. These descriptions ascribed combinations of moral character, personality, and sometimes disparaging assumptions about individuals to physiological attributes.

During the Middle Ages, literature on temperament was less prominent. However, mental health hospital treatment for some of the pathology symptoms (e.g., depression, cycling moods) linked to original temperament theory appeared as early as the eighth century. Those treatment facilities are mentioned in medieval Islamic medical records, with one of the first mental health hospital units reportedly located in Baghdad (Syed, 2002). Physicians were trained in the early Greek temperament philosophies of Hippocrates and Galen, as well as others, and embraced humane treatment practices for mental health symptoms. Clinical training included an emphasis on identifying many of the physical characteristics that Greek literature had associated with temperaments (e.g., yellow jaundiced skin, melancholy) as well as clinical observation of behavior. Medical diagnosis and treatment for perceived emotional illnesses within hospitals later emerged in Persia during the 11th century (Syed, 2002) and in Europe during the 13th century (Shorter, 1997).

In the 1600s, with the advent of the pre-modern period, governments in Europe began systemically establishing public hospitals and often included physicians who treated mental health illnesses (Shorter, 1997). Unfortunately, many early institutions lacked effective or dignified treatment for mental health issues and engaged in a variety of ill-conceived and sometimes punitive treatments.

Medicine, including surgery, could be practiced without formal education, competency exams, or licensure by a variety of persons, including barbers (Fu, 1998). These practices resulted in poor outcomes and often patients were institutionalized for a lifetime. Interpretations of temperament and other mental health or personality qualities were left to laypersons and self-proclaimed healers. This period in European history is noted to have lacked enlightenment on understanding human behaviors related to personality or mental health and yielded few major philosophical or scientific advancements in treatment. However, the continued prominence of temperament ideas in identifying human behavior patterns for everyday life is evident through the popular culture of that era. Temperament prototypes were the inspiration for both protagonists in literature and playwrights' characters in many theatrical works. For example, several of Shakespeare's (1564/1616) manuscripts depicted Galen's four humors; Hamlet as the melancholy prince, Sir John Falstaff as the phlegmatic knight, Lady Macbeth as the choleric villainess, and Viola as the sanguine heroine (Fahey, 2008).

Reform in the 1700s encouraged physicians to seek better methods of understanding and treating mental health symptoms. The term psychiatry originated with Johann Christina Reil in 1808, and the medical specialization in mental health treatment became firmly established across Europe at that time (Marneros, 2008). The institutionalization of public service hospitals marks a critical juncture in psychology, as many were associated with university training centers. This alignment fostered renewed study of psychological concepts accompanied by rigorous training standards for practice. From the late 1800s to the 1920s the number of mental health patients in Europe grew exponentially. By the early 1900s, asylums also had emerged in the United States with thousands of patients and an expanding interest in psychological theories and effective treatments (Shorter, 1997).

Modern 19th and 20th century psychiatrists brought a resurgence of interest in the concept of temperament. New hypotheses reflected an emphasis on tendencies and dominant qualities. Temperament perspectives now included references to personal traits, behavioral concepts, self-regulatory factors, and motivational attributes. Today, definitions of temperament are multi-dimensional with sophisticated and more complex theory. A number of quantitative temperament measures also have emerged since the 1950s and validation of test constructs is now subject to the rigor of scientific methods. Research on temperament has evolved to include international and interdisciplinary studies, conducted across the fields of developmental and child psychology, psychiatry, and educational psychology (Goldsmith & Rieser-Danner, 1992).

As with many psychological premises, consensus on a definition for temperament is still evolving. There are variations in defining temperament due in part to training and dominant psychological perspectives of the individual theorists (e.g., psychoanalytic, developmental, behavioral, or biological). However, the metamorphosis of theories has lead to commonly accepted agreement on several important factors. First, temperament has a biological basis and individual differences are evident early in life (Bates, Wachs, & Emde, 1994). Secondly, these predispositions are relatively stable while also influenced by environmental factors (Goldsmith & Rieser-Danner, 1986; Chess & Thomas & Chess, 1984, 1986). Thirdly, temperament is perceived as bidirectional as specific attributes can elicit particular responses from others (Chess & Thomas, 1984, 1986; Thomas & Chess, 1977, 1989). Temperament also is perceived as somewhat malleable as personal behavioral choices can be altered based on an understanding of one's own temperament qualities (Myers & Myers, 1980; Oakland, Glutting, & Horton, 1996; Tegalsi, 1998). Lastly, temperament is related to but not synonymous with personality. It may in fact, shape the early foundations for later development of personality based on one's temperament-related propensities (Costa & McCrae, 2001; McCrae et al., 2000). Kagan and Snidman (2004, p. 218–219) describe temperament as a possible biologically based reactivity sequence on an individual's quality of mood, through a series of physiological responses (e.g., circuitry between heart, blood vessels, muscles, amygdale, and prefrontal cortex). A person experiences these responses holistically creating a *feeling tone* or *quality of mood* that if mild elicits interpretation such as fatigue but if aversive provokes "an emotion, that in our culture, invites an interpretation of a personal flaw."

In addition to the areas of agreement regarding temperament, there also are a number of divergent perspectives. Major points of disagreement include the extent to which temperament is heritable, biologically based, or malleable, which has implications for the efficacy of influencing temperament through educational or therapy approaches. The boundaries between definitions of personality and temperament also are sometimes nebulous or overlapping, which makes distinguishing components for measurement challenging. In addition, there are numerous proposals as to which specific components comprise temperament dimensions (Goldsmith et al., 1987). A review of all the proposed temperament qualities is beyond the scope of this text. In fact, Goldberg (1982) proposed over 900 elements that could be included in his conceptualization of temperament. The next section will review several predominant theories. Broad definitions of temperament as compared to personality are provided in Rapid Reference 1.1.

≡ *Rapid Reference 1.1*

Comparing Definitions: Personality Versus Temperament

Personality

Personality is defined as, "enduring patterns of perceiving, relating to, and thinking about the environment and oneself that are exhibited in a wide range of social and personal contexts" (American Psychiatric Association, 2000, p. 686).

"Personality is the sum total of the physical, mental, emotional, and social characteristics of an individual. Personality is a global concept that includes all those characteristics that make every person an individual, different from every other person. Personality is not static; it is developed over the years and is always in the process of becoming" (Rice, 1992, p. 228).

Temperament

"Temperament refers to the characteristic phenomena of an individual's emotional nature, including his susceptibility to emotional stimulation, his customary strength and speed of response, the quality of his prevailing mood, and all the peculiarities of fluctuation and intensity of mood, these phenomena being regarded as dependent upon constitutional make-up and therefore largely hereditary in origin" (Allport, 1961, p. 34).

We (Buss and Plomin) "define temperament as a set of inherited personality traits that appear early in life. Thus, there are two defining characteristics. First, the traits are genetic in origin, like other psychological dispositions that are inherited (e.g., intelligence). Second traits appear in infancy—more specifically, during the first year of life—which distinguishes temperament from other groups of personality traits, both inherited and acquired" (Goldsmith et al., 1987, p. 508).

We (Thomas and Chess) "conceptualize temperament as the stylistic component of behavior—that is, the *how* of behavior as differentiated from motivation, the *why* of behavior, and abilities, the *what* of behavior. A group of individuals—children and adults—may have the same motivation and a similar level of ability for a particular task or social activity. But they may differ markedly as to how they perform in terms of their motor activity, their intensity and quality of mood expression, their ease of adaptability, their persistence, or their degree of distractibility in the process of functioning. These later characteristics, among others, would represent components of temperament" (Goldsmith et al., 1987, p. 508).

Contrasting Definitions of Personality and Temperament

Personality refers to a wide variety of personal qualities, demeanor characteristics including social appeal and expressive energy, traits, cognitive attributions, emotional response patterns, behaviors, and temperament that together form a unique constellation recognized by others as the individual's persona. However, any of these factors separately also can be identified as personality variables common to many persons. It is the unique combination and degree of expression of personality traits that is specific to the individual rather than the actual traits. The temperament components of personality are considered predispositions with a stronger biological basis than personality traits, are developmentally evident earlier, and are less mediated by environmental influences. However, temperament theory does acknowledge the reciprocal nature of biological and environmental influences as well as the brain's plasticity in generating or sustaining neural connections that can shift temperament qualities over time. Temperament may be conceptualized as a foundational substrate for the subsequent development of personality through its effect on response instincts and thus the self-selection of environmental experiences (e.g., personal interactions, activities) that will further strengthen or diminish predispositions.

CLASSIC TO MODERN HISTORY OF TEMPERAMENT THEORY

A review of the development of temperament theory can provide further insights into the concepts that form the foundations for current research and assessment instruments. The earliest known writings on temperament date to the work of Hippocrates (460–370 B.C.) and Plato (427–347 B.C.). The influence of this work is again evident several years later in the orations of Plato's student, Aristotle (384–322 B.C.). As philosophers who melded their viewpoints from the science, literature, early medicine, and politics of their era, they often made broad conclusions that paired temperament with other attributes. As an example, in his writings, Aristotle paired melancholy temperament with genius, noting that men of greatness were always by nature melancholy (Akiskal & Akiskal, 2007).

Hippocrates was a physician who conceptualized the body as having four critical fluids (i.e., phlegm, blood, yellow bile, and black bile) that moderated health and wellness. The four components could result in both positive and negative effects. However, this was dependent on maintaining the appropriate balance within the human body. Hippocrates perceived an imbalance, excess or shortage of one of the four fluids would result in a variety of physical and/or behavioral symptoms (Hippocrates, trans. 1939; 1988; 1994).

Nearly 500 years later, Galen (130–200 A.D.), also a physician, further delineated Hippocrates' concept of four humors as physical and emotional characteristics of four temperaments, he called choleric, phlegmatic, melancholic, and sanguine (Galen, trans. 1992; Hergenhahn, 2001; Hippocrates, trans. 1939). Individuals were considered fools and choleric if they were irascible exhibiting irritability, quick tempered, easily angered, and readily changed moods. The phlegmatic temperament was denoted as slow, lethargic, pale, weak, mild-mannered, and prone to fantasy as well as somatic complaints (e.g., gas, epilepsy). Extreme happiness, malaise, sadness or depression was deemed a melancholic temperament. The fourth temperament, sanguine, was described as being a gracious speaker, loving, hairy, and optimistic (Galen, trans. 1992; Hergenhahn, 2001). Interest in temperament theory again piqued at the beginning of the 20th century with the advent of psychiatry as a profession. In 1921, three influential psychiatrists, from the psychoanalytic tradition, each published theories of temperament based on their clinical observations of patients and interpretations of behavioral patterns. These theorists included Ernst Kretschmer (1888–1964), Hermann Rorschach (1884–1922), and Carl Jung (1875–1963). Ernst Kretschmer's theory of temperament was titled *Physique and Character* (i.e., Körperbau und Charakter). His early work linked temperament with physical attributes, as Hippocrates and Galen had. Kretschmer proposed three body types; thin (i.e., asthenic), athletic (later combined with asthenic and called asthenic/ leptosomic) or overweight (i.e., pyknic) and delineated associated traits as well as potential psychopathologies. He attributed friendliness and gregarious personality traits to overweight persons with a propensity toward manic-depressive illness for those who were obese. Introversion and a timid demeanor were associated with the thin or athletic body type and if pathology were present it manifested similar to the negative symptoms of schizophrenia (Kretschmer, 1936; Pedrosa-Gil, Weber, & Burgmair, 2002). Ernest's theory did not garner wide acceptance, although a variation by William Sheldon (1898–1977) appeared in the 1940s. Sheldon (1940, 1954) adapted Kretschmer's three body physique type theory, arguing for three somatotypes that he termed Endomorphy, Mesophorphy, and Ectomorphy. Each somatotype was named by its perceived relationship to one of the three embryonic cell layers that later evolve to support specific body systems (i.e., endoderm or inner skin supporting digestive functions, mesoderm or middle skin the precursor to muscle and circulatory system development, and ectoderm or outer layer contributing to nervous system development). The Endomorphic (endoderm) had a soft body with a rounded shape and underdeveloped muscles. Associated traits included a Viscerotonia temperament that loves food and comfort, is tolerant, displays even emotions, is sociable, and has a good sense of humor. The Mesomorphic (mesoderm) body was toned, muscular, and overly mature with good posture. Their temperament qualities (Somatotonia) were described as adventurous with a desire for power and dominance, courageous, and competitive. The last type, Ectomorphic (ectoderm) was described as thin, delicate, tall, and stoop-shouldered. The Ectomorph was considered to have Cerebrotonia temperament qualities including sensitivity, introversion, self-consciousness, and emotional restraint with a propensity for artistic ability. Sheldon (1954) tried to create a systematic approach to measuring male body types that he titled the *Atlas of Men*; however, his system and theory lacked wide acceptance. Over time, interest in body types as a marker for temperament waned, whereas endorsement for psychological types in temperament flourished.

Both Rorschach (i.e., *Psychodiagnostik*) and Jung (i.e., *Psychological Typen*) published manuscripts on temperament that included the concepts of introversion and extroversion. Rorschach, although disavowing any endorsement or similarity to Jung's ideas, claimed he could provide an objective measurement of introversion and extroversion (Wehr, 1971). Prior to this assertion, temperament qualities were attributed to patients based solely on interviews, observations, and the clinical judgment of the psychiatrist. Rorschach's test was one of the first attempts at measurement of temperament. However, studies of the instrument as an assessment of introversion-extroversion were not supported (Brawer & Spiegelman, 1964).

PSYCHOLOGICAL TEMPERAMENT TYPES

Throughout the 21st century, several temperament theories and subsequent measures were developed based on a dichotomous conceptualization of temperament. These theories proposed a variety of dimensions that measured opposing qualities and resulted in ascribing typologies or categorical distinctions. Measures typically include forced choice items for two contrasting characteristics on each dimension and yield scores that vary from a mild to strong preference for one of the two qualities. The scores place individuals within a category and the overarching combination of preferred categories result in a typology that is considered as the best level of interpretation rather than the continuous score.

Carl Jung's Theory of Temperament

Carl Jung's theory of temperament evolved from his clinical practice in a Zurich psychiatric hospital and observation of patients. After a number of years of collecting notes on his patients' behaviors, he perceived reoccurring patterns of personal qualities that correlated with particular psychopathology or adjustment problems. His writings discussed how extroversion patients more frequently experienced aggressive or outwardly demonstrative behaviors (Jung, 1921/1971). In patients with hysteria, despite their emotional state, they maintained awareness of the external environment and interacted with the therapist, thus were considered extroversion. In patients with schizophrenia, Jung thought introversion was dominant as they withdrew from the world around them (Storr, 1991). Jung (1915/1954, 1920/1926, 1930/1933, 1928/1945, 1943/1953, 1954/1967, 1921/1971) mentions the historical underpinnings of his theory as associated with the early ideas from Hippocrates, Galen, Ostwald, and others. However, he differentiated his temperament theory as a psychological typology.

The foundation of Jung's temperament concepts are based on two attitudes, introversion and extroversion and four psychological functions (see Rapid Reference 1.3). An attitude is described as "the psyche to act or react in a certain way" (Jung, 1921/1971, p. 414). Jung did not characterize patients as unidimensional or only capable of exhibiting just introversion or extroversion in their behavior. He postulated that each individual possesses the ability to both introvert and extrovert; however, the individual has acquired a propensity to exhibit one of the attitudes over the other (Jung, 1921/1971; Storr, 1991). As this attitude is preferred, it is utilized more often, and thus becomes increasingly more skilled than the other attitude. He noted, "There is no such thing as a pure extrovert or a pure introvert . . . those are only terms to designate a certain punction, a certain tendency" (Evans, Leppman, & Bergene, 1968). Jung also was careful to explain these qualities without judgment, noting introversion and extroversion qualities may be expressed in positive or negative behaviors depending on the personality and disposition of the individual (Wehr, 1971). Introversion and extroversion also can be conceptualized along a continuum in addition to categorically. Individuals may vary from strongly introverted to slightly introverted or from strongly extroversion to slightly extroversion.

Introverts are interested more in their own thoughts and their inner world of feelings. Thus they may shrink away from interest in others or objects. They acquire energy from within, prefer solitude or small groups, are introspective, hesitant in new circumstances, and prone to making decisions cautiously. Extroverts are more attuned to the environment. They are outgoing, foster attachments quickly, and have concern regarding others' expectations (Jung, 1921/1971; Wehr, 1971).

Jung's temperament theory of psychological type also identified two additional dichotomies that created four psychological functions: sensation-intuition and thinking-feeling (Jung, 1921/1971). Each of the functions may be exhibited in an extroversion or introverted manner. Within each dichotomy, one function was described as well developed and used on a conscious level while the alternate function is not well developed or used on a conscious level (Jung, 1920/1926). Therefore, only one opposing function (e.g., thinking or feeling and sensation or intuition) can be operating on a conscious level at any particular time.

In describing the two functions responsible for how one prefers to acquire or assess information, Jung labeled the dimensions "sensation" and "intuition." He also conceptualized these as opposing styles. He wrote, "Sensation is just as antagonistic to intuition as thinking is to feeling" (Jung, 1930/1933, p. 106). The dichotomy of sensation and intuition are considered irrational decision-making styles (Jung, 1921/1971). Intuition is a quick and holistic manner of assimilating information that gleans insight from experiences and unconscious perceptions. Intuition can infer meaning from perceptions of nebulous ideas, broad theories, and patterns with lesser attention to details or facts. Jung noted, "In intuitives a context presents itself whole and complete, without our being able to explain or discover how this context came into existence" (Jung, 1921/1971, p. 453). In contrast, sensation function prefers direct experience, facts, and physical evidence. It is concerned with external stimuli (i.e., acquired through the five senses). Real-life experience is more dominant and sensation is a conscious perception.

Thinking and feeling were defined as rational functions (Jung, 1921/1971) for decision making. Persons using the thinking function carefully deliberate their decisions with a preference for utilizing facts, logic, and objective data. They most value broad principles of justice and truth when pondering judgments. Feeling is a more subjective process that makes decisions based on a personal values system (e.g., empathy, well-being of others). This value creates a sense of liking, disliking, or overall mood that may incorporate experience and leads to accepting or rejecting a choice. "Feeling is a kind of judgment, differing from intellectual judgment in that its aim is not to establish conceptual relations but to set up a subjective criterion of acceptance or rejection" (Jung, 1921/1971, p. 434). Because the laws of reason are used in establishing subjective value, Jung (1921/1971) noted that feeling is a rational quality. Depending on the pairing of combinations of temperament components, an individual could be one of eight temperament types. Jung considered four of these types to be rational and four to be irrational.

Jung's Rational Types
Extroversion-thinking, introverted-thinking, extroversion-feeling, and introverted-feeling were considered to be rational types. In describing his ideas, Jung made comparisons to influential personalities of his era. He considered Charles Darwin, with his emphasis on scientific evidence and fact, to be an example of the extroversion-thinking type. Immanuel Kant, with his emphasis on subjective reality and rationalist philosophy, was provided as an example of

the introverted-thinking type. Both are strongly influenced by ideas, but the extroversion-thinking type is interested in objective data and will follow ideas externally. The introverted-thinking type is influenced by subjective ideas and will ponder those inwardly (Jung, 1921/1971). Jung considered the extroversion-feeling and introverted-feeling types to be found most commonly among women. Later research would confirm this hypothesis (see Chapter Two). These types are guided by a personal value system comprised of subjective feelings and place strong value on harmony.

Jung's Irrational Types

Jung's four irrational types are (a) extroversion-intuitive, (b) introverted-intuitive, (c) extroversion-sensing, and (d) introverted-sensing. His caricature of an introverted-intuitive type is that of a person who is a solitary dreamer or artist and engages in mystic ponderings. His description of the extroversion-intuitive is one of marked dependence on the external, seeking new possibilities. Each is strongly influenced by subjective factors and ideas. In contrast, the extroversion-sensing seeks external facts, concrete objects, and reality while the introverted-sensing studies or ponders such evidence.

DON'T FORGET

Carl Jung's Rational and Irrational Types

Carl Jung's rational and irrational types can be either introverted or extroversion. The distinguishing dimensions were thinking or feeling to be considered a rational type and sensation or intuition for irrational types.

Rational Types	Jung's Irrational Types
Extroversion – Thinking	Extroversion – Sensation
Extroversion – Feeling	Extroversion – Intuition
Introverted – Thinking	Introverted – Sensation
Introverted – Feeling	Introverted – Intuition

Jung's Falsification of Type

In conjunction with his theory of psychological types, Jung described a phenomenon he called falsification of type. He suggested that the best psychological health is promoted when persons can express and be recognized for their natural preferences and external forces do not dictate behaviors contrary to these preferences. Jung noted that persons who could utilize both qualities of a dimension when appropriate while maintaining their own personal strengths were best adjusted. As an example, if the work demands of an individual who may be introverted are consistent with introverted tasks, he or she is more likely to be successful, especially if the individual could extrovert when required for social situations. However, if an introverted person was constantly required to function in extroversion ways at work (e.g., high demand for public speaking engagements) or other social obligations, this becomes exhausting and soon the negative effects of relentless stress ensue (Jung, 1921/1971).

Jung's ideas on temperament were only one portion of his life's work that also included analytical therapy techniques. There are several institutes that continue that work today (i.e., C.G. Jung Institute of New York, http://www.junginstitute.org) in the United States. His temperament theory enjoyed a significant period of acclaim following its publication in the 1920s and became the foundation for development of several current temperament and personality measures.

Myers and Briggs Theory of Temperament

At the same time that Jung had published his *Psychological Types*, Katharine C. Briggs (1875–1968) was endeavoring to identify common personality factors for highly accomplished individuals through extensive reviews of biographies. She became intrigued with Jung's work adding a fourth dimension, judging and perceiving (see Rapid Reference 1.3). Judging or perceiving were concepts to describe how individuals structure their lives as related to the outside world (Myers & Myers, 1980). Persons with a judging orientation prefer a self-regimented lifestyle, routinely engage in planning, are organized, prefer schedules, and seek closure on projects and tasks. Persons with a perceiving orientation prefer spontaneity, keeping options open, and are often highly tolerant, curious, and readily adaptive (Myers & Myers, 1980).

In the summer of 1942, Briggs and her daughter Isabel Briggs-Myers (1896–1980) began developing test items for an instrument to measure Jung's psychological types. Subsequently, the Myers-Briggs Type Indicator® (MBTI) was published in 1962 (Myers & Myers, 1980). The MBTI combines Jung's three temperament dimensions and adds Briggs's fourth dimension to yield interpretations for 16 types (see Rapid Reference 1.2). Each of the 16 types can be interpreted holistically or within a more complex and sophisticated understanding of which dimensions are dominant, auxiliary, or tertiary. Detailed guidelines for administration, scoring, and interpretation of the MBTI are available in the *Essentials of Myers-Briggs Type Indicator Assessment, Second Edition* (Quenk, 2009).

Katherine Briggs's partnership with her daughter Isabel continued throughout her lifetime, initiating decades of research on the utility of the MBTI. Unlike

≡ *Rapid Reference 1.2*

Myers-Briggs Type Indicator (MBTI) Psychological Types

ISTJ	ISFJ	INFJ	INTJ
ISTP	ISFP	INFP	INTP
ESTP	ESFP	ENFP	ENTP
ESTJ	ESFJ	ENFJ	ENTJ

Note. I = introverted, E = extroversion, S = sensing, N = intuition, T = thinking, F = feeling, J = judging, P = perceiving

some measures of personality, they conceptualized the MBTI as primarily a method for understanding others differences rather than an instrument to measure pathology. They intended for the MBTI to help "parents, teachers, students, counselors, clinicians, clergy, and all others who are concerned with the realization of human potential" (Myers & Myers, 1980, p. xiii). The concepts of Jungian and Myers/Briggs temperament typology are now widely recognized, even appearing in a variety of secular media from George Balanchine's ballet *The Four Temperaments*, to television series such as *Northern Exposure*, and endorsements by Dr. Niles Crane's character in the sitcom series *Fraser*. Thus, whether through historical theatre of Shakespeare or modern technology media, our muses continue to recognize temperament qualities in everyday life and imbue those traits upon their characters.

The MBTI measure is utilized among a variety of psychologists (e.g., clinical, rehabilitation), as well as counselors, social workers, and other mental health providers. Today industrial/organizational (IO) psychologists also incorporate the measure into a variety of career assessments, employee training, and team-building programs for numerous Fortune 500 companies. In fact, the MBTI is reported by its publisher, Consulting Psychologists Press (CPP), to be the most widely administered personality assessment in the world with distribution of over two million copies annually. Sample reports are available online (https://www .cpp.com/products/mbti/index.aspx).

The Center for Applications of Psychological Type (CAPT) was founded by Isabel Briggs-Myers and Mary H. McCaulley in 1975. It is currently located in Gainesville, Florida, and offers online bibliography searches for over 10,000 MBTI entries, sample reports, web-based MBTI test administration, as well as subscription to the *Journal of Psychological Type* (http://www.capt.org/about-capt/home.htm).

≡ Rapid Reference 1.3

Jungian and Myers-Briggs Dichotomies

Energy Orientation (Attitudes)

Extroversion (E)

Renew energy from external or outer world of people and objects, outgoing, foster attachments quickly, share ideas readily

Introversion (I)

Renew energy from inner world of thoughts and introspection, prefer solitude or small groups, self-reflection

Perception or Learning Processes (Functions)

Sensing (S)

Acquire information from five senses; real-life, concrete experiences dominate; practical, realistic, pragmatic, detail oriented

Intuition (N)

Holistic assimilation of information; value insight, ideas, theories, interest in patterns with lesser attention to details

Decision-Making Process (Functions)

Thinking (T)

Deliberate decisions based on facts, logic, objective data; emphasize principles of justice and truth in decision, seek fairness

Feeling (F)

Decisions made with emphasis on subjective values such as empathy and well-being of others, seek harmony

Environment or Lifestyle Orientation (Attitudes)

Judging (J)

Prefer structure in daily interactions with outer world; like routines, organization, schedules, planning ahead; seek closure on projects

Perceiving (P)

Prefer to approach the outer world in a spontaneous and flexible manner, tolerant, adaptive, like to keep options open

Keirsey Theory of Temperament

In the 1970s, David West Keirsey (born 1921), an educational psychologist and eventually chair of the California State University, Fullerton, Counseling Department, published a text providing a short, self-scoring, temperament measure, *The Keirsey Temperament Sorter*. The instrument yielded the MBTI 16 types (Keirsey & Bates, 1978). However, he argued for a modified interpretation of the original Jung-Briggs-Myers temperament model that groups the 16 types into four clusters for interpretation. Keirsey (1998, p. 15, 18) noted this structure was suggested by Myers and better reflected what Keirsey perceives as a four-type theoretical construct based on the work of multiple theorists (i.e., Ernst Kretschmer, Eduard Spranger, Eric Adickes, and Eric Fromm). Although he acknowledges each of the four temperaments within a cluster have differences, the overarching similarities are considered more important and definitive. In fact, Keirsey and Bates proposed that, "the real usefulness of the types comes not in memorizing the sixteen portraits, but in understanding the temperamental base of the types" endorsing Hippocrates' idea that four core types exist (Keirsey & Bates, 1978, p. 26). The styles were described figuratively as similar to the characteristics manifest by four Greek mythology entities: Dionysus, Prometheus, Epimetheus, and Apollo. The four clusters included sensing-judging, sensing-perceiving, intuition-thinking, and intuition-feeling. Over the next 20 years, Keirsey (1998) refined his temperament theory and published the revised *Keirsey Temperament Sorter®-II* (p. 4–11) as well as a shorter version, the *Keirsey Four-Types Sorter* (p. 348–350). His current model often is utilized in business and there is a modified self-administered short version available online (http://www.keirsey.com). The new model also ascribes new names to the four categories: Artisan, Guardian, Rational, and Idealist (see Rapid Reference 1.4). These are consistent with Plato's original four temperament types and based more on individuals' function within society. The names help facilitate understanding of the temperament profiles for laypersons that have little or no theoretical knowledge of temperament theory.

When referenced within this model (Keirsey, 1978, 1998), those with sensing-perceiving preferences are characterized as artistic, athletic, easy-going, tolerant, open-minded, adaptable, and persuasive. They enjoy exploring new experiences, discovery, and have a strong play ethic and need for freedom. The sensing-judging temperament is characterized as dutiful, responsible, conservative, stable, patient, dependable, and highly productive with a strong work ethic. They need a sense of belonging and traditions, thus are often caregivers. They thrive in well-defined roles, routine, and prefer to learn in a sequential manner. The intuition-thinking temperament is described as rational, analytical, systematic, curious, scientific, and research-oriented. They have a strong drive for success, competency, high standards and achievement. They also can be inquisitive, perfectionistic, and at times compulsive. They tend to emphasize work before recreation and even carry over their achievement drive to hobbies or leisure activities (e.g., self-imposed golfing expertise). The intuitive-feeling temperament is friendly, sympathetic, insightful, creative, intuitive, caring, and attuned to the needs of others. Their core value is personal integrity and self-actualization. They are often quite passionate about social causes and the impact of actions on humanity. Keirsey and Bates also make reference to the effects of temperament as observed in children, marriage compatibility, and note frequency patterns of particular temperaments by career.

≡ Rapid Reference 1.4

Keirsey Temperament Sorter Types (1978 & 1998)

Sensing-Perceiving (Dionysian–1978) Artisan–1998	Sensing-Judging (Epimethean–1978) Guardian–1998	Intuition-Thinking (Promethean–1978) Rational–1998	Intuition-Feeling (Apollonian–1978) Idealist–1998
ESTP	ESTJ	ENTJ	ENFJ
ISTP	ISTJ	INTJ	INFJ
ESFP	ESFJ	ENTP	ENFP
ISFP	ISFJ	INTP	INFP

TEMPERAMENT THEORY EMBEDDED IN BROAD PERSONALITY MEASURES

In addition to unitary measures of temperament, there are many well-established personality instruments that incorporate one or more dimensions from temperament theory. Dimensional approaches provide continuous measures that can be interpreted as the strength of a characteristic. Although personality instruments are not the core topic of this text, a brief discussion of some major instruments is provided. There are evaluations, especially if pathology is suspected, where including these measures as a supplement to traditional temperament measures can provide additional insight. These measures differ from the temperament measures discussed thus far in a number of ways. First, many are considered atheoretical as the inclusion of items and scales was first determined based on empirical statistical methods rather than preconceived philosophical constructs. Secondly, they measure a broader spectrum of personal traits than temperament measures do. In addition, they often include characteristics noted as symptoms of pathology and are utilized in mental health diagnoses based on the Diagnostic and Statistical Manual of Mental Disorders (DSM) criteria. They may also provide support for treatment planning. The instruments typically yield continuous scores rather than categorical, and this facilitates comparisons of particular traits to clinical populations as well as evidence of improvement for treatment outcomes.

In the early 1930s, at about the same time that Freud (1856–1939) and Jung (1875–1961) were establishing their concepts of temperament within psychodynamic perspectives, others were exploring new quantitative methods for the study of personality. Two key developments of this era were the catalyst for several advances in personality theory, statistical analysis methods, and the lexical hypothesis premise. Sir Francis Galton (1809–1882), Karl Pearson (1857–1936), and Charles Spearman (1863–1945) all made significant early contributions to correlation and multivariate factor analyses techniques (Wiggins, 2003). These strategies were originally applied to the study of intelligence and then later utilized in measuring constructs of temperament and personality. A student of Spearman, Raymond Cattell (1905–1998) embarked on a lifetime career to identify a taxonomic system for the core components of personality structure. He utilized a method originally discussed by Galton, Klages, Baumgarten, Allport, and Odbert: the lexical tradition. This method proposed that the important and obvious tenets of personality characteristics would already be evident in modern language, as over the years society would have a need to label these qualities in order to have discourse regarding them. This method is deemed by some researchers to be atheoretical, as the factor analyses determine the constructs rather than a prior theoretical proposition of characteristics. However, others argue the lexical process itself inherently assumes some theoretical assumptions about language development naturally encompassing psychological constructs and a subjective selection process when clustering terms that may be influenced by individuals' theoretical underpinnings (John, Angleitner, & Ostendorf, 1988).

The lexical hypothesis procedure started in 1936 with Gordon Allport (1897–1967) and his graduate student Henry Odbert documenting every descriptive word in the dictionary related to personality (originally 550,000 words, later refined to approximately 18,000 terms). Beginning in 1943, Cattell further reduced Allport and Odbert's list to clusters, grouped the words by traits, and later applied multivariate statistical methods to confirm those trait clusters through three types of data: Life records, self-report questionnaires, and behavioral tests. The feasibility of these types of procedures were made possible through the advent of computer technologies that had not been available to prior researchers. Cattell eventually identified 35 core variables and five global scales that later resulted in the 1949 publication of the "Sixteen Personality Factors Questionnaire" (16PF) (Cattel & Schuerger 2003; Pervin, 1990; Wiggins, 2003). The 16PF is now in its fifth edition (Cattell, Cattell, & Cattell, 1993; Cattell, Cattell, Cattell, & Kelly, 1999). The five global scales include extroversion, anxiety, tough-mindedness, independence, and self-control (see Rapid Reference 1.6). For a detailed review of administration and interpretation, see *Essentials of 16PF Assessment* (Cattel & Schuerger 2003).

Fiske, Tupes, and Christal conducted new research from Cattell's trait variables, also confirming five factors, later coined the "Big Five" or five-factor-model (FFM) (Goldberg, 1981; Pervin, 1990). Robert McCrae and Paul Costa's research had similar results and they labeled their factors neuroticism, extroversion, openness, agreeableness, and conscientiousness (McCrae & Costa, 1985a; 1985b; 1989). They subsequently created the Revised NEO Personality Inventory (NEO-PI-R) to measure these domains (Costa & McCrae, 1992). From the 1960s through the 1980s multiple theorists, utilizing a variety of methods and test items, also found five factors very similar to those of Cattell, thus building a preponderance of evidence in support of the five-factor model (FFM) of personality (Goldberg, 1981). It is important to note that most of these theories include a measure of an extroversion-introversion scale consistent with Jung's interpretation of this construct. More importantly, across measures, the extroversion-introversion scale is one of two that consistently accounts for the most variance in five-factor theories. The confirmation of extroversion-introversion as a high loading factor across nearly 10 measures provides supportive evidence for the validity of this construct (for an in-depth review see Pervin 1990). Wiggins (2003) and McCrae and Costa (1989) also note considerable conceptual overlap between several of the other MBTI dimensions and Big Five personality theories to temperament (see Rapid Reference 1.6).

Hans Eysenck (1916–1997) conceptualized personality as strongly biologically based and originally proposed two factors: extroversion-introversion and neuroticism-stability (Eysenck & Eysenck 1958, 1975b). Excitability versus inhibition and arousal were considered explanatory factors for extroversion (Strelau & Eysenck, 1987). He summarized his extroversion-introversion characteristics as based on the need, or lack thereof, for external stimulation or arousal. He proposed an optimal or balanced level of arousal at which individuals function best. Extroverts who were underaroused would be prone to boredom and thus seek out external stimulation. Continual overarousal in introverted persons could result in the need to seek out quiet settings that renewed tranquility. The example is given that introverted individuals perform difficult tasks better than extroverts in circumstances with low or moderate stimulation and stress, whereas the opposite is true for extroverts (Strelau & Eysenck, 1987). This balance or homeostasis concept is similar to Jung's original theory of extreme temperament qualities most likely resulting in maladaptive characteristics (Jung 1921/1971). A number of physiological measures now exist which permit researchers to test these proposed brain/temperament relationships utilizing brain waves and heart rate to objectively establish cortical arousal patterns.

Eysenck considered the limbic system's (visceral brain) effect on inhibition and disinhibition to be responsible for the neuroticism-stability dimension (Strelau & Zawadzki, 1997; Zuckerman, 1997). Persons with low inhibition or control of their emotions were more vulnerable to even low levels of stress and more likely to exhibit neurotic behaviors. Whereas persons with good inhibition or control of their emotions had high activation thresholds for stress and were more likely to be calmer thus exhibiting stability. Depending on the combination of traits, individuals might be stable-extroverts, unstable-extroverts, stable-introverts, or unstable-introverts, and these attributes were considered similar to Galen's earlier four temperament types (see Rapid Reference 1.5).

≡ Rapid Reference 1.5

Eysenck Two-Factor Model

	Extroversion	**Introverted**
Emotionally Stable	outgoing, carefree, sociable (Sanguine)	passive, peaceful, calm, thoughtful (Phlegmatic)
Emotionally Unstable (Neurotic)	restless, excitable, impulsive (Choleric)	anxious, pessimistic, unsociable (Melancholic)

In collaboration with his wife, Sybil Eysenck, a third factor, psychoticism-socialization, was added to the theory in the 1970s. Psychoticism-socialization measured the propensity for psychotic or aggressive features and testosterone levels were considered the contributing physiological marker (see Rapid Reference 1.6). Subsequently, the Eysenck Personality Questionnaire (EPQ) was published in 1975 and revised in 1985, Eysenck Personality Questionnaire—Revised (EPQ-R) (Eysenck & Eysenck, 1975b; Eysenck, Eysenck, & Barrett, 1985). Additionally, the Eysenck Personality Profiler was published in 1995 (Eysenck, 1995).

Originally, the Eysencks conducted exploratory factor analyses on the responses from the administration of several questionnaire instruments with a variety of scales in determining their "Super Three" theory of personality. The neuroticism and extroversion factors correlate strongly with the counterparts of Big Five (i.e., Five-Factor

Model) theory (see Rapid Reference 1.6). However, psychoticism is only modestly (and negatively) correlated with agreeableness and conscientiousness (Block, 1977; Eysenck, 1986; Eysenck & Eysenck, 1985; McCrae & Costa, 1985b).

Lastly, there are a number of broad personality measures, such as the Minnesota Multiphasic Personality Inventory (MMPI-2), that also include narrow scale measures (e.g., social introversion) of some temperament qualities, especially related to social withdrawal or extreme introversion. For a detailed review of

≡ Rapid Reference 1.6

Alignment of Major Personality Theories and Temperament Scales

Big 5 Personality Theories	1949 Cattell, 16PF	Extroversion-Introversion	Anxiety	Tough-Minded-ness	Independence	Self-Control
	1961 Tupes & Christal	Surgency (talkative, assertive, energetic)	Emotional Stability	Culture	Agreeableness	Dependability
	1985 Costa & McCrae, NEO-PI-R	Extroversion	Neuroticism	Openness	Agreeableness	Conscientiousness
	1981 Goldberg	Surgency	Emotional Stability	Intellect	Agreeableness	Conscientiousness
Super 3	1985 Eysenck, Eysenck EPQ	Extroversion	Neuroticism	Psychoticism		
MBTI	1956 Myers, Briggs, MBTI	Extroversion-Introversion		Intuition – Sensing	Feeling – Thinking	Judging – Perception
EAS	1975, 1984 Buss & Plomin EASI & EAS	Activity and Sociability	Emotionality			Impulsivity (later dropped this dimension as it overlapped w/ others)

administration and interpretation of the MMPI-2, see *Essentials of MMPI-2 Assessment* (Nichols, 2001). This measure was originated by Starke Rosecrans Hathaway (1903–1984), a professor in clinical psychology, and John Charnley McKinley (1891–1950), a psychiatrist, at the University of Minnesota. Their goal was to create a measure to help assess mental health patients. They began development by compiling over 500 true/false items related mostly to mental disorder symptoms and then comparing scores from normal persons to those with specific mental health diagnoses. This factor analysis procedure, called empirical criterion keying, resulted in identifying response patterns that could distinguish psychiatric patients from control subjects. This procedure follows what some consider to be a medical model. The instrument has considerable focus on pathology rather than normative qualities. Therefore, utility is somewhat more informative for clinical clients (Tellegen, Ben-Porath, McNulty, Arbisi, Graham & Kaemmer, 2003). In general, personality measures designed for clinical populations correlate highly with other personal maladjustment and mental health syndromes. Therefore, they may not be the best measures of core temperament qualities, such as introversion or extroversion, for the general population (Nichols, 2001).

TEMPERAMENT THEORY AS APPLIED TO THE ASSESSMENT OF CHILDREN

Most early historical temperament theory was conceptualized based on the behaviors of adults, although many early theorists did acknowledge the manifestation of temperament qualities in early childhood. In his writings, Jung (1928/1945, p. 303) notes, "The differentiation of type begins often very early, so early that in certain cases one must speak of it as being innate." He further explained that infants' adaptation to their surrounding environment, especially how readily they interacted with objects and others, was an early indicator of extroversion. In describing introversion in children, he noted their shyness, thoughtful reflection before acting, and their fearfulness of unknown objects as key indicators (Jung, 1928/1945).

Children's Psychological Temperament Type Theory

Most of the temperament and personality measures discussed thus far recognize the early emergence of temperament, and have published adolescent and child versions. The most widely used instrument, the MBTI, is recommended for ages 14 and over (Myers, McCaulley, Quenk, & Hammer, 1998). A parallel instrument, the Murphy-Meisgeier Type Indicator for Children (MMTIC) was created by Elizabeth Murphy, a psychologist, and Charles Meisgeier, a chair of the Educational Psychology Department at the University of Houston (Meisgeier & Murphy, 1987). As an educator, Murphy first became interested in the applications of the MBTI for children after reading David Keirsey's book, *Please Understand Me* (Horsch, 2008; Keirsey & Bates, 1978). She later completed her dissertation at the University of Houston, investigating applications of the MBTI for children, which led to her coauthoring the MMTIC. Meisgeier's interest in type was related to his career advocating for special education services and the need to better understand children's learning abilities. The current version of the MMTIC yields temperament types based on Jungian-Briggs-Myers theory for children ages seven to 18, grades two through 12, and a number of MMTIC teacher resources are available that reflect psychological type theory (Murphy & Meisgeier, 2008). Keirsey also offers an online version of his instrument, the Keirsey Temperament Sorter®-II, Student Version.

In the early 1990s Thomas Oakland, a professor in the Educational Psychology Department at the University of Texas at Austin; Joseph Glutting, a professor at the University of Delaware; and Connie Horton, a psychologist and faculty member at the Illinois State University developed the Student Styles Questionnaire (SSQ). The SSQ is a temperament measure for children and youth

CAUTION
....

Myers-Briggs Type Indicator® (MBTI) Terms as Compared to SSQ Terms

The SSQ and MBTI are based on the same theoretical constructs and can be interpreted similarly; however, the names of two dimensions differ on the SSQ. The consistency in theory is an advantage for longitudinal research utilizing the SSQ for young children and the MBTI as they reach adult age. For individual psychological reports that may compare temperament over time, it will be important to provide an explanation for the parallel terms between the childhood SSQ measure and the adult scores on the MBTI.

MBTI	SSQ
Extroversion – Introverted	Extroversion – Introverted
Sensing – Intuitive	Practical – Imaginative
Thinking – Feeling	Thinking – Feeling
Judging – Perceiving	Organized – Flexible

ages eight to 17 (Oakland, Glutting, & Horton, 1996). The measure is based on Jungian-Briggs-Myers theory with a strong emphasis on minimizing harmful labeling practices and enhancing both an understanding of others and personal development. In addition, the manual provides learning styles applications for the classroom and personal as well as family relationship building strategies. Positive and potentially negative temperament characteristics are discussed as strengths and weaknesses rather than pathology. The authors indicate they relabeled the temperament terms on two dimensions to provide more declarative and accurate descriptors for the preferences that better communicate attributes and facilitate positive interpretations (Oakland, Glutting, & Horton, 1996, p. 3). On the SSQ, the Jungian terms of sensing and intuition are labeled practical and imaginative. The Myers-Briggs terms of judging and perceiving are referred to as organized and flexible. Three interpretation methods are provided including the eight basic styles (i.e., extroversion-introverted, practical-imaginative, thinking-feeling, organized-flexible), the Keirsian model (i.e., practical-organized, practical-flexible, imaginative-thinking, imaginative-feeling) and the MBTI 16-type combinations.

Temperament Theory Embedded in Broad Personality Measures for Children

A number of researchers have provided empirical support for the existence of the core five-factors in adolescents as well as children (Digman, 1989; John, 1990; John et al., 1994). Many of the five-factor model personality theory instruments also have adapted versions for children and youth that include some temperament components, particularly extroversion or social introversion measures. The 16PF Personality Questionnaire: Fifth Edition (Cattell, Cattell, & Cattell, 1993) and a short version, the 16PF Select Questionnaire (Cattell, Cattell, Cattell, & Kelly, 1999), are based on Cattell's theory and intended for ages 16 through adulthood (Cattel & Schuerger 2003). Adaptations for children and adolescents include the Early School Personality Questionnaire for ages six through eight (Coan & Cattell, 1959; Cattell & Coan, 1976), the Children's Personality Questionnaire for ages eight through 12 (Porter & Cattell, 1968), and the High School Personality Questionnaire (Cattell, Cattell, & Johns, 1984), later renamed the Adolescent Personality Questionnaire for ages 12 through 18 (Schuerger, 2001). The NEO-PI-R may be administered to adolescents, ages 17 through 18, as well as adults (Costa & McCrae, 1992). The Five Factor Personality Inventory for Children is designed for ages nine through 18 (McGhee, Ehrler, & Buckhalt, 2007). The parallel child version of the Eysenck Personality Questionnaire (EPQ), the Revised Junior Eysenck Personality Questionnaire (JEPQ-R), can be administered to ages seven through 17 (Eysenck & Eysenck, 1975a). The Minnesota Multiphasic Personality Inventory (MMPI-2) also offers an adolescent version, the MMPI-A. For a detailed review of administration and interpretation of the MMPI-A see *Essentials of MMPI-A Assessment* (Archer & Krishnamurthy, 2001). As noted earlier, broad personality measures typically only include narrow measures of temperament dimensions and scales may correlate highly with other constructs related to pathology. Therefore, consideration of these measures as a supplement in temperament assessment is most relevant to evaluations where mental health diagnoses exist and/or maladaptive functioning is evident.

Children's Biobehavioral Temperament Measures

The interest in measuring temperament for even younger children, including infants and toddlers, established its original theory base during the 1950s through the 1980s, resulting in several new perspectives. In contrast to child self-report measures of psychological type, these theories measure different constructs. They have a greater emphasis on physiological phenomena related to observable behaviors in infants, toddlers, and young children. Changes in assessment methods included an emphasis on parent questionnaires, interviews, and observational data.

Some researchers argue that the temperament qualities exhibited by infants and toddlers may in fact be the truly innate conceptualization of temperament qualities and the core building blocks of individual personality (Costa & McCrae, 2001). The primary rationale for this premise is that during infancy and the toddler stage children are the most egocentric and have the least communication skills (both receptive and expressive), thus lesser environmental influence on the expression of their temperament qualities. As they enter early childhood and assuredly by adolescence, there are an inestimable number of interactions with others and the environment. Developmentally, this is a highly vulnerable period when individuals are most dependent on others, most malleable, and highly susceptible to the sanctions of others. The interactions exert a bidirectional effect on personality development often called dynamic interactionism (Costa & McCrae, 2001, p. 3; Magnusson, 1990).

Alexander Thomas and Stella Chess Temperament Theory

Alexander Thomas (1914–2003) and his wife, Stella Chess (1914–2007), two psychiatrists at the New York University Medical Center in 1956, began research that provided a framework for understanding children's temperament, both normal and aberrant, that was based on behavioral characteristics (see Rapid Reference 1.7) (Thomas & Chess, 1989). They began their work, the New York Longitudinal Study (NYLS), in the early 1950s by gathering data on children from infancy.

Their methods included observations, parent questionnaires, and later teacher interviews. In reviewing their data, they identified nine traits: activity level, rhythmicity, approach-withdrawal, adaptability, threshold of responsiveness, intensity of reaction, quality of mood, distractibility, and attention span/persistence (Cole & Cole 1996; Thomas & Chess 1989). Two instruments, the Parent Questionnaire and the Teacher Temperament Questionnaire (TTQ), resulted from this work (Thomas & Chess, 1977).

The activity level of children was measured by calculating a ratio between active and non-active times. Rhythmicity was determined by reviewing the regularity of several child daily activities (e.g., sleeping, feeding, and elimination). The child's approach or withdrawal traits were measured by recording initial responses to novel stimuli, such as objects or persons. Some children were inclined to seek out the new experience further whereas others became fearful. A child's propensity to approach new circumstances is considered positive; whereas, reticent or withdrawal behaviors are considered negative. Once a new stimulus is presented, the child's adaptability is judged by the ease with which the child habituates or adjusts to the stimuli. The threshold of response measured the level of stimuli needed to elicit a response. For example, some children require a significantly louder noise to wake them than others do. Intensity of reactions relates to the child's energy level of response. The quality of mood contrasts a child's propensity for pleasant responses (e.g., joy) with the number of unpleasant responses (e.g., crying, unfriendly). Distractibility and attention span/persistence measure how easily a child can be diverted from an activity and the length of time a child can maintain concentration.

Chess and Thomas also provided pioneering work in linking particular temperament trait clusters with long-term outcomes, thus providing additional evidence for the importance of understanding child temperament. As the children in the study became older, Thomas and Chess (Chess & Thomas, 1984, 1986; Thomas & Chess, 1977, 1989), identified three core temperament patterns: easy, slow-to-warm, and difficult. Forty percent of children had an easy temperament, 15 percent demonstrated a slow-to-warm pattern, 10 percent were in the difficult category, and about 35 were noted as exhibiting blended styles. Children with an easy temperament established regular routines quickly, were cheerful, and adapted easily to new circumstances. The parents described these children as very content and easygoing. The slow-to-warm children were noted as cautious with strangers, lethargic, more often negative in mood, and exhibited slow adjustment to new experiences. Children with the difficult behavioral pattern experienced irregular routines with problematic sleep cycles, were slow to adapt to new stimuli, and more often reacted negatively.

In reviewing long-term outcomes, easy children had the best prognosis. Nearly half of the slow-to-warm children experienced psychological adjustment

≣ *Rapid Reference 1.7*

Thomas & Chess Nine Behavioral Dimensions

Activity Level	Typical level of movement, calculate ratio of active to nonactive time
Rhythmicity	Predictability and regularity of daily biological activities (e.g., sleeping, feeding, and elimination), is a routine or schedule naturally established
Approach/ Withdrawal	Infant's initial responses to new stimuli (e.g., meeting a new person, new object, jack-in-box toy), are responses fearful or exploratory
Adaptability	How easily a baby's first response to a stimulus is modified, how quickly does infant adjust or habituate (e.g., first experience with solid food)
Threshold of Responsiveness	Intensity required to elicit a response (e.g., level of noise required for a response, does mildly wet diaper prompt response)
Intensity of Reaction	Energy level evident in the response (e.g., does child have a mild frown or cry vigorously if displeased, grin or robustly smile if pleased)
Quality of Mood	Comparison of the ratio of positive responses (e.g., smiles, laughter) to negative responses (e.g., unhappy, unfriendly)
Distractibility	How easily child is distracted or redirected (e.g., how quickly can the introduction of a toy or pacifier change her/his focus)
Attention Span/ Persistence	Once activity is started, how long is attention maintained (e.g., stare at a new toy, lose interest in toy mobile)

problems during their lifespan. Nearly 70 percent of children identified as having a difficult temperament experienced negative effects as they matured (Chess & Thomas, 1984; Thomas & Chess, 1977; Thomas, Chess, & Birch, 1968). The longitudinal design of their research made important contributions to understanding the value of early child temperament assessment and risk factors for intervention. The authors also acknowledged that early temperament qualities do not have a perfect correlation with long-term outcomes. Some children with no indicators of unfavorable temperament qualities did later exhibit poor outcomes and some with early risk factors did not develop behavioral difficulties.

In addition to their identification of early temperament patterns and long-term outcomes, Chess and Thomas also made another valuable contribution to the understanding of child-parent interactions as related to temperament through their concepts of "goodness of fit" and "poorness of fit" (Thomas, Chess, & Burch, 1968). When the parents and child have similar temperaments, a good match exists and the child more naturally and effortlessly meets the expectations of the parents. With goodness of fit, children have greater freedom to be at ease in their environment and direct their energy toward further developing their own preferences. By sharing common temperament drives, the parents more intuitively understand the child, are more likely to naturally embrace and foster the child's strengths, and these factors create a harmonious setting for the child's formative years.

Although conflicts are more likely to exist if the parent's and child's temperaments do not match, this is not always the case. Having differences in temperament would not automatically infer conflict if the parents were able to acknowledge and appreciate the child's differences, allowing her or him to express those needs. Circumstances that presented incompatibility between the child's temperament pattern and the parents' expectations or the environment demands were noted to have a "poorness of fit." This point is illustrated by comparing the two samples of children in New York who were utilized in the Thomas and Chess (1977) studies. The original NYLS included children from primarily middle-income homes and Euro-American descent and the second sample was comprised of children from working-class and Puerto Rican descent. As an example of the implications for goodness of fit, it was noted that children who had irregular sleep patterns and were arrhythmic were not problematic for parents of Puerto Rican descent as they were more accommodating than parents of Euro-American descent in regards to the child complying with their schedules. Therefore, at age five, arryhthimicity was only predictive of adjustment difficulties for the children of Euro-American descent (Thomas & Chess, 1977; Thomas, Chess, Sillen, & Mendez, 1974).

The risk factors associated with poorness of fit are directly related to the relentless stress that can be created when parents and children have competing temperament needs on a daily basis. When a parent places high conformity demands for behaving in ways at odds with the child's style, the child loses opportunities to develop their own inherent strengths and increases risk for maladaptive temperament expressions (e.g., irritability, externalized aggressiveness). As noted by Chess and Thomas (1986, p. 9), "a psychologically determined behavior disorder in a child or adult develops out of a substantial incompatibility between the individual's capacities and coping abilities and the expectations and demands of the environment." As noted before, many years earlier, Jung termed this distortion "falsification of type," noting the exhaustion it caused within an individual and the risk for poor psychosocial adjustment (Jung, 1921/1971). Later Myers and Myers (1980) described the phenomenon of conflict between child-parent temperaments as resulting from the assumption by parents that the child's differences reflect an inferiority. As noted recently, Kagan and Snidman (2004, p. 218–219) suggest society may interpret these differences as personal flaws.

William Carey Measurement of NYSL Dimensions

Carey, a pediatrician, reviewed the Thomas and Chess interviews research and operationalized interview data to form parent questionnaires, based on the nine behavioral qualities and three temperament patterns (i.e., easy, slow-to-warm, difficult, pattern). The measures included the Revised Infant Temperament Questionnaire (RITQ) for ages 4 to 8 months, the Toddler Temperament Scale for ages 1 to 3, The Behavioral Style Questionnaire for ages 3 to 7, and the Middle Childhood Temperament Questionnaire for ages 8 to 12 (Hegvik, McDevitt, & Carey, 1982; McClowry, Hegvik, & Teglasi, 1993; McDevitt & Carey, 1978). Sanson and his colleagues later created a short form of the Revised Infant Temperament Questionnaire (SITQ) based on their factor analyses of results from a large study using the RITQ (Sanson et al., 1987). Their factor analyses supported five dimensions rather than the original nine (i.e., approach, cooperation/manageability, rhythmicity, activity/reactivity, threshold). The Toddler Temperament Scale was created by Fullard, McDevitt, and Carey (1984) to measure NYLS dimensions for ages 1 to 3 years. Another comprehensive review of the NYLS data also resulted in support for five factors and creation of the Dimensions of Temperament Scales (DOTS). The DOTS was later revised (DOTS-R) and it provides parallel questionnaire forms for infants, children, and adults through several scales (activity level-general, activity level-sleep, approach-withdrawal, flexibility-rigidity, attention span-distractibility) (Lerner et al., 1982). Carey's instruments were an important contribution to temperament research as they provided a quantitative methodology for other clinicians to assess the nine temperament components (Carey, 1982, 2000).

Arnold Buss and Robert Plomin Temperament Theory

In the early 1970s Buss (1989) and Plomin (Buss & Plomin, 1975) also created a theory of temperament based on analysis of the NYLS research. They first paraphrased the NYLS interview protocols creating items with a five-point rating scale and then conducted factor analyses to determine if there was empirical support for nine independent factors. They found only attention span/persistence emerged as an obvious factor; however, some items across the constructs did appear to load forming a cluster for what they termed sociability and emotionality. Buss and Plomin were strongly convinced that evidence of temperament must first meet five criteria: heritability, stability, retention to maturity, adaptive value, and be present as a trait in animals (thus substantiating an evolutionary adaptive function). From their continued extensive studies, they identified four qualities: activity, emotionality, sociability, and impulsivity that appeared to be supported both by their five criteria and the factor analyses. They subsequently published the EASI Temperament Survey (EASI). Emotionality encompassed autonomic nervous system functions including arousal, tempers, fearful responses, and mood swings. Sociability was defined as one's affiliations or desire to interact with others. Activity measured level of energy and impulsivity involved inhibition, motivation, and impulse drives. A later analysis of EASI data resulted in publication of the Colorado Childhood Temperament Inventory (CCTI) (Rowe & Plomin, 1977). Their theory was again revised to include a sixth primary temperament criteria, presence of the trait early in life, and subsequently impulsivity was dropped from their scale. They renamed the questionnaires, the EAS Temperament Survey for Children and the EAS Temperament Survey for Adults (Buss & Plomin, 1984).

Other Biobehavioral Temperament Theorists

The refinement of temperament perspectives continues to evolve as evidenced by national and international forums that have brought leading researchers together over the years to debate these issues (Goldsmith et al., 1987; Strelau & Angleitner, 1991). Since Thomas and Chess's seminal work with infants, other scholars continue to investigate biobehavioral constructs in early childhood. Rothbart has proposed reframing temperament through concepts of reactivity and self-regulation in infants (Rothbart & Derryberry, 1981; Strelau, 1983). She developed the *Infant Behavior Questionnaire* (Rothbart, 1981) as a measure of these constructs. Goldsmith and Campos (1986) defined temperament in lieu of primary emotions (e.g., fear, anger, sadness, pleasure). They published the Toddler Behavior Assessment Questionnaire (TBAQ) and also designed the Laboratory Temperament Assessment Battery (LAB-TAB) which provides standardization procedures for infant and toddler assessment within a laboratory setting (Goldsmith, 1996).

Others argued for conceptualizing children in respect to their impulsivity and flexibility as overcontrollers, undercontrollers, or resilients (Block & Block, 1980; Caspi 1998). Overcontrollers are described as having strong ego-control resulting in rigidity and the ability to suppress emotional impulses. In contrast, undercontrollers typically act on their impulses. Resilients have a balanced ability to quickly adapt and modulate impulse control based on what the immediate circumstances mandate. Research utilizing Big Five model personality measures indicates overcontrollers are lower on extroversion and emotional stability qualities as well as psychological well-being factors. They report high conscientiousness corresponding with high academic achievement and lower delinquency and bullying participation among teens. Agreeableness and openness are modest as are social skills. Undercontrollers indicate elevated extroversion and lower scores for agreeableness and conscientiousness. As might be anticipated, this group also demonstrates lower academic achievement, peer-acceptance, and higher behavioral problems and delinquency among teens. The third category, resilients, have mean Big Five scores that are higher on all five scales: extroversion, emotional stability, conscientiousness, agreeableness, and openness. Likewise, intelligence, academic performance, social skills, general psychological adjustment, and self-esteem are higher. Delinquency and bullying indicators were lower (Scholte, van Lieshout, de Wit, & van Aken, 2005).

Neisworth, Bagnato, Salvia, and Hunt (1999) created the Temperament and Atypical Behavior Scale (TABS), an instrument that measures attachment, reactivity, and self-regulation characteristics. The measure yields four scales (Detached, Hyper-sensitive/active, Underactive, and Dysregulated) and is interpreted in lieu of early childhood indicators of developmental dysfunction for ages 11 to 71 months. Kagan (1994, 2009) proposed a strong reciprocal relationship between biology and environment influences that yields inhibited and uninhibited temperaments. Inhibited children (approximately 20 percent of children) are considered vulnerable to anxiety-related difficulties. They exhibit a quiet watchfulness, shyness, and stay at the perimeter of social interactions. Uninhibited children (approximately 35 to 30 percent of children) are spontaneous in social interactions, smiling and laughing readily with others. Over time, he noted most (approximately 75 percent) of children remained above the mean on these attributes if they were inhibited and below the mean if they were uninhibited, suggesting these traits were somewhat stable. Throughout the last several decades, he has conducted a number of electroencephalogram (EEG) and functional magnetic resonance imaging (fMRI) studies to identify hypothesized underlying psychophysiological correlates, particularly related to the amygdale. His work continues today as he encourages a broader scope of research with collaboration between biology, psychology, and humanities in understanding the shaping influences in human development (Kagan, 2009).

In Summary

The earliest speculations about temperament date to the time of Hippocrates and four clusters of behaviors and attitudes comprised the categories: choleric, phlegmatic, melancholic, and sanguine. These rudimentary concepts became the catalyst for several more sophisticated psychological type theories of temperament with some minor variation in interpretations. Based on modern sampling techniques, factor analysis of constructs, as well as reliability and validity standards, several well-recognized assessment instruments for adults and children have emerged

≡ *Rapid Reference 1.8*

Temperament Theories & Instruments Timeline

350 B.C.E.	Hippocrates, Four Humors
150 A.D.	Galen, Four Temperaments (Choleric, Phlegmatic, Melancholic, Sanguine)
1921	Ernest Kretschmer, *Physique and Character* (Asthenic, Leptosomic, Pyknic)
	Rorschach, *Psychodiagnostik* (Extroversion/Introversion measure)
	Carl Jung, *Psychological Type* (Extroversion/Introversion, Sensing/Intuition, Thinking/Feeling)
1940	William Sheldon, *Atlas of Men* (Endomorphy, Mesophorphy, Ectomorphy)
1940s	Katherine Briggs (adds Judging/Perceiving to Jung's theory)
1942–1944	Isabel Briggs-Myers develops MBTI test items
1949	Raymond Cattell, *16PF Questionnaire*
1956–1975	MBTI published as research instrument first, then available to public
1950s–1970s	Alexander Thomas and Stella Chess, NYLS (activity, rhythmicity, approach-withdrawal, adaptability, threshold of responsiveness, intensity of reaction, quality of mood, distractibility, attention span/persistence)
1978, 1998	David Keirsey & Marilyn Bates, *Keirsey Temperament Sorter and Keirsey Temperament Sorter®-II* (Artisan, Guardian, Rational, Idealist)
1978, 1982	William Carey devised measurement instruments for NYLS dimensions
1975, 1984	Arnold Buss & Robert Plomin, *EAS Temperament Survey*
1996	Thomas Oakland, Joseph Glutting, & Connie Horton, *Student Styles Questionnaire* (SSQ)

(e.g., MBTI, Keirsey Temperament Sorter®-II, MMTIC, and SSQ). There are numerous personality measures that also include temperament constructs such as extroversion and introversion. Research has indicated strong support for this construct, particularly among five-factor models (e.g., 16PF, NEO-PI-R) and the super-three model (i.e., EPQ). Additionally, there are some personality measures (e.g., MMPI-2) designed to differentiate pathology that have subscales related to social withdrawal or introversion and may be useful supplemental measures in a temperament battery, especially if maladjustment is a concern.

A complimentary line of temperament inquiry for early childhood was established by Thomas and Chess. They delineated nine biobehavioral dimensions in infants with three patterns—easy, slow-to-warm, and difficult—that are predictive of long-term adjustment outcomes. The goodness-of-fit paradigm was another important contribution from their work as it investigates the reciprocal implications between parental reactions and child temperament. In efforts to apply factor analyses methods to confirm the nine NYLS dimensions, others validated only some of the components: activity, emotionality, sociability, and impulsivity. Recent theorists have proposed redefining innate temperament constructs based on core physiological attributes that determine behavioral responses. Proposed paradigms include measures of reactivity and self-regulation; impulsivity and flexibility as overcontrollers, undercontrollers, or resilients; or inhibited and uninhibited temperaments. With the advent of modern research methods, there is a call for cross-discipline research that further investigates heritability factors, biological evidence, stability of traits, as well as crosscultural evidence for temperament constructs.

 TEST YOURSELF

1. **Which temperament dimension was added to the original Jung theory by Myers and Briggs?**
   (a) Thinking-Feeling
   (b) Extroversion-Introversion
   (c) Judging-Perceiving
   (d) Sensing-Intuition
2. **The Keirsey Temperament Sorter®-II yields which four descriptive types?**
   (a) Artisan, Guardian, Provider, Realist
   (b) Artisan, Guardian, Rational, Idealist
   (c) Administrative, Quizzical, Rational, Industrious
   (d) Administrative, Guardian, Provider, Realist
3. **Galton, Pearson, and Spearman all contributed to the eventual development of personality assessments through which of the following?**
   (a) Lexical hypothesis guidelines
   (b) Super Three theory framework

(continued)

(c) Publishing temperament measures

(d) Development of advanced statistical methods

4. **Which of the following instruments are both consistent with Five-Factor Model?**

   (a) 16PF and MMPI-2

   (b) NEO-PI-R and 16PF

   (c) EPQ and EAS

   (d) EAS and SSQ

5. **Which of the following instruments are designed to measure temperament in children?**

   (a) MMTIC, MCTQ, CCTI, SSQ

   (b) SSQ, MMPI-2, MMTIC, RITQ

   (c) RISK, TTS, RITQ, MBTI

   (d) MBTI, MMPI-2, MMTIC, SSQ

6. **What major contributions did Thomas and Chess make to temperament theory?**

   (a) Falsification of type, goodness of fit, poorness of fit

   (b) Super three, five-factor model, falsification of type

   (c) Three body types, inhibited and uninhibited, reactive type

   (d) Goodness of fit, nine temperament dimensions, three temperament patterns

7. **Which of the following is *not* a modern area of investigation for temperament theory?**

   (a) Reactivity and self-regulation

   (b) Inhibited and uninhibited

   (c) Endomorphy, mesophorphy, and ectomorphy

   (d) Overcontrollers, undercontrollers, resilients

8. **Which of the following constructs frequently emerges across temperament and personality measures?**

   (a) Sanguine

   (b) Psychoticism

   (c) Impulsivity

   (d) Extroversion-introversion

Answers: 1. c; 2. b; 3. d; 4. b; 5. a; 6. d; 7. c; 8. d

Two

EMPIRICAL FOUNDATIONS FOR TEMPERAMENT THEORY

Thus far, this text has discussed the historical evolution of major temperament theories. In considering theoretical paradigms, it is equally important to consider empirical evidence that validates or challenges those theories. This section will review some of the research that provides overarching support for temperament theory. Ideally in psychology, theorists are able to accurately identify all components of a construct—those elements that can be accurately measured, are somewhat consistent over time, and clinicians can confidently utilize screening or evaluation data for effective prevention and intervention. Bronson (1974) describes this as the continuity-predictability model. The common themes for temperament evidence include heritability studies, biological correlate studies, stability analysis, and crosscultural investigations. However, there are always challenges to applying Bronson's premise, and temperament is no exception. In temperament assessment, some of the challenges include competing theories with differing constructs, the wide variation of maturation rates in early childhood as compared to more stable traits in adulthood, and very different qualities measured from infancy to adult temperament measures. A discussion of the limitations and future research areas for temperament theory and its assessment is provided in Chapter Five.

DON'T FORGET

Changes in Temperament Constructs

Infants, toddlers, and children mature rapidly and subsequently the manifestation of behaviors or emergence of preferences that constitute temperament also change.

EVIDENCE FROM HERITABILITY STUDIES

Since the inception of psychological studies of human development, debates have flourished over the relative contributions of nature versus nurture. The use of heritability studies to address the nature-nurture paradigm first originated with Francis Galton (1822–1911). In psychology, nature is considered the genetic components that predispose functioning, whereas nurture is comprised of the environmental influences, including family and socialization processes, that foster personal traits. Research with twins is considered the strongest supporting evidence for heritability. These investigations often compare fraternal (dizygotic) twins who are reared together in the same environment and those who are separated and reared apart, as well as identical (monozygotic) twins who are either reared together or apart (Hergenhahn, 2001). Early heritability research in psychology indicated strong support for factors such as height and intelligence. In fact, some heritability studies found genetic heritability rates for intelligence at about 70 percent ($h^2 = .71$). Later studies included heritability analysis of personality traits and found significant correlations for shared genetics accounting for 50 to 60 percent of the variance. Surprisingly, family environment effects for persons who are not related, such as adopted children, is estimated at only 5 percent. Other environmental influences that are not shared by family members, such as friendships or random life circumstances (e.g., injuries, trauma), may account for up to 45 percent of variance (Bouchard, 1984; Bouchard, McGue, Hur, & Horn, 1998; Tellegen et al., 1988).

Psychological Temperament Type Model

Bouchard and Hur (1998) conducted one of the few heritability studies for temperament that utilized psychological type theory. They administered the Myers-Briggs Type Indicator® (MBTI) to 61 identical (monozygotic) twins and 49 fraternal (dizygotic) twins reared apart. On two of the four dimensions, extroversion-introversion and thinking-feeling, heritability was about .60. The heritability for the other two dimensions, sensing-intuition and judgment-perception, was close to .40.

Early Childhood Biobehavioral Models

In considering heritability research for early childhood biobehavioral models of temperament, Goldsmith and Irving Gottesman (1981) noted strong support for heritability in measures of activity level among twins. In a study of 12,898 twins, Florderus-Myrhed, Pedersen, & Rasmuson (1980) found about half of the phenotype variation reflected in heritability factors (e.g., extroversion in males .54, females .66). In examining their three temperament qualities of emotionality (identical .63, fraternal .12), activity level (identical .62, fraternal −.13), and sociability (identical .53, fraternal −.03), Buss and Plomin (1984, p. 122) found identical twins were very similar, whereas fraternal twins were not. They propose that their scale of emotionality is similar to the neuroticism scale and their sociability scale is similar to extroversion scales on other personality measures (Buss & Plomin, 1984, p. 115).

Temperament Embedded in Personality Models

Researchers have found support for all five factors of the Big Five personality theory with estimates of heritability accounting for significant portions of phenotype variance across peer and self-reported measures (peer-reported $h^2 = .57$ to $.81$; self- and peer-report $h^2 = .66$ to $.79$) (Jang, McCrae, Angleitner, Riemann, & Livesley, 1998; Riemann, Angleitner, & Strelau, 1997). Based upon the prevalence of heritability data for personality measures, some researchers have suggested that extroversion and neuroticism may indeed be *"super traits"* (Buss & Plomin, 1984, p. 115; Loehlin, 1982) as they demonstrate the strongest heritability even when utilizing a variety of instruments (e.g., Eysenck Personality Inventory, California Psychological Inventory).

Limitations

Acknowledging the limitations of heritability studies is an important consideration when interpreting research results. Studies of twins reared apart have several unique factors; first there is a possible placement selection bias as adoption procedures vary considerably by region. Some agencies require a rigorous process often including financial reviews, career stability checks, home environment reviews, as well as parental interviews and sometimes observations of prospective parent/child interactions. Other agencies only require parental screening measures. It is likely adults who are socially gracious, outgoing, well-educated with higher incomes and possessing a poised demeanor as well as infants with an easy temperament would be advantaged in the more rigorous matching processes. Secondly, underrepresentation is also problematic as parents who place their child for adoption or parents who adopt represent a restricted range of variables in regards to ethnicity, income, and education levels (Goldsmith, 1989). More recent social perspectives on adoption can also favor placing twins together or with extended family and this has further limited the number of subjects to recruit for twin studies who are reared apart.

Another inherent problem in this type of research is the dependence on parental report. It is possible parents expect and therefore report more similarity between identical twins and more differentiation between fraternal twins. Some researchers have debated if the typically low correlations on parent-reported temperament measures for fraternal twins are actual evidence for parental bias. A series of detailed debates on this topic are provided by Rothbart, Bates, Saudino, and others (Hwang & Rothbart, 2003; Rothbart & Bates, 1998; Saudino, 2003).

Goldsmith (1989, p. 125) also suggests consideration for interpretation of results in lieu of possible interactions between genetic and environmental effects delineating three types of correlations: passive, evocative or reactive, and active. Additionally, studies typically do not control for other family variables such as number of siblings, parental years of experience with parenting, or placement of child among siblings (e.g., youngest). Presumably, adoptive parents would more frequently be first-time parents and thus the subject child may be an only child.

Lastly, McCrae and Costa (2001, p. 15) propose that there is great difficulty in distinguishing the effects of biology and environment as individual adaptations to their environment create a behavioral prototype that can be self-sustaining creating a cumulative continuity. As an example, a child with an irritable disposition is likely to elicit poor interactions with others and respond accordingly, thus perpetuating the cycle.

CAUTION

Limitations of Heritability Research

There are several limitations inherent in heritability studies that must be considered when interpreting research results: sources of adoption placement bias in twin studies, potential for bias in parental reports, interactions between genetic and environmental effects, lack of control for family variables, and the effects of behavioral prototypes.

EVIDENCE FROM BIOLOGICAL CORRELATES

Biological correlate studies typically measure one or more physiological attributes as well as administer a measure of the psychological constructs of interest. The variables are selected based on a hypothesized relationship. If the relationship between these measures is strong there may be support for a possible causal pathway or contributing factor. Therefore, these studies can be utilized to test theoretically proposed relationships in temperament. However, even with strong correlations, there can also be other explanations for the relationship besides causation, such as confounding variables. Therefore, caution is always warranted in interpreting these data.

Psychological Temperament Type Models

There is a body of research related to a variety of biological correlates and psychological temperament qualities as defined by the Myers-Briggs Type

Indicator® (MBTI). In considering evidence of biological correlates for extroversion and introversion, numerous studies have investigated brain functioning. Several researchers have found lower cortical arousal, lower limbic site activity, lower reported rates of hypertension, and lower heart disease among extroverts when compared to introverts (Kagan & Snidman, 1991, 2004; Shelton, 1996; Sternberg, 1990; Wilson & Languis, 1990). The lower cortical arousal level among extroverts is thought to account for their continual quest to seek out stimulation from the environment and others. In contrast, introverts have a higher cortical arousal level and this would be consistent with their inclination to withdraw in order to renew their energy.

Greater activity in the left hemisphere of the brain has been noted for persons preferring sensing styles and greater activity in the right hemisphere for those preferring intuitive styles (Hartman, Hylton, & Sanders, 1997; Newman, 1985). In presuming a brain lateralization paradigm, some models hypothesize the left brain processes information sequentially consistent with preferences for facts and linear logic. The right brain is hypothesized to process in a simultaneous manner consistent with the intuitive preference for discovering ideas holistically. Cautions are noted regarding brain lateralization theories as there is considerable variation in the dominance of brain functions, especially by gender and handedness. Individuals who prefer sensing also more frequently report stress and related coronary heart disease as well (Shelton, 1996). Hartman, Hylton, and Sanders (1997) studied the judging and perceiving dimension with a subject pool of 232 students. Those reporting a judging style preference exhibited increased right-brain activity. When comparing students who preferred perceiving, increased activity in left-brain structures was indicated.

Early Childhood Biobehavioral Models

In a broad review of temperament, Rothbart, Chew, and Gartstein (2001) note three biological areas of study for early childhood temperament. They propose the limbic system is critical to reward stimuli and thus approach or withdrawal behaviors. It may also be involved in arousal states, especially fear and anxiety that signal danger and thus prompt withdrawal. Irritability and rage are noted to be reliant on neural pathways, which may be related to the most problematic difficult temperament. Opiate projections are perceived as related to prosocial behaviors and thus may account for the underpinnings of easy and social temperaments in infants.

Consistent with the MBTI research on adult extroversion and introversion, longitudinal studies of children identified as prone to shyness or timidity through observation and parental survey methods also indicate higher adult cardiovascular rates (Kagan & Moss, 1962). In studies of inhibited children followed from age 21 months to age four, higher heart rates where noted when they were presented tasks as compared to children in the uninhibited group. Behaviorally, the inhibited children also remained more reticent, quiet, and solitary when observed in kindergarten classrooms (Garcia-Coll, Kagan, & Reznick, 1984). At age 12, the same inhibited children were more likely to have symptoms of social anxiety, whereas the uninhibited were more sociable, outgoing, and jovial (Schwartz, Snidman, & Kagan, 1999). This again is consistent with the arousal hypothesis as an explanation for extroversion and introverted behavioral manifestations.

In considering threshold of response factors, Snidman and Kagan (1994) conducted a number of other studies utilizing cortical arousal, brain stem, and autonomic response measures in comparing high-reactive and low-reactive children. They found greater activation of the right hemisphere, increases in cortical arousal on electroencephalogram (EEG) measure of brain activity, and larger evoked potentials for several discrete measures in children who were high-reactive. For a detailed review of Snidman & Kagan's work, including resting heart rate, blood pressure, spectral analysis of heart rate, EEG power, Wave 5, and event-related potential measures, see The Long Shadow of Temperament (2004). Additional studies have investigated hypothesized correlations between the serotonin transporter gene (5-HTTLPR) and social withdrawal/anxiety traits; however, results did not support this conclusion. Studies of dopamine and estrogen receptors as genetic contributors to temperament qualities show promise and are ongoing (Prior, Sanson, Smart, & Oberklaid, 2000).

Temperament Embedded in Personality Models

A number of studies have been designed to investigate brain function correlations with personality measures. Canli (2006) provides a review of such studies in genomic imaging of introversion and extroversion. In a study presenting pleasant pictorial stimuli (e.g., foods, happy people), and utilizing functional magnetic resonance imaging (fMRI), differences were noted for cortical regions activated in attentional neural systems for extroverts as compared to introverts. Other studies have noted extroverts attend differently from introverts to stimuli associated with reward, and it is hypothesized this may account for the tendency of extroverts to be more interested in outside stimuli (Derryberry & Reed, 1994). Amygdala activation was also noted to vary between introverts and extroverts when presented positive emotional pictures using persons with happy faces. Variations in dopamine D4 receptor gene was found for persons reporting extroversion qualities. Additionally, the presence of at least one 7-repeat allele also correlated with high self-report ratings of extroversion as well as greater novelty seeking behavior (Canli, 2006). Extroverts in general are noted to seek out new experiences more that introverts. In contrast, absence of the 7-repeat allele was noted for studies of infants with distressed or irritable temperaments (Auerbach et al., 1999, 2001).

Limitations

Again, in reviewing correlational studies it is always important to note that correlations do not always support causation. A number of mitigating or confounding variables may be inherent in the interpretations of these methods. Correlational studies in infancy and toddlers can be especially complex as some temperament qualities are hypothesized to be related to cortical structures that mature at different and rapid rates. Thus a correlate found at one point in time may no longer have a primary influence a few months later, so correlations would not necessarily be meaningful over time. As many infant and toddler studies include laboratory observations, data may also have effects based on this unfamiliar setting and interactions with raters can introduce error.

CAUTION

Limitations of Biological Correlates Research

The old adage, "correlation does not equal causation" is critical to remember in understanding research based on correlational studies. A correlation supports a relationship between variables but does not prove that one causes the other, thus should be considered cautiously.

EVIDENCE FROM CONTINUALITY AND STABILITY OF TEMPERAMENT

In general, personality and temperament qualities are thought to be stable over time, although not as stable as other measures such as intelligence. Understanding the stability of traits is important as it has implications for how malleable an attribute may be and the probability of changing the trait if it is maladaptive. When traits are consistent there is the opportunity for cumulative effects for several reasons. First the attribute can become well rehearsed, prohibit other more adaptive actions, and eventually become habitual and thus more resistant to change. Secondly, there are reciprocal interactions based on individual's moods, characteristics, and subsequent behaviors. If maladaptive, these actions will in turn elicit negative behaviors that become cyclical. It is also important to the concept of measurement that constructs be at least stable enough to ensure accuracy in their measurement.

Psychological Temperament Type Models

A large study of 7,902 students, ages eight through 17, utilizing the Student Styles Questionnaire (SSQ) examined the stability of self-reported temperament preferences (Bassett, 2004). Across the sample, students generally preferred extroversion to introversion, imaginative (i.e., intuition in MBTI) rather than practical, and organized (i.e., judging on MBTI) qualities rather than flexible. On the thinking-feeling dimension, there was a predominately male preference for thinking and female preference for feeling. This gender difference on the thinking-feeling scale temperament distribution is consistent with an overwhelming body of evidence in psychological type research for adults as well (Myers, McCaulley, Quenk, & Hammer, 1998).

In investigating the stability of these preferences over time, the majority of students preferred extroversion, and this increased temporarily from ages 8 to 13. Between ages 8 to 10 students temporarily reported an increased preference for imaginative (i.e., intuition) styles, which returned to the prior balanced preference between imaginative and practical for ages 10 to 15 before increasing again. Male preference for thinking was consistent from ages 8 to 17, whereas females indicated a steadily increasing preference for feeling with age. The pattern for organized (i.e., judging) and flexible (i.e., perceiving) preferences is balanced from ages 8 to 15 and then increasing in organized preferences from ages 15 to 17. These data suggest psychological type temperament qualities that are stable over the long term with a primarily pre- and early-adolescence fluctuation. Several cross-national studies have also found these temporary fluctuation at maturation points when comparing children from Romania, Greece, Nigeria, and South Korea (Oakland & Hatzichristou, in press; Lee, Oakland & Ahn, in press; Oakland, Illiescu, Dinca, Maiorescu, & Dempsey, 2009).

Early Childhood Biobehavioral Models

In their longitudinal study, Thomas and Chess (1986) found that six of their nine measures (i.e., activity level, rhythmicity, adaptability, threshold of response, intensity of reaction, quality of mood) of temperament had significant correlations over a one year time span (.30), although this decreased with additional years (at five years .10). Approach/withdrawal, distractibility, and attention span/persistence were not significant. In their research of the difficult child pattern, the majority of subjects experience negative long-term effects. Children in the slow-to-warm category also experienced adjustment problems throughout their lifespan further supporting the stability of these traits (Chess & Thomas, 1984; Thomas & Chess, 1977; Thomas, Chess, & Birch, 1968).

The Fullerton longitudinal study, an 18-year effort beginning in 1979, measured temperament from ages one through 17. Several parent and child self-report ratings based on the original NYLS theory were administered as well as adolescent personality measures. Stability of the difficult temperament pattern from toddler to adolescence was moderately high (.61 to .64). These teenagers were more likely to have negative moods, low adaptability, high activity levels, more intense reactions, more withdrawal, and subsequent externalizing behavioral difficulties (Guerin, Gottfried, Oliver, & Thomas, 2003). However, it should be noted sociability, which is typically a factor in difficult temperaments, was not consistent in parent ratings and the difficult profile in the Fullerton study is not totally aligned with the Thomas and Chess difficult temperament category. Stability of specific traits in the NYLS model were also tested in the Fullerton study. Of the nine dimensions, stability of rhythmicity-predictability, negative mood and threshold were significant on most instruments; activity, approach/withdrawal, intensity, and distractibility had moderate stability, and adaptability and persistence were low. Approach-withdrawal indicated a significant change in ratings from ages 8 to 12, and then returned to stable.

Additional studies by other researchers for a variety of the early childhood dispositions defined by Thomas and Chess also have supported stability of some traits. McDevitt found significant consistency from infancy up to age five for the three temperament patterns: easy, slow-to-warm, and difficult (Buss & Plomin, 1984, p. 144; Thomas & Chess, 1986, p. 289). In assessing irritability and cheerfulness of infants, Stifter and Fox (1990) found parent ratings to be stable for over five months. Although, by adult standards this may be a short period of time, it should also be noted, infancy is the most variability time of development and maturation. Caspi's research of children with hesitant approach and social withdrawal also found these traits were persistent to adulthood as subjects continued to describe themselves as cautious, reporting they married and established careers later than the subjects noted as sociable (Caspi, Elder, & Bern, 1988; Caspi & Silvia, 1995). International studies of Canadian, Dutch, and Icelandic toddlers have concluded temperament traits are stable through elementary or middle school age. (Cote et al., 2002; Hart et al., 1997; Kagan & Snidman, 2004; Rimm-Kaufman et al., 2002; Stams, Juffer, & van Ijzendoorn, 2002). In a series of newer detailed studies, Kagan and Snidman (1994) explored several other components including fearfulness with outcomes indicating less stability for these characteristics over time.

Temperament Embedded in Personality Models

Research on the five-factor model of personality for adults indicates traits, although still subject to change, are most stable after age 30 and to a lesser degree between ages 18 and 30 (Costa & McCrae, 2001; Siegler et al., 1990). A model proposed by McCrae and Costa (2001, p. 10) suggests initial temperament qualities are biologically based and there are "characteristic adaptations" that result from environmental and personality factors, such as cultural conditioning, personal strivings, attitudes, and effects on self-concept. A component they labeled "objective biography" includes emotional reactions and behaviors that occur at important junctures in life often influenced by external events (e.g., mid-career shifts). These maturational or critical role change points in life may account for personality changes in adulthood.

Limitations

In considering longitudinal research that correlates early child and later adolescent or adulthood temperament characteristics, a variety of instruments must be utilized over time due to maturational changes in how attributes are expressed. This results in variations in how constructs are defined and, when different instruments are used, may result in significant differences in underlying theoretical focus for test items. As an example, infant measures tend to be biobehaviorally focused based on Thomas and Chess dimensions or EAS factors, whereas adult measures may rely on five-factor model or psychological type. In considering withdrawal, it may be defined by lack of responsiveness to a caregiver for an infant, lack of play interactions for a toddler, and then later by parent or self-report as poor peer interactions. In large longitudinal projects, such as the Australian Temperament Project, dozens of differing instruments are utilized across the course of the study. These instruments also vary in the rigor of psychometric properties. Therefore, it is difficult to be certain the same constructs are being measured across the time span. Goldsmith (1989) noted the selection of particular infant versus toddler instruments can effect research findings even when measuring the same construct as item wording and maturational expectations differ in how a trait will be expressed.

Rothbart and Bates (1998) suggest a number of difficulties with basing conclusions of temperament stability on parental reports. First, the studies utilize single-point measurements rather than a mean of multiple measures that might establish a behavioral baseline. The same informant (usually mothers) completes the ratings; therefore they may be subject to informant bias. Consideration for longitudinal studies utilizing multiple informants is encouraged as fathers, teachers, or peers for older children may offer broader insight. The authors caution that other explanations, such as nonlinear effects for temperament, interactions with cultural or context factors, the additive effects of particular temperament quality clusters, and personal characteristics of parents, should be further investigated. As an example, some research has indicated that parents within low economic levels rate their children as more difficult and higher-income families report less problematic behaviors (Prior, Sanson, Smart, & Oberklaid, 2000). This may suggest other hypotheses accounting for confounding variables especially related to difficult temperaments. Such confounds include larger family sizes, greater financial strain, some negative community environment factors (e.g., crime, poor housing, lack of childcare), and general cumulative stressors in low-income families.

CAUTION

Limitations Related to Temperament Stability

Although temperament is thought to be moderately stable over time, qualities are not as consistent as other characteristics such as intelligence. In addition, the theoretical constructs of temperament and subsequent test instruments can vary considerably in what behaviors they are measuring across the lifespan.

EVIDENCE FROM CROSS-CULTURAL STUDIES

One of the core foundations of developmental psychology is the understanding that biologically based trajectories of growth are typically consistent across all groups of people. Children progress in predictable sequences of acquiring attachment, motor skills, language, physical prowess, and cognitive processes across nations. However, there are also differences across cultures and for subgroups within a culture. Gender differences in muscle structure and height are examples of a consistent cross-cultural and cross-national subgroup difference. Different ideas of the value in making decisions based on collectivist or individualistic perspectives are an example of a cross-national difference in a social construct. Biologically based phenomena are thought to remain relatively consistent across humanity, whereas socially constructed behaviors are more subject to cultural influences. Anthropologists have long recognized and investigated this phenomenon. The study of temperament utilizing cross-cultural and cross-national samples can provide additional understanding of the proportional contributions of genetics and socialization processes as well as the stability of traits.

Psychological Temperament Type Model

For the purposes of discussing cross-cultural research related to psychological type, a discussion of two instruments—the MBTI for adults and the SSQ for children—is provided. As reviewed by Myers, McCaulley, Quenk, and Hammer (1998), the original MBTI Manual (Myers & McCaulley, 1985) summarized three studies with African-American and Japanese students supporting the MBTI constructs of temperament (Carlson & Levy, 1973; Myers, 1977). Kirby and Barger (1996) also provide a review of studies supporting reliability and validity for the MBTI temperament model across cultures, and there is evidence from both English-speaking and non-English-speaking cultures outside the United States. Similar distributions of extroversion, introversion, sensing, and judging qualities were noted for a limited number of studies. However, the authors suggest caution in utilizing the instrument in countries with collectivist cultures as construct validity of the MBTI needs further research within those countries.

The SSQ constructs are based on Jungian-Myers-Briggs theory and yield temperament types for children comparable to those on the MBTI. Cross-cultural research for the Student Styles Questionnaire (SSQ) within the United States includes several studies of racial-ethnic groups. Stafford and Oakland (1996) found their four-factor structure was supported with generally independent factors and consistent item loading for factors across African-American, Hispanic-American, and Anglo-American samples. Item functioning studies indicated similar results for Hispanic-American and Anglo-American. However, significant differential item functioning was noted on one scale (i.e., organized-flexible) when African-American and Anglo-American subjects were compared and suggest a need to review language/meaning for those items.

Recent cross-national research with the SSQ includes over a dozen countries and lends additional support for four psychological temperament type constructs. Benson, Oakland, and Shermis (2008) analyzed SSQ data across eight countries to determine if the same four bipolar dimensions (i.e., extroversion-introversion, practical-imaginative, thinking-feeling, organized-flexible) and factor loadings were evident. A strong fit for the theoretical model was noted when comparing samples from Australia, the People's Republic of China, Costa Rica, Philippines, the United States, and Zimbabwe suggesting strong support for these four dichotomous dimensions. In investigating the model fit for samples from Palestine (Gaza) and Nigeria, there was overlap in items from two dimensions: Extroversion-introversion and organized-flexible. Thus, further research is needed to investigate possible language and/or cultural factors. It was also noted the sample from Palestine may be less valid as the area was engaged in military conflict with Israel at the time and duress was experienced by the children.

It is interesting to note that in comparing data from 13 countries for extroversion-introversion, practical-imaginative, and organized-flexible dimensions, some strong similarities emerge. Notably, children from most countries prefer an organized style in their daily lives (see Figure 2.1). This may have implications for

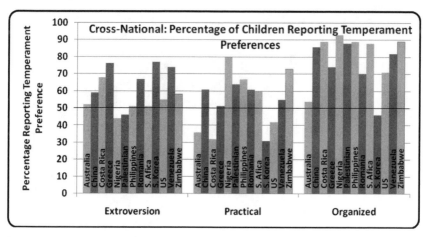

**Figure 2.1   Cross-National: Percentage of Children Reporting
Temperament Preferences**

Note: Compilation of data from studies of 13 countries (Faulkner, 2002, 2009; Oakland,
Alghorani,&Lee,2007;Lee,Oakland,&Ahn,in press;Leon,Oakland,Wei,&Berrios,2009;
Oakland & Callueng, 2009; Oakland, Faulkner, & Bassett, 2005; Oakland & Hatzickristou,
in press; Oakland, Illiescu, Dinca, & Dempsey, 2009; Oakland & Lu, 2006; Oakland &
Mata, 2007; Oakland, Mogaji, & Dempsey, 2006; Oakland, Mpofu, & Sulkowski, 2008;
Oakland, Pretorius, & Lee, 2008).

classroom structure and educational strategies as discussed in Chapter Six. On
the extroversion-introversion dimension close to 50 percent of students reported
preferences for extroversion rather than introversion, although variability across
nations is also present. The most variability across the countries was on the practical-imaginative scale.

Gender data are evident, in most countries, with more males reporting a thinking
rather than feeling preference as compared to females. There were two exceptions:
South Korea and Zimbabwe (see Figure 2.2). This consistent gender difference
is noted in multiple studies utilizing the MBTI as well (Myers et al., 1998). Many
temperament scales do not yet provide a wide range of cross-cultural and cross-
national studies and these examples demonstrate the additional insights that are
afforded with such data.

Early Childhood Biobehavioral Models

The stability of inhibited versus uninhibited temperament factors appears to be
consistent across culture, although the preponderance of particular traits may

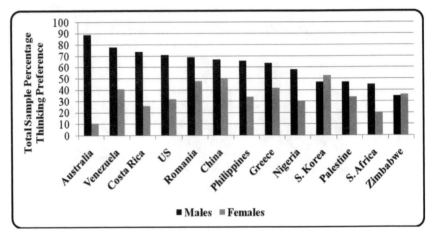

Figure 2.2 Total Sample Percentage Thinking Preference

Note: Compilation of data from studies of 13 countries (Faulkner, 2002; Oakland, Alghorani, & Lee, 2007; Lee, Oakland, & Ahn, in press; Leon, Oakland, Wei, & Berrios, 2009; Oakland & Callueng, 2009; Oakland, Faulkner, & Bassett, 2005; Oakland & Hatzickristou, in press; Oakland, Illiescu, Dinca, & Dempsey, 2009; Oakland & Lu, 2006; Oakland & Mata, 2007; Oakland, Mogaji, & Dempsey, 2006; Oakland, Mpofu, & Sulkowski, 2008; Oakland, Pretorius, & Lee, 2008).

vary cross-culturally. In a study comparing Chinese-American and Caucasian infants, Kagan found withdrawal and inhibited characteristics to still be evident two years later (Kagan, Kearsley, & Zelazo, 1978). The study contrasted children in both groups who were reared at home and who attended daycare. Regardless of whether they stayed at home with their mothers or attended childcare, Chinese-American toddlers more frequently stayed closer to their caregivers, were more cautious in playing with new peers, and cried more readily if the caregiver was removed. Goldsmith (1989) notes the opposite was true in a comparison of Japanese and Euro-American mothers and infants. Japanese babies were less active and vocalized less than Euro-American infants. As an example, Freedman (1974) and Kagan (et al., 1994) found that when purposefully disturbed, Chinese-American infants were less reactive and vocal than African-American, Anglo-American, or Irish babies.

The Australian Temperament Project (original N=2,443; retained 67% of sample, N=1650) is one of the most extensive and recent longitudinal studies following infants through the age of 18 (Prior, Sanson, Smart, & Oberklaid, 2000).

The program was designed to investigate outcomes including behavior problems, learning difficulties, substance use, social competence, social responsibility, and positive peer support. It was modeled on the Thomas and Chess (1977) dimensions and utilized the Carey and McDevitt questionnaires format. Approximately every two years, a series of temperament, behavioral, and social-emotional measures were administered. Each two years starting from infancy through age 18, parents completed questionnaires. Teacher questionnaires were added at ages five or six through ages 11 or 12. Self-report measures were included by age 11 or 12 through age 18. At age 15, the five-factor Personality Questionnaire was utilized as a self-report measure of temperament.

Findings indicate from ages 4 to 8 months through age 16, two original Thomas and Chess constructs remained evident: approach and activity level. A negative reactivity construct (related to irritability) and persistence (related to rhythmicity) were also noted across ages. More extreme ratings of temperament qualities were the most stable over time with more variation in children whose ratings were mild or moderate on a characteristic. Consistent with prior studies, the children with difficult temperaments exhibited the most problematic behaviors over time. In considering children with Attention Deficit Hyperactivity Disorder (ADHD), those with early hyperactive problems and a difficult temperament had the worst prognosis and highest risk for anti-social types of behavior. In contrast to prior research, a high activity level was more predictive of an easy rather than difficult style. Shy, inhibited children were most at risk for anxiety disorders. In comparing their data with samples from the United States, Greece, and the People's Republic of China, they found Chinese and Greek infants had lower activity levels as well as more negative mood.

Temperament Embedded in Personality Models

Evidence for temperament constructs in cross-cultural studies can been found across several aspects: Analytical factor studies that support the same constructs for translated instruments and well-documented group differences in customary responses or values that are collaborated in cultural literature. There is strong cross-cultural support for the five-factor models of personality. A number of researchers have found support for the five-factor model even when utilizing differing data sources, instruments, and languages (John, 1990; John, Angleitner, & Ostendorf, 1988). McCrae and Costa (2001) found adult traits on the five-factor model stable, particularly after age 30 for samples in Germany, Italy, Portugal, Croatia, and Korea. Similar findings were noted for studies in Estonian, Filipino, Chinese, and English language test versions (McCrae, Costa, del Pilar, Rolland, &

Parker, 1998). In comparing the adult version of the Eyzenck Personality Questionnaire (EPQ) and the Junior version (J-EPQ) for large samples in Hungary, Spain, Japan, New Zealand, Hong Kong, Singapore, Canada, Denmark, Greece, and Yugoslovia, strong support for the super-three theory was noted (Eysenck & Eysenck, 1985).

In the Australian longitudinal study the Five Factor Personality Questionnaire was utilized to measure temperament for teenagers and then compared to early predictor factors based on Thomas and Chess dimensions (Prior, Sanson, Smart, & Oberklaid, 2000). The Five Factor Personality Questionnaire measures extroversion, agreeableness, emotional stability, conscientiousness/self-control, and intellect/openness. Results indicated early measures of sociability and activity were positively correlated with extroversion and approach also was positively correlated with emotional stability. Reactivity was inversely related to agreeableness and emotional stability was negatively related to reactivity. As would be expected, negative reactivity was predictive of later behavioral problems. In girls, negative emotionality (e.g., moodiness, crankiness, intense emotions, anger) coupled with low persistence at ages 3 to 4 was predicted to be a risk factor for eating disorders. Depression risk factors included early low sociability scores and negative reactivity. A cluster of temperament risk factors and environmental elements were the best predictor of hard core drug addictions: negative reactivity, low persistence, low agreeableness, and conscientiousness coupled with delinquency and aggression.

Limitations

Paunonen and Ashton (1998, pp. 152–153) suggest 10 limitations to consider in cross-cultural and cross-national studies, especially when differences are found. The first concern is poor test translation to ensure equivalent meaning. There are colloquialisms and nuances of vocabulary use that do not translate appropriately, as well as terms that do not have equivalent forms in other languages (e.g., a pie may be translated as a tart in some languages). Thus, merely translating a test word-by-word may not be sufficient. Back-translation techniques have been recommended to address this limitation. The process includes translating the original instrument by a person fluent in the target language and then another blind translation by a different individual from the target language back to the original language. If the meaning remains the same there is more confidence in how the test items are understood by those evaluated. A second issue is lack of item relevance between cultures. This can occur when items are related to laws, customs, or local climates and terrain. Trait distributions may differ, test factor structure may differ, and causal or predictive value of a trait may differ by culture. Different response styles, especially in lieu of perceived socially desirable answers, may effect validity. For example, in some cultures an outgoing, gregarious personality is highly valued, whereas other cultures may value a calm and yielding demeanor. Test formats (e.g., true/false, Likert scale) may be differentially perceived and test developers in different countries also utilize different statistical methods in establishing reliability and validity data. Test constructs may also lack relevance to a particular culture or just not exist in that group. To ensure results from cross-cultural and cross-national studies are most relevant, researchers should address these considerations in the methodological design of their investigations.

CAUTION

Limitations in Cross-Cultural Studies

Cross-cultural studies are subject to several limitations, including lack of equivalence of translated terms, item relevance across cultures, possible differing factor structures in the same test instruments when administered across cultures, and variation in the rigor of statistical methodologies to establish reliability and/or validity for use of a translated instrument.

In Summary

There is evidence from a variety of sources supporting the three temperament theory groups discussed in this text: psychological temperament type, biobehavioral temperament models, and personality models with embedded temperament constructs (i.e., big-five and super-three theories). Heritability studies indicate identical twins are significantly more alike on temperament qualities than fraternal twins, suggesting support for a genetic basis for attributes. A number of correlational studies support differences in brain activity, especially related to arousal for extroversion and introversion. Temperament constructs from the psychological temperament type and personality measure groups appear to be moderately stable over time with fluctuations coinciding to major maturational points. Some biobehavioral measures of temperament qualities appear stable, although for shorter duration and not as strongly as measures of adolescent and adult temperament. Cross-cultural research suggests the same four psychological type constructs and five-factor as well as super theories of personality are supported. Thomas and Chess's three patterns of early childhood temperament also appear to be supported cross-culturally in lieu of long-term outcomes. There is less support for their original nine dimensions. However, new methods of brain research are promising additional insights for arousal studies. In addition, cross-national research continues to emerge that will further enhance understanding of the socio-cultural influences on temperament development.

≡ Rapid Reference 2.1

Key Research Findings

- Evidence from twin studies supports a genetic basis for temperament.
- Physiological arousal differences between introverts and extroverts are supported by correlational studies.
- Longitudinal research suggests temperament is moderately stable over time.
- Cross-cultural research utilizing factor analyses provides some support for the four constructs (dimensions) in psychological type theory.
- Early childhood temperament patterns have some correlation with long-term outcomes, especially more problematic patterns such as slow-to-warm or difficult temperament.

 TEST YOURSELF

I. The strongest evidence for heritability is found in:

(a) Adoption studies of non-related children

(b) Laboratory medical tests

(c) Twin studies, reared together and apart

(d) Sibling studies for large families

2. Heritability rates are highest for:

(a) Temperament qualities

(b) Personality attributes

(c) Gender

(d) Intelligence

3. Which of the following are true across a number of biological correlate studies?

(a) Lower cortical arousal and lower limbic site activity is noted for extroverts

(b) Higher cortical arousal and lower limbic site activity is noted for introverts

(c) Intuitive individuals have the highest coronary disease rates

(d) Uninhibited children experience the highest heart rates in task studies

4. Gender difference in psychological temperament type is most prevalent for:

(a) Extroversion–introversion

(b) Sensing–intuition (practical-imaginative)

(c) Thinking–feeling

(d) Judging–perceiving (organized-flexible)

5. Temperament traits in individuals typically are:

(a) Strongly stable, remaining the same after age two

(b) Moderately stable through childhood with dramatic changes in adulthood

(c) Stable for extreme scores but unstable for moderate scores

(d) Moderately stable with fluctuations at some maturational points

6. Which of the following are *not* true for cross-cultural research?

(a) Four factor constructs of psychological temperament type are supported

(b) Long-term outcomes for children who are withdrawn, inhibited, or difficult are similar

(c) Five-factor and super-three models of personality theory are supported

(d) All nine dimensions of the NYLS study are supported

7. Which of the following is a technique to ensure valid cross-cultural testing?

(a) Likert scales for items

(b) Back-translation of tests

(c) Administering multiple measures

(d) Electroencephalogram

8. Who is credited with the continuity-predictability model?

(a) Freud

(b) Bronson

(c) Jung

(d) Kagan

Answers: 1. c; 2. d; 3. a; 4. c; 5. d; 6. d; 7. b; 8. b

Three

VALIDITY AND RELIABILITY IN TEMPERAMENT ASSESSMENT

As reviewed in Chapter One, there are a wide range of temperament measurements from which to choose when designing an assessment. The initial considerations for selection of particular instruments are guided by the clinician's theoretical framework, type of data preferred, and the presenting referral concerns to be addressed. For infant, toddler, and early childhood evaluations, instruments may be limited to those in the NYLS, or arousal theoretical frameworks. Chess and Thomas (1986, p.5) propose four purposes for behavioral temperament data that clinician's often encounter. Those include indentifying (a) strong traits that although within normal range may appear deviant to others and thus interfere with adaptation, (b) exaggerated traits due to a poor interaction between the individual and environment that become maladaptive, (c) intensively negative individual-environment interactions resulting in behavioral disorders, and (d) the mental health disorders or physical handicaps for which temperament qualities effect the manifestation of symptoms. Professionals may utilize these data both to better identify problematic child temperament qualities and goodness-of-fit related to parent/child interactions as well as design therapy goals.

For elementary-age children, adolescents, and adults, a range of assessment instruments based on psychological temperament type are available. Briggs, Myers, Keirsey, Oakland, and others endorse temperament assessment as a means for promoting self-awareness and understanding among individuals regarding differences that can be primarily perceived as personal strengths (Keirsey, 1998; Myers, McCaulley, Quenk, & Hammer, 1998). They also acknowledge lesser developed traits may substantiate areas for further development or weakness, if severe. This perspective elicits interpretation of the data for broad applications such as personal growth, career planning, marital counseling, and within industry, data are used for team building among personnel. When viewed within the context of temperament influence on learning styles, the data can inform educational strategies for children as well as parents', caregivers', and teachers' understanding of differences (Oakland, Glutting, & Horton, 1996). If the temperament assessment is part of a broad personality evaluation, includes concerns for pathology, or has forensic implications, instruments within the five-factor or super three models may also be beneficial. Regardless of the hypotheses focus of the assessment battery, ethical use of the instruments is paramount.

CONSIDERATIONS IN ASSESSMENT METHODS

Once the theoretical framework and purpose of the temperament data interpretation is decided, the professional must consider the best methods of data collection when comparing instruments. Each method has both strengths and limitations, which are discussed briefly in this section. Interviews and observation methods are most common in the NYLS framework. Some rating scales also may be included. Among these instruments, the clinician has options of interviewing or rating scales for parents, caregivers, or daycare and school teachers with consideration for how well the informant knows the child and how fair their opinions may be. Observations may be conducted in labs, clinics, or home settings and protocols will vary based on the environment. Psychological type instruments are typically self-report rating scales, thus the reading level and self-reflection of the client are important considerations. Self-ratings are also frequently utilized in five-factor personality models. If maladaptive or pathological tendencies are suspected, forthrightness of the individual in answering questions should be a consideration when selecting instruments, as some provide scales to detect self-serving response patterns.

Observations

In temperament assessment, observational data is most common when assessing infants or toddlers rather than older children. Temperament observational assessment methods differ from general behavioral assessments in several ways. First they are not anecdotal or unstructured observations of naturally occurring events but rather follow a strict protocol. This analog observational technique is systematic in measuring targeted discrete behaviors, often elicited by a specified set of tasks or stimuli presentations. Behaviors should be operationally defined to minimize inference, assure raters can accurately distinguish actions, and facilitate data coding. Measurement of low intensity and subtle behaviors is especially problematic (Bates, 1989). Observer training, explicit coding matrices, and interrater agreement checks can minimize scoring errors. Analog measures can be subject to *observer reactivity*, if there are variations in the examiner's attentiveness as well as her/his interaction style with the child. Often even young children can perceive nuances in verbal tones as well as nonverbal cues from others, and thus examiners may inadvertently elicit actions. Scripts and feedback including review of recordings of the examiner can help reduce unintentional cueing. The rigid nature of these exams can be a limitation of this method as it creates a propensity for *situational specificity of behavior*, particularly if the elicited behaviors are uncommon to daily life events (Merrill, 2008). Protocol assessments are not ecological in nature and thus do not consider complex interactions within the broader context or interactive environment in which most behaviors occur.

A strength of the observation method is the versatility of settings in which observations can be conducted (e.g., home, laboratory, daycare). Home or school settings are generally thought to yield more naturalistic responses as they provide stimuli within the context and expectations the child encounters on a regular basis. Laboratory observations provide a greater opportunity to control the environment, eliminating extemporaneous stimuli, and apply some strategies particularly useful for research (e.g., videotaping, recording, timing interactions, measuring physiological response such as heart rate). However, when observing parent-child interactions within a laboratory, caregivers may be less at ease and thus alter their typical behavior patterns (Bates, 1989).

Questionnaires and Surveys

Parent or caregiver questionnaires have a variety of formats from open-ended to very direct questions. Checklists are close-ended and typically require parents to mark a preset list of items that apply to the child in a true/false manner, whereas questionnaires require extended answers. An advantage of questionnaires is that they permit caregivers to elaborate on issues relevant to the particular child. If administered as an interview, they also permit the examiner to query items of interest and request elaboration. Both forms tend to be inexpensive; however, questionnaires that are administered in an interview format require extensive professional time, thus considerable cost.

Bates (1989) points out a number of issues to contemplate when utilizing parental questionnaires or rating scales. The respondent must have (a) adequate comprehension of the instructions and questions, thus reading level is an important consideration; (b) the caregiver must have significant exposure to the child over time to form general impressions of behavioral patterns, thus recent changes in caregiver can present inaccurate data; (c) an objective and accurate memory that is not influenced by selective recall is vital, therefore parents with an inadequate bond or bias (positive or negative) can present unreliable data; (d) the respondent must not be under duress as experiencing significant life stress or personal mental health issues may skew a respondent's answers; and (e) caregivers who have accurate perceptions of the reference group (e.g., other children the same age) are better able to make norm comparisons.

Strengths of caregiver surveys include awareness of very young behaviors prior to school entry, knowledge of intimate bonding relationships (e.g., parent-child bond, sibling interactions), observation of more covert or less frequent behaviors over time, and awareness of daily care functions (e.g., toileting habits, feeding, grooming). Limitations of parental reports include the fact that caregivers observe behavior in response to their own interactions with the child; these are reciprocal in nature and influence each other. Parents also have a smaller comparison sample than others outside the home who observe many children the same age, and parents are not privy to child behaviors under the task demands of a group setting such as daycare or school classrooms. Caregivers interpret behaviors within their own cultural and personal values context; whereas teachers observe a child's ability to adapt to a wider range of influences.

Rating Scales

Rating scales are more prescriptive than questionnaires and surveys and can readily yield norm-referenced data. Some forms can be administered to multiple informants—parents, teachers, and by self-report—thus providing multiple perspectives. Temperament rating scales are more typically completed by parents or teachers for very young children and self-report for students or adults. The scales assume a level of discernment as to the frequency and severity of behaviors utilizing Likert scales (e.g., seldom, often) thus parents or teachers need to be very familiar with the child. Like parent questionnaires, rating scales also have the advantage of exploring low frequency and covert behaviors that are not easily observable (Sattler & Hoge, 2006).

Bias of responses is an important consideration when administering rating scales (Martin, Hooper, & Snow, 1986; Merrill, 2008). Respondent bias can occur through response patterns such as halo effects, leniency/severity, and central tendency. Halo effect is created by overly positive or negative ratings from informants based on qualities other than those relevant to the test instrument. For example, a child who is perceived by a teacher as especially endeavoring or frustrating may elicit less objective ratings. Leniency and severity ratings occur when the informant has a general propensity to be overly kind or derogatory in their assessment of others. If a rater has particularly low or high frustration tolerance for particular behaviors, this may occur. Central tendency responses tend to rate behaviors in the middle of a Likert scale (e.g., sometimes, average) rather than utilizing a wider range of choices (e.g., never, always, often).

In the case of self-report measures, individuals also are subject to forms of response bias. *Social desirability* is a term used to describe the tendency of some respondents to answer questions in what they perceive to be socially acceptable ways. This may occur purposefully to present one's self in a particularly positive manner or inadvertently if the individual perceives there is a correct response. Overly negative responses can be a result of faking if the individual desires to be perceived in that way. This is more common when maladaptive behavior, pathology, or malingering are present (Merrill, 2008). Self-report scales are also subject to a central tendency response pattern and scales that build in nonsense items may help in identifying central tendency. Some rating scales will include validity scales that alert examiners to these forms of bias, although this is much more common in diagnostic and pathology instruments than temperament measures.

Rapid Reference 3.1

Assessment Methods Pros and Cons

Observations

+ Facilitates systematic data collection following a strict protocol
+ Measures discrete behaviors
+ Coding provides quantitative data for analyses
+ Inter-rater agreement checks can control bias
+ Technique can be utilized in variety of settings (e.g., home, lab)
+ Can videotape to ensure multiple reviews of behavior
+ Laboratory observation can permit equipment for physiological measures

− Laboratory observations are an unnatural setting that may elicit atypical responses
− Caregivers may change their interaction patterns when observed or videotaped
− Infrequent and low-intensity behaviors may be overlooked
− Subject-observer reactivity
− Situational-specific behaviors may not generalize well

Questionnaires and Surveys

+ Permit parents to elaborate on items, providing additional information
+ Permit examiner to query answers of interest

+ Inexpensive forms
+ Caregivers know early history
+ Caregivers are aware of home and private behaviors

− Interviewing can be time intensive, thus expensive in terms of personnel costs
− Parents may have selective recall or biases
− Caregivers interpret behaviors in lieu of their own value system
− Caregivers have limited norm comparisons to other children the same age
− Parents with low reading levels or experiencing significant stressors may be less reliable informants

Ratings Scales

+ Provide norm-reference scores
+ Can acquire and compare data from multiple informants and settings
+ Measures frequency and severity of behaviors
+ Can provide information on covert behaviors

− Parent and teacher forms are subject to several forms of respondent bias
− Self-report forms also are subject to bias (e.g., social desirability, malingering)
− Dependent on reading skills

STANDARDS FOR PSYCHOLOGICAL TESTING

The American Psychological Association Ethical Principles for Psychologist and Code of Conduct and the National Association for School Psychologists Principles for Professional Ethics provide in-depth standards and guidelines that delineate best practices in psychological assessment. Broad standards include practicing within one's own competency, thus temperament assessment should only be conducted by appropriately credentialed individuals with training in these measures. Integrity, professional and scientific responsibility, respect for others' rights, concern for others' welfare, and social responsibility are also required in practice decisions. Acquiring consent and ascent for testing, confidentiality, maintaining test item security, and rigorous selection criteria for instruments are also ethical obligations.

Any specific instrument considered should be critiqued in lieu of its fundamental psychometric properties. Evidence of reliability and validity are core standards for the use of any educational or psychological measure. Thus, a review of the concepts of reliability and validity are provided in the chapter. A table with examples of these data for major instruments is provided at the end of the chapter (see Table 3.1). The *Standards for Educational and Psychological Testing*, published by the American Educational Research Association (AERA), American Psychological Association (APA), and the National Council on Measurement in Education (NCME) is a definitive guide on test guidelines (1999). Professionals can acquire validity and reliability studies from the assessment instrument manuals, independent research publications that have tested validity components, as well as test reviews from sources such as the *Mental Measurements Yearbook* published by the Buros Center for Testing (http://www.unl.edu/buros/).

Validity in Temperament Assessment

Validity establishes the empirical evidence for the extent to which a particular instrument measures the theoretical constructs upon which it is based. It provides the rationale upon which interpretations about the test are made, and there are several sources of data that can confirm validity. The *Standards for Educational and Psychological Testing* (AERA, 1999) recommendations for validity evidence include test content, response processes, internal structure, and relationships to other variables.

Evidence Based on Test Content

The content of a test includes the instructions, test item vocabulary and stimulus, the tasks required, the overall themes, and the answer formats. These should represent the concepts measured by the test in adequate breadth, depth, and proportion. When a particular construct or skill is measured it is important to consider the hierarchy or multiple components of that skill and assure all levels are adequately addressed. It is equally important to review items for irrelevant content that may have been inadvertently included. Test content validity is often established through expert panel reviews. For example, in designing a temperament measure, persons who have expertise in temperament theory may review test content to be sure items align with temperament components and that instructions are concise enough not to introduce error. If a team was designing an instrument to measure the Thomas and Chess's NYLS nine dimensions, items would be written for each of the areas: activity level, rhythmicity, approach-withdrawal, adaptability, threshold of responsiveness, intensity of reaction, quality of mood, distractibility, and attention span/persistence. In general when proposing temperament instruments, it would be important to consider the challenges in overlapping theory between temperament and personality traits and how those might be distinguished. Often multicultural expert panels representing ethnicity groups and both genders are obtained to assure item wording is not offensive or subject to differential interpretations. The reading level of the instrument should also be reviewed to ensure respondents are not confused by the vocabulary or content of questions. The specific processes involved in determining test content of a temperament instrument should be available in the manual for review.

Response Processes
Response processes evidence is less relevant to temperament measures and more pertinent to achievement tests. It involves analyzing the extent to which an examinee is utilizing the strategies that should be evoked by the test items. For example, if the questions are based on algebraic equations, examiners may wish to see the math process by which the individual arrived at an answer to ensure the test items are eliciting the conceptual processes intended. Some methods of establishing process include interviewing examiners about the strategies they utilized in arriving at answers to decipher whether a particular method was used. Judges may also observe eye movements and response times to infer the thinking process involved for test items. The use of laboratory observers for infant and toddler temperament exercises may incorporate some response processes techniques. For example, clinicians can assure the child is engaged in the process required through observation of eye movement (i.e., tracking a stimulus). If individuals are able to arrive at correct answers without employing the techniques that the test items were designed for, those items are often discarded as they may reflect strategies that were not intended (e.g., memorized responses, using a different strategy, incidental knowledge, picture cues in the stimulus).

Evidence Based on Internal Structure
Internal structure evidence specifics the degree to which items and their proposed scales support the theoretical framework proposed by the test. If a test is unidimensional then items should be homogeneous and one construct should emerge from factor analyses of the test responses (AERA, 1999). If the test proposes to measure multiple factors, items should be heterogeneous, loading on appropriate scales. In considering Jungian-Myers-Briggs theory, four dimensions are theoretically hypothesized: extroversion-introversion, sensing-intuition, thinking-feeling, and judging-perceiving. Thus, during development an analysis of responses to measures based on this theory should yield the proposed four factors. Several studies have validated these factors for the MBTI, MMTIC, as well as the SSQ (Murphy & Meisgeier, 2008; Myers, McCaulley, Quenk, &

Hammer, 1998; Oakland, Glutting, & Horton, 1996). As reviewed in Chapter One, evidence for validity based on internal structure has been established for several personality measures with temperament components (e.g., five-factor and super-three models) as well. In some cases factor analyses do not support the originally hypothesized factors and test developers or researchers may need to review items more closely for test content or consider other viable theoretical constructs. A prior discussion of Sanson and his colleagues' factor analyses of the original NYLS nine temperament dimensions for infants/toddlers ultimately found support for five dimensions rather than the original nine creating the impetus for a new infant instrument, the SITQ (Sanson et al., 1987). Differential item functioning is another important consideration for internal structure validity. The theoretical framework should not only be investigated for the sample as a whole but for subgroups of individuals as well (e.g., ethnicity, gender, clinical samples). Differential item functioning can be a tool to investigate appropriateness for use of a test with specific subgroups. There are circumstances when differential item functioning is consistent with the intended multidimensionality of the instrument (e.g., diagnostic instruments, differentiating clinical from nonclinical populations) (AERA, 1999).

Evidence Based on Relations to Other Variables

The relationship to variables outside of the test can provide strong evidence for the validity of a measure. When scores on an instrument representing particular theoretical constructs are compared to other measures that also measure the same attributes, the relationship should be significant and positively correlated (i.e., convergent evidence). As an example, when comparing the four dimensions of the MBTI to other personality instruments (e.g., *California Psychological Inventory, Millon Index of Personality Style*) with similar scales (e.g., extroversion-introversion, feeling/openness) positive correlations in scores were indicated. In contrast, when comparing unrelated scales or instruments, the expectation is that scores should not be similar. This principle, called discriminant evidence, proposes that inverse relationships or insignificant relationships can also provide validity support. Test-criterion relationships are an additional form of evidence related to outside variables as they investigate how

DON'T FORGET

Value of Discriminant Evidence

Validity support is also found when inverse or insignificant relationships are indicated for variables that indeed should not be similar.

well a test predicts a particular outcome (i.e., criterion) variable. Predictive studies related to Thomas and Chess's three temperament patterns (i.e., easy, slow-to-warm, difficult) and the original questionnaires they formed have been used in establishing validity for their measurement perspectives broadly, although studies of the nine dimensions were not supported. (Sanson et al., 1987; Thomas & Chess, 1977).

Reliability in Temperament Assessment

Reliability refers to how consistent or dependable test scores are when the test administered is repeated and presumes the constructs being measured are somewhat stable (AERA, 1999). A number of precautionary measures are taken to ensure that tests are administered in the same manner to all participants, thus reducing error during testing. These measures include strict administration sequences, scripted instructions, identical stimuli presentation, as well as rigid timing when required. However, variations remain often based on individual examinee circumstances from one day to the next (e.g., mood, alertness, anxiousness, general health). Therefore, scores are perceived to have some measurement error, which can be minimized by the examiner's diligence in following good rapport and standardization procedures.

The AERA (1999) delineates three types of reliability coefficients that can be utilized to provide evidence of reliability. The first method compares scores on parallel or alternate forms of a test (e.g., Form A, Form B). This particular method is often found in achievement measures and not typical of temperament instruments. The second method, test-retest, requires administration of the same test to the same individual after a period of time (e.g., 30 days). Scores are compared to yield reliability coefficients. Temperament rating scales often utilize the test-retest method in establishing reliability of scores. The third procedure, internal consistency coefficients, tests relationships between items or item cluster scores within the test.

In considering the validity and reliability of temperament instruments it is important to note that many of the instruments, particularly related to early childhood assessment, are older measures. Thus, original methodologies in design of the instruments was not as thorough or rigorous as current testing standards and, therefore, not reflected in manuals. Although many of the instruments are still utilized, there are significant limitations in the availability of validity and reliability data (see Table 3.1). Limitations will be discussed further in Chapter Five. Research studies following the publications of these tests may provide additional reliability and validity information.

Table 3.1 Select Temperament Measures

Instrument	Description of the Test Psychometric Properties	Population/Format Reliability & Validity
Baby Behavior Questionnaire (BBQ), Bohlin, Hagekull, & Lindhagen, 1981	54 items, caregiver questionnaire, ages 3–10 months, 7 factors: intensity/activity, regularity, approach-withdrawal, sensory sensitivity, atten-tiveness-manageability, sensitivity to new food	Internal Consistency (Cronbach Alpha) .51 to .71
Brazelton Neonatal Behavioral Assessment Scale (BNAS), Brazelton 1973, Brazelton & Nu-gent, 1995	Age birth – 1 month, factors: habituation, orientation, motor performance, range of state, state regulation, autonomic regulation, abnormal reflexes	Interobserver reliability .85 to 1.00
Behavioral Style Questionnaire (BSQ), McDevitt & Carey, 1978	100 item questionnaire, based on Thomas & Chess NYLS nine dimensions, ages 3–7, parent rating scale	Coefficient alphas range .47–.84 and .84 for total instrument; test-retest at one month interval range .67–.93 (overall r = .89)
Carey Temperament Scales (CTS), McDevitt & Carey, 1978 (reprint 2000)	86–110 items, ages infants/children, 1 month to 12 years-old, 5 questionnaire Likert scale formats (1–4mo, 4–11mo, 1–2yr, 3–7yr, 8–12yr) for caregivers, measures nine temperament quali-ties: activity, rythmicity, approach, adaptability, intensity, mood, persistence, distractibility, and threshold; Sample of 200–500 infants or children, primarily Euro-American in eastern US area	Test-retest reliability ranges from .64 to .94 with highest reliability at ages 3 and older (no inter-rater reliability provided); Authors note high construct validity based on substantial body of research supporting Thomas & Chess theo-retical framework and longitudinal research establishing long-term outcome correlates (e.g, New York Longitudinal Study)

Children's Behavior Questionnaire (CBQ), Rothbart, Ahadi, & Hershey, 1994	Parental questionnaire, ages 3–7, Subscales: activity level, anger/frustration, approach-anticipation, attentional focusing, discomfort, falling reactivity-soothability, fear, high-intensity pleasure, impulsivity, inhibitory control, low-intensity pleasure, perceptual sensitivity, sadness, shyness, smiling and laughter	unavailable
Colorado Childhood Temperament Inventory (CCTI), Rowe & Plomin, 1977	Utilizes Thomas & Chess dimensions and EASI factors: sociability, emotionality, activity, attention span-persistence, soothability, reaction to food.	unavailable
Dimensions of Temperament Survey – Revised Child (DOTS-R), Windle, 1988; Windle & Lerner, 1986	54-item questionnaire, ages early childhood to young adult, measure has two versions with same questions (Parent rating scale and child self-rating scale) as well as teacher form, based on Thomas & Chess NYLS nine dimension although scales are somewhat different: activity-general, activity-sleep, approach, flexibility, positive mood, rhythmicity-sleep, rhythmicity-eating, rhythmicity-daily habits, task orientation	Cronbach's alphas range from .54–.81

(continued)

Table 3.1 (Continued)

Instrument	Description of the Test Psychometric Properties	Population/Format Reliability & Validity
EAS Temperament Survey for Children, (EAS) and *EAS Temperament Survey for Adults,* Buss & Plomin, 1984	20 items, intended for research at any age including child-adolescents, Factors: emotionality, activity, sociability, subscale shyness	Internal consistency (Cronbach Alpha) ranges from .48 (sociability) to .79 (shyness) when tested with 18–50 month other children
Early Infancy Temperament Questionnaire, (EITQ), McDevitt & Carey, 1978	76 items, ages 1–4 months, 9 NYLS dimensions: activity, rhythmicity, approach, adaptability, threshold, mood, intensity, persistence, distractibility	Internal Consistency (Cronbach Alpha) .49–.71
Infant Behavioral Questionnaire (IBQ), Rothbart, 1981	96 items, ages 3–12 months, (some research for ages 2 weeks to 19.5 months), six factors: activity, distress to limits, fear, duration of orienting, smiling and laughter, soothability	Interobserver reliability range .45 (direction of orienting) to .60 (activity); Internal Consistency (Cronbach Alpha).67–.84
Infant Characteristic Questionnaire (ICQ) Bates, Freeland, Lounsbury, 1979	32 items, based on difficulty temperament factors, ages 4–7 months, 13–24 months, Four Factors: fussy/ difficult/demanding, unadaptable, persistent (later labeled resistant to control), unsociable	Interobserver reliability range .29 fussy/ difficult to .58, unpredictable; Internal Consistency (Cronbach Alpha) .39–.79
Infant Reactivity Inventory (IRI), O'Boyle & Rothbart, 1996	45 items, age 4 months, 1 factor: distress to sensory stimulation	Two studies of Internal Consistency (Cronbach Alpha) .84, .91

Instrument	Description	Reliability/Validity
Laboratory Temperament Assessment Battery (LAB-TAB), Goldsmith & Rothbart, 1988	Age 6 months, also used for infants/toddlers, designed for video-taped laboratory observation, scales: fearfulness, anger proneness, pleasure/joy, interest/persistence, activity level	unavailable
Laboratory Assessment of Infant Temperament (LTS), Matheny & Wilson, 1981	Ages 3, 6, 9, 12 months, laboratory videotaped assessment, factors: emotional tone, attentional activity, orientation to staff	Interobserver reliability.65 (orientation to staff) to .92 (emotional tone); Internal Consistency (Cronbach Alpha) .80–.91
Middle Childhood Temperament Questionnaire (MCTQ), Hegvik, McDevitt, & Carey, 1982	99 item parent rating scales, based on Thomas & Chess NYLS nine dimensions, ages 8–12; TTQ is companion teacher form	Coefficient alphas range .71-.87 (median r = .81); Test-retest over average 75 days .88; McClowry, Hegvik & Teglasi, 1993 found support for less than nine factors
Myers-Briggs Type Indicator® (MBTI); McCaulley, Myers, Quenk, & Hammer, 1998	Ages 14 and older, five forms [M/M self-score = 93 items (most commonly used); G/G self-score = 126 items; Q/Step II = 144 items for executive coaching uses], 7th grade reading level, item response theory scoring method, measures temperament on four dichotomous scales based on Jungian/Myers-Briggs theory and yielding 16 types: extroversion/introverted, sensing/intuitive, thinking/feeling, judging/perceiving, sample of 3,009 (for form M) over age 18, U.S. Census matched for gender, and ethnicity groups defined as black/white/other	New form M: Reliability (if continuous scores are used) is generally >.90, Four-week test-retest identifying type based on four dimensions is reported as 65% consistent. Convergent studies (e.g, MBTI & California Psychological Inventory or Big Five Personality domains); Confirmatory factor analysis supports four-factor model; Studies of brain activity patterns associated with temperament dimensions are also provided by authors.

(continued)

Table 3.1 (Continued)

Instrument	Description of the Test Psychometric Properties	Population/Format Reliability & Validity
New York Longitudinal Scales Adult Temperament Questionnaire (ATQ), Althanasou, 2003	Sample of 135 NYLS participants ages 20–30; the author notes as this norming sample is based on a longitudinal study, sample stratification by gender, ethnicity, and age is not provided	Concurrent validity studies are noted with earlier versions of the ATQ; author also notes high construct validity based on substantial body of research supporting the theory
Revised Infant Temperament Questionnaire (RITQ) McDevitt & Carey, 1978	95 items, completed by parents, ages 4–8 months, nine Thomas & Chess NYLS dimensions: activity, rhythmicity, approach, adaptability, threshold, mood, intensity, persistence, distractibility	Interobserver reliability .00 (Persistence) to .59 (Rythmicity)
Short Form of the Revised Infant Temperament Questionnaire (SITQ), Sanson et al., 1987	30 items, ages 4-8 months, 5 factors: approach, irritability, rhythmicity, activity-reactivity, cooperation-manageability	Internal Consistency (Cronbach Alpha) .57–76
Student Styles Questionnaire (SSQ), Oakland, Glutting, & Horton, 1996	Ages 8–17, four dichotomous scales from Jungian/Myers-Briggs theory. T-scores for extroversion/introverted, practical/imaginative, thinking/feeling, organized/flexible, self-report format, 69 items, ≤ 30 minutes. Sample of 7,902 students ages 8–17 stratified on age, sex, race/ethnicity, geographic region, & school type. Sample representative 1990 U.S. Census	7-month test-retest reliability coefficient: extroversion/introverted = .80; practical/imaginative = .67; thinking/feeling = .70; organized/ flexible = .74; convergent studies (e.g., SSQ & Children's Values), divergent studies (e.g., SSQ & achievement)

Teacher Temperament Questionnaire – Short Form (TTQ), Thomas & Chess, 1977; Keogh et al., 1982	23-item short form, based on factor analysis of the TTQ by Thomas & Chess; retained eight scales with three factors: task orientation, personal-social flexibility, & reactivity, MCTQ is the parent form	Based on factor analysis of TTQ 64 items resulting in retaining eight dimensions
Temperament Assessment Battery for Children-Revised (TABC-R), Martin & Bridger, 1999	48 items, modified form of TTQ, six of NYLS dimensions yielding three factors: activity, distractibility, persistence	Internal consistency range .82 – .86, test-retest over 6 months .79 and .85 (2 samples)
Temperament and Atypical Behavior Scales (TABS) Neisworth, Bagnato, Salvia, & Hunt, 1999	Ages 11 to 71 months, a screener is available as well as a 55-item full battery, yields t-scores on four scales; detached, hyper-sensitive/active, underreactive, and dysregulated, & temperament/ regulatory index score	All four scales Eigenvalues > 1, discriminant validity between children with/without disabilities supported, corrected split/half reliability = .95

Note: Tables compiled from manuals noted in the tables as well as Guerin, Gottfried, Oliver, & Thomas, 2003; Reynolds & Kamphaus, 1990, 2003; Singer & Zeskind, 2001; Teglasi, 1998)

Test Fairness and Diversity Issues

The purposes of temperament assessment include identifying risk factors for developmental outcomes, identifying personal strengths and limitations related to learning or personal interactions, identifying maladaptive temperament expressions to guide therapy, and career counseling. Fairness in evaluation is a critical consideration if instruments are to fulfill these purposes for all individuals equally well. A measure is considered fair when "examinees of equal standing with respect to the construct the test is intended to measure should on average earn the same test score, irrespective of group membership" (AERA, 1999). First, fairness requires that all examinees have comfortable, distraction free, and adequate testing environments. The evaluation setting should be selected by the examiner with these factors in mind. Equal opportunity for rapport-building and respect from the examiner, equal opportunity to demonstrate ability, and equal access to materials must be ensured. For temperament measures, practice items are not utilized, thus strict test security can guarantee that some participants do not have an unfair familiarity with items. Many of the standardization instructions for administration of instruments, including verbatim directions, query statements, gestures, and timing, are designed to facilitate fairness. Confidentiality also must be maintained. Validity measures including differential item functioning and predictive studies are designed to alert test developers to items that may be interpreted differently by groups or differing association patterns correlating with long-term outcomes. Some researchers argue, in comparison studies of test scores and criterion measures, the regression slopes and standard errors of estimate should be the same across groups (AERA, 1999).

DON'T FORGET

Fairness

Fairness should ensure that scores from persons of different groups who possess the same attribute to the same degree should obtain, on average, the same scores.

Additional considerations are required for persons from diverse linguistic backgrounds and persons with disabilities. Tests developed in English within the United States are most appropriate for administration to native English speakers within the United States. The International Test Commission (2000) provides guidelines for adaptations of measures in different linguistic or cultural settings. Although other countries also may be proficient in English, there are nuances in the language that differ (e.g., idioms) as well as cultural differences that can impact test scores. For bilingual students who are proficient in English, there can also be effects for language as particular types of vocabulary (e.g., technical terms) may be better developed within one language than the other. When examinees are not proficient in English, tests may be administered through bilingual examiners who are familiar with the culture and can translate test items. Caution is noted for translations in that not all languages have equivalent terms for some concepts or vocabulary. Utilizing interpreters when a bilingual examiner is not available may also be an option. There is the potential for examiner variables (i.e., changes in administration, nonverbal expressive cueing) that can effect scores and behaviors with interpreters. Therefore, training the interpreter in test item presentation guidelines would be beneficial. In marketing or research of test instruments to other countries, some have advocated for back-translation techniques (see Chapter Two) to reduce error in how individuals perceive the meaning of test items. Nonverbal forms of temperament rating scales are not feasible for persons with severe language deficits, thus temperament instruments may be inappropriate, especially self-report forms. In temperament evaluation with infants and toddlers, observational and parental report methods can provide important information that is not as dependent on the examinee's language skills as self-rating scales are. Accommodations and variations in test administration for persons with physical disabilities (e.g., hearing devices, assistive technology, reading items) may be warranted and should be acknowledged in evaluation reports.

CAUTION

Test Translations

When utilizing bilingual examiners, it should be noted that not all languages will have equivalent terms for specific vocabulary in test items. In addition, nonprofessional interpreters may inadvertently interject variations in wording, gestures, intonation, or expressions that effect test scores.

In Summary

A variety of assessment methods are available for temperament measurement including observations, questionnaires, surveys, and rating scales. Each offers both advantages and limitations that are considered when designing an evaluation or research project. Observations can be utilized in a variety of settings including laboratories that permit control of variables as well as measurement techniques for physiological responses. Limitations include observer reactivity and situational specificity of behavior effects. Questionnaires, checklists, surveys, and interviews can be presented in closed- or open-ended question formats. They can provide information on low frequency and covert behaviors as well as insights into relationships with family members. Limitations include the reciprocal nature of child/caregiver effects, parents limited comparison for behaviors of children at particular ages, as well as the expense of interviews conducted by professionals. Rating scales offer norm-reference data, self-report formats, but are subject to several forms of bias: halo effects, leniency/severity, central tendency, social desirability, and malingering.

National standards for test development including validity, reliability, as well as fairness are set by AERA, APA, and NCME. Sources of evidence for validity include test content, response processes, internal structure, and relationships to external variables. Reliability can be established through alternate form, test-retest, and internal coefficient analyses. Considerations in test fairness include equal respect, equal access, equal opportunity to demonstrate ability, and critical review of differential item functioning as well as predictive criteria. Language proficiency is an important consideration in test selection and accommodations may be provided for disabilities. However, most temperament measures offer few translated instruments and very limited assistive technology versions (e.g., computer administration).

 TEST YOURSELF

I. Which of the following are limitations of observation methods?
  (a) Observer reactivity and matrices coding
  (b) Central tendency and matrices coding
  (c) Situational specificity of behavior and observer reactivity
  (d) Teacher bias and situational specificity of behavior

2. According to Bates, all of the following are important considerations in questionnaires except:
  (a) Comprehension of instructions/questions
  (b) Age of the caregiver
  (c) Caregiver duress
  (d) Selective recall

3. Rating scales are subject to what forms of bias?
  (a) Halo, central tendency, social desirability
  (b) Central tendency, situational specificity of behavior
  (c) Observer reactivity, halo, leniency
  (d) Leniency-severity, five-factor model

4. Evidence for test validity includes:
  (a) Evidence based on external variables, test-retest
  (b) Internal structure, test content

(c) Response processes, number of test items

(d) True/false formats, internal structure

5. **Which of the following are evidence for reliability?**

(a) Expert review, response processes

(b) Test content, test-retest

(c) Parallel forms, selective recall

(d) Internal efficiency coefficients, test-retest

6. **Standardization procedures include:**

(a) Distraction-free testing environment, selective scale hierarchy

(b) Confidentiality statements, halo effects

(c) Verbatim instructions, standard query items

(d) Expert review, situational specificity

7. **Cautions to ensure fairness in testing may include all of the following except:**

(a) Random scale order administration

(b) Differential item functioning analyses

(c) Back-translation techniques

(d) Standardized administration

8. **Caution is warranted in using interpreters in test administration based on:**

(a) Age of the interpreter, language of the translation

(b) Breech of standardization rules, gender

(c) Difficulty of the test items, gender

(d) Nonverbal expressive cueing, breech of standardization rules

Answer: 1. c; 2. b; 3.a; 4. b; 5. d; 6. c; 7. a; 8. d

Four

INTERPRETING TEMPERAMENT MEASURES

TRAITS VERSUS STATES AND STABILITY OF TEMPERAMENT

The beginning of this chapter will discuss issues related to interpreting temperament measures in lieu of the differences between states and traits, as well as scores that are perceived as best interpreted as continuous rather than dichotomous. Each topic has implications for how temperament data are utilized. States are defined as general moods and demeanors that are subject to quick and frequent change, sometimes within a matter of minutes. States are transient, short-term, and highly dependent on current circumstances, environments, and events. One might describe them as snapshots that describe feelings at a moment in time. In fact, they may change instantly, when the individual is removed from the event or stimulus. They are not highly predictable either, as differing circumstances can elicit the same moods and multiple exposures to similar circumstances can elicit very differing moods.

In contrast, traits are distinguishing characteristics and enduring attributes that constitute consistent response patterns over time. Traits may actually interpret the states, as in the example of a trait of optimism that interprets most circumstances in a positive manner. Cognitive behavioral therapy is thought to change behaviors in this manner, by changing the automatic attributions and thought patterns that influence responses to daily circumstances. Traits are also thought to have a biological basis as in the examples of height and weight. The identification of traits has evolved through years of research and is based on scientific methods including multivariate factor analysis. The level of a trait can be measured quantitatively in relationship to another person's rating of the same trait, demonstrating individual differences. They are thought to have causal connections as research has demonstrated relationships between specific traits and long-term outcomes (Butcher, 2002). In addition, traits are moderately stable over time as demonstrated by test-retest reliability studies. Evidence from the continuality and stability of temperament was reviewed in Chapter Two. Unlike states, which are situation-specific, there is evidence that traits are cross-situational, and this is established through observational studies as well as multiple informant ratings that observe persons in differing context with differing demands (Shapiro & Skinner, 1990). As noted by Strelau and Angleitner (1991, pp. 349–355), researchers have identified numerous personal traits related to temperament, and there are over 25 trait-based adult assessment measures (see Rapid Reference 4.1). Some of the measures are utilized for research purposes that include measurement of physiological arousal states variables. Trait-based measures have the advantage of being able to indicate the degree to which a trait is present and with stratified norms provide a comparison to other individuals. This type of measurement is very important in establishing pathology.

> # CAUTION
> ....
> ### State versus Trait
>
> The terms state and trait are not synonymous. Traits are attributes with an enduring pattern over time and across circumstances. They can influence temporary mood states as traits denote perspectives in cognitive and behavioral approaches to interpreting circumstances and events.

Understanding the difference between a state and trait is also important for how interventions, treatment, or personal growth goals are approached. Given their stability, traits are not changed easily, and in times of duress or surprise, persons may revert to innate qualities. Therefore, if temperament traits are the subject of change, individuals will need to know the process takes some time and effort.

INTERPRETING CONTINUOUS VERSUS DICHOTOMOUS VARIABLES

As noted previously, many temperament measures, particularly those for early childhood or those based on biobehavioral models of arousal, are interpreted based on strengths or deficits of traits. In fact, some authors point out that one of the purposes of assessment, particularly continuous variables, is to provide a norm-reference that ensures enough variability to accurately identify subgroups within a population (Teglasi, 1998). However, the psychological temperament type theories propose interpretation based on a prototypal model. The instruments are designed with forced-choice items that sort individuals into dichotomous categories. This approach does not interpret scores in lieu of high or low qualities but rather which category responses are indicated. The clarity indexes on the MBTI are interpreted as how "clearly a respondent prefers one of two opposite poles of a dichotomy" rather than an abundance or lack of the trait (Myers et al.,

≡ *Rapid Reference 4.1*

Additional Temperamental Traits and Adult Measures Across Theories

Strelau and Angleitner (1991) identified 80 possible adult temperament traits across theories and assessment instruments. These are some of the additional temperamental traits that are not discussed in major instruments reviewed in this text.

Additional Temperamental Traits: active avoidance, ascendance, boredom susceptibility, dominance, ergonicity, experience seeking, plasticity, recurrence, social tempo, solidity, trait-pleasure, and venturesomeness.

Additional Adult Temperament Assessment Measures: Adolescent Temperament List (ATL), Affect Intensity Measure (AIM), Barratt Impulsiveness Scale (BIS), Gray-Wilson Personality Questionnaire (GWPQ), Guildford-Zimmermann Temperament Survey (GZTS), I_7 Impulsiveness Questionnaire (I_7 Questionnaire), Irritability and Emotional Susceptibility Scales (IESS), Marke-Nyman-Temperamentskala (MNT), Mehrabian Temperament Scale (MTS), Structure of Temperament Questionnaire (STQ), The Reactivity Scale (RS), Sensation-Seeking Scale Form IV (SSS IV), Sensation Seeking Scale Form V (SSS V), Stimulus Screening Questionnaire (SSQ), Strelau Temperament Inventory – Revised (STI-R), Temperament Inventory (TI), Temporal Traits Inventory (TTI), Thurstone Temperament Schedule (TTS), and the Vando Reducing-Augmenting Scale (RAS).

1998, p. 5). Millon (1990, p. 349) notes, "a type simply becomes a superordinate category that subsumes and integrates psychologically covariant traits, which in turn represent a set of correlated habits, which in their turn stand for a response displayed in a variety of situations." He also noted, "types are higher-order syntheses of lower-order dimensional traits; they encompass a wider scope of generality. For certain purposes, it may be useful to narrow attention to specific traits; in other circumstances, a more inclusive level of integration may be appropriate" (p. 350). An example of the premise of adjusting level of interpretation to meet the individual's needs is noted in Rapid Reference 4.2.

Categorical approach also is applied in psychiatry, psychology, and medicine where persons either meet criteria for a diagnosis or do not meet the criteria. The use of categories provides clinicians a quick taxonomy and a common nomenclature for communicating the profile of individuals succinctly. In the field of medicine, patient lab results and other symptomology indicators are often interpreted to meet diagnosis criteria when a critical mass of data support a uniform pattern that are predictive of an illness trajectory and prognosis (e.g., diabetes). Although, it is acknowledged that individuals will manifest symptoms and outcomes somewhat differently. In applying this principle to a mental health diagnoses example, an adolescent either has a diagnosis of Oppositional Defiant Disorder (ODD) or does not. All teenagers are not perceived as possessing high, medium, or low ODD characteristics.

Categorical interpretations of prototypal temperament assessments are not intended to imply homogeneity, as there are many items within each scale and persons may endorse varying combinations of those items, yet scores still represent a preponderance of preferences for the set of attributes or behaviors representing that trait. Returning to the mental health example of ODD, there are eight symptoms in this diagnosis, and to meet criteria an individual only has to exhibit four (ODD criteria are noted in the next paragraph). DSM symptom clusters are based on extensive literature reviews, prior analyses of large data sets, and field trials of the criteria providing evidence that although all symptoms may not be presented by one individual they are covariant (APA, 2000; Joyce & Dempsey, 2009).

313.81 Oppositional Defiant Disorder: A. A pattern of negativistic, hostile, and defiant behavior lasting at least six months, during which four (or more) of the following are present: (1) often loses temper, (2) often argues with adults, (3) often actively defies or refuses to comply with adults' requests or rules, (4) often deliberately annoys people, (5) often blames others for his or her mistakes or misbehavior, (6) is often touchy or easily annoyed by others, (7) is often angry and resentful, (8) is often spiteful or vindictive. B. The disturbance in behavior causes clinically significant impairment in social, academic, or occupational functioning. C. The behaviors do not occur exclusively during the course of a Psychotic or Mood Disorder. D. Criteria are not met for Conduct Disorder, and, if the individual is age 18 year or older, criteria are not met for Antisocial Personality Disorder (APA, 2000, p. 102).

Therefore, it is possible that two persons with an ODD diagnosis may not share a single symptom in common; however, each has a behavior repertoire that is consistent with maladaptive oppositional and defiant functioning. In addition, the behavior pattern is related to a core set of causal factors and impairment outcomes. Frances and Widiger (1986, p. 251) provided the following explanation for use of categories in diagnostic procedures.

A number of practical implications follow from a prototypic orientation. Diagnostic categories are defined by polythetic (multiple and optional) criteria sets rather than monothetic criteria sets (that is, membership will require only the satisfaction of five of eight criteria and not five of five). This means that the diagnosis can be met by many (in this case 93) different combinations of individual criteria items. A measure of prototypicality for each patient can be established by simply identifying the number of criteria items possessed by the patient, with the patient who meets all eight of eight being considered the most prototypic.

As also noted by Frances and Widiger (1986), emerging prototypes can combine categorical and dimensional aspects. "A prototypal model also acknowledges that some symptoms or combinations of symptoms are more important to the diagnosis than others and should therefore be given greater weight. One can do this by having the essential symptoms be necessary while the rest are optional (p.251)." As noted above in the ODD example, criteria A, B, C, and D must also be met in addition to the 4 of 8 symptoms. The necessity of A, B, C, D criteria are given a greater emphasis than any of the eight symptoms singularly and some describe this as a hybrid model.

In many ways categorical interpretations permit a taxonomy for contextualizing the multi-faceted complexities of human behavior. This difference in

---

≋ Rapid Reference 4.2

Student Styles Questionnaire Interpretation Options

Eight Basic Types

Extroversion-Introverted, Practical-Imaginative, Thinking-Feeling, Flexible-Organized

Four Keirseian Combinations

Practical-Organized, Practical-Flexible, Imaginative-Thinking, Imaginative-Feeling

Sixteen Style Combinations

Extroversion-Practical-Thinking-Organized; Extroversion-Practical-Thinking-Flexible

Extroversion-Practical-Feeling-Organized, Extroversion-Practical-Feeling-Flexible

Extroversion-Imaginative-Thinking-Organized, Extroversion-Imaginative-Thinking-Flexible

Extroversion-Imaginative-Feeling-Organized, Extroversion-Imaginative-Feeling-Flexible

Introverted-Practical-Thinking-Organized, Introverted-Practical-Thinking-Flexible

Introverted-Practical-Feeling-Organized, Introverted-Practical-Feeling-Flexible

Introverted-Imaginative-Thinking-Organized, Introverted-Imaginative-Thinking-Flexible

Introverted-Imaginative-Feeling-Organized, Introverted-Imaginative-Feeling-Flexible how temperament trait measurements are interpreted is especially important as dichotomous variables that yield types are not necessarily intended to represent indicators of pathology or mental health wellness (Myers et al., 1998, p. 4–5). Test instrument authors provide guidelines on interpretation for their respective measures and are an important reference, as some encourage more than one perspective for interpretation. As an example, the SSQ may be interpreted in three ways (see Rapid Reference 4.2); the eight basic types, the four Keirseian combinations, or the 16 style combinations (Oakland, Glutting, & Horton, 1996).

Some researchers have proposed hybrid models that include both dichotomous variables resulting in categorical decisions combined with continuous variables that specify severity of key symptoms. This approach emphasizes that some symptoms may be more influential in predicting outcomes. This type of model is evident in many diagnoses of the DSM-IV-TR that have subtype specifiers and feature designations. The hybrid principle is not prevalent in temperament assessment interpretation at this time.

In Summary

In some theories traits are perceived as dimensional biophysical dispositions with only one end of the scale having clinical applications (Millon, 1990). This is the interpretive perspective of many of the early childhood and biobehavioral measures (e.g., attention span/distractibility). Viewed through the lens of temperament traits as curvilinear, both ends of the spectrum on a dimension represent more risk for pathology and/or if pathology is present it is exhibited in a manner consistent with the extreme preference. As Jung noted in his clinical observations, extreme introverts were more likely to present pathology as depression or in internalizing manners. Categorical perspectives interpret clusters of traits representing dimensions that are indicative of enduring behavioral patterns and thinking perspectives. This paradigm acknowledges the heterogeneity of categories while still maintaining the integrity of the categories' schemas as predictable dispositions. Traits are perceived as neutral, each representing strengths that are adaptive. Opposing traits may be less prevalent and an area to cultivate. It is difficult to predict the future architecture of temperament theory and if that may evolve to include more hybrid models (e.g., succinctly combining dimensional and categorical through weighted item interpretations).

BEST PRACTICES IN MULTI-FACETED ASSESSMENT

Assessments can serve multiple purposes, and the approach to selecting methods and test batteries will be guided by the (1) presenting reasons for initiating the evaluation, (2) theoretical orientation and training of the examiner, (3) hypotheses that develop during assessment, (4) any diagnoses that emerge, (5) information needed to design intervention or treatments, and (6) the requirements of the intended audience for the findings and final report. Each of these components are discussed below.

(1) Referrals for evaluations can be self-generated by individuals who wish to better understand their own characteristics, strengths, and weaknesses in an effort to enhance their own performance. Career counseling can be an example of a positive psychology application. Positive psychology orientations seek to use scientific principles in helping to identify the virtue in persons and foster those characteristics. Individuals may also seek evaluations as a result of duress if they are experiencing mental health, coping, or interpersonal distress. Examples may include families with parent-child conflicts or marriage partners experiencing discord. Evaluations also may be prompted by referrals between professionals who are concerned about a patient or client's functioning and impairment. These types of referrals are more common in mental health settings and based on a medical model that identifies deficits for treatment. Psychiatric, psychological, counseling, and rehabilitation evaluations are possible examples. These can be self-referred but also may be involuntary. The majority of psychoeducational referrals are prompted by school personnel out of concern for poor academic achievement or behavioral and social-emotional issues that are negatively impacting performance. Children and adolescents rarely self-refer. Assessments may also be generated through the legal system and related to custody, abuse/neglect, or adjudication issues. These are a few examples of evaluation purposes and of course the questions to be answered by each will be significantly different. Temperament data can inform aspects of each of these types of referrals; however, that decision is reserved for the examiner's professional judgment and the unique circumstances of the evaluation.

(2) The theoretical orientation and training of the examiner will be a deciding factor in which instruments and types of data are acquired. Training standards are set by many national organizations such as the Accreditation Council of Graduate Medical Education, American Psychological Association, Council for the Accreditation of Counseling and Related Educational Programs, Council

on Rehabilitation Education, and the National Association of School Psychologists. Each field will reference broad medical and psychological principles; however, the focus of practice will be specific to the populations and needs they serve. Training programs within each field also will vary as to concentration on theoretical constructs and related assessment measures taught. Therefore, the selection of specific instruments will be guided by the expertise and training of the individual practitioner. Ethical practice also requires that service providers remain current on developments in their field after initial training, and this should include acquiring updated training on new instruments as they emerge and limiting selection of instruments to those demonstrating sound psychometric properties. Best practices dictate rigorous consideration for the fairness and cultural diversity impact of assessment results as well (AERA, 1999; Merrill, 2008).

(3) Based on clinical intake interviews and initial referral data, examiners will generate hypotheses about the patient, client, or student's needs and design an initial evaluation battery. However, as data are collected other questions and needs may become evident that require additional measures, and this also will guide the examiner's subsequent choices of assessment instruments. If the new questions are outside the training of the practitioner, referrals to others with that specialized training are initiated. Therefore, it is important that professionals not only have expertise in their own field but also have awareness of the services in related fields and a willingness to collaborate.

(4) When a preponderance of assessment data appear to support a diagnosis, supplemental instruments and often syndrome specific or narrow assessment tools are used to confirm symptom criteria are met. Additional measures also may be utilized to rule out other disorders. Assessment choices may consider data sources that document an initial baseline for comparison later in evaluating intervention or treatment outcomes.

(5) Ultimately, assessment should inform services that will be provided and thus clarity and specificity in delineating exact points of intervention or treatment is required. This may require prioritizing needs to determine sequence of treatment focus or discussing a hierarchy of skills to denote entry intervention points (Batsche, Castillo, Dixon, & Forde, 2008; Christ, 2008).

(6) Lastly, the requirements of the intended audience for the findings also will influence assessment components and the final report structure. As examples, evaluation supporting diagnoses often must delineate specific symptoms as well as their severity and impact. Diagnoses can provide access to reimbursement sources. Evaluations supporting school interventions may be required to document state eligibility components for access to special education. Some adult temperament assessments coupled with training workshops can provide certifications in leadership and team-building skills. Forensic evaluation components may be dictated by local, state, and federal agencies.

DON'T FORGET

Assessment Battery Design

Selection of assessment instruments should always be based on the referral question(s), utilizing measures with sound psychometric properties, and inform treatment, intervention, or positive psychology goals.

In general, best practices for a thorough assessment requires a multi-faceted approach. Data should review multiple traits, utilizing multiple sources, and multiple methods across multiple settings and periods of time (AERA, 1999; McConaughy & Ritter, 2008). The purposes of these provisions are to ensure that conclusions are not drawn prematurely based on insufficient information, to avoid potential one-rater biases, and also to establish duration, intensity, and impact of some traits. Multiple traits may include several temperament dimensions. Multiple sources may include a comparison between father/mother or self-ratings and interviews, if applicable. Multiple methods in temperament assessment may consist of a cross comparison between observations, interviews, and rating scales. Observational and interview methods are particularly suited for establishing the consistency of temperament qualities over time and in multiple settings.

Once data is collected it must be integrated with consideration for both convergent and divergent information (Beutler & Groth-Marnat, 2003). The integrative approach is designed to provide a more comprehensive understanding of the individual within the context of how he/she behaves in his/her daily life in response to environmental demands. In considering temperament for very young children, multiple informant ratings scales (e.g., two caregivers) that are similar provide stronger evidence based on aggregation principle. Ratings that are very different may alert examiners to rater bias or differing demands across settings.

The culminating product from an evaluation will be communicating results in a therapeutic manner through both written and oral formats (Sattler & Hoge, 2006). Components of a well-written report include the referring concern, question, or purpose. This is typically followed by a history based on interviews with parents and caregivers, teachers, or the client. Background information is important for several reasons. It provides health and developmental information that may be relevant to disabilities, diagnoses, medications, cognitive abilities, and language development. Social-emotional history can reveal family factors, interests, goals, motivations, attachments, relationship interaction patterns, cultural impact factors, and prior treatment or interventions (both effective and ineffective). Personal accomplishment history will review learning difficulties, achievements, attendance patterns, educational attainment, employment history, and criminal incidents. All of these elements provide a more holistic view of the individual and context for temperament impact on their functioning (Lichtenberger, Mather, Kaufman, & Kaufman, 2004). One caution in gathering history data is to weigh what is pertinent to the evaluation and avoid unnecessarily invasive questions (e.g., income, intimacy details), omitting any embarrassing information that has no relevance to the purpose of the evaluation or intervention. Following the history, the core report will provide assessment data, diagnostic impressions, and end with recommendations. It is important that the report avoids unnecessary technical terms and communicates clearly to persons who may be less familiar with assessment. Some instruments offer multiple computer-generated analyses reviews which are adapted for specific readers (e.g., teacher, parent, adolescent). These overviews differ in how technical the information is and emphasize the applied aspects of assessment.

Oral communication of results can be equally important and are often provided as a psychoeducational or counseling component of the evaluation. Guidelines for oral communication include providing candid information with sensitivity to cultural factors and the well-being of the client. For parents of children with significant temperament risk factors this can be especially important, as parents will need strategies to improve interactions and also will need to know potential long-term outcomes if traits are interfering with appropriate functioning. Laypersons typically do not understand statistical scores (e.g., standard scores, t-scores) and thus categorical descriptions or percentiles may be more meaningful. Assessment results conversations are most productive if the conversation is reciprocal and individuals can ask for clarification or add their opinions. Adequate time to help clients process the new information shared also is important, and some individuals may not be ready to accept all results immediately, thus the opportunity for follow-up calls or questions later may be helpful. Recommendations and interpretations regarding results should always remain within the evidence supported, not predict beyond the data, and be linked to applied solutions. In addition, communicating results is an opportunity to educate persons and also may be therapeutic if presented with a best practices counseling approach (Kamphaus, 2001).

DON'T FORGET

Oral Communication of Assessment Results

Tips for verbally communicating assessment results include utilizing, sensitivity, cultural awareness, forthright information, nontechnical terms, adequate time for processing, and an emphasis on therapeutic outcomes.

🐟 TEST YOURSELF 🐟

1. **Mood states may be defined as:**
   (a) Moderately stable, cross-situational personal attributes that persist over time
   (b) Biologically based genetic predispositions for behavior
   (c) Temporary, transient moods that are dependent on the circumstances
   (d) Quantitatively measurable with multivariate factor analysis

2. **Traits are defined as:**
   (a) Moderately stable, cross-situational personal attributes that persist over time
   (b) Unstable, cross-situational personal qualities that change with circumstances
   (c) Temporary, transient moods that are dependent on the circumstances
   (d) Highly stable pathology that can easily be changed

3. **Which of the following statements are *false* regarding continuous variables?**
   (a) Can be quantitatively measured
   (b) Provide a norm comparison
   (c) They are thought to have causal connections
   (d) They are interpreted only as categories

4. **Which of the following statements is *false* regarding instruments measuring categorical variables?**
   (a) Often utilize dichotomous, forced-choice items
   (b) Sort persons into group designations
   (c) May utilize Likert scale formats
   (d) They are interpreted only as linear, quantitative scores

5. **Ergonicity, recurrence, and social tempo are:**
   (a) Relevant to interpreting temperament in relation to Freud's ego concepts
   (b) Items measured on introversion scales
   (c) Temperamental qualities in some adult temperament measures
   (d) Related to the temperament intervention therapies

6. **Which of the following statements is *false* regarding report history information?**
   (a) History data can assist in understanding behavior and traits within a social context
   (b) All information gathered during assessment must be documented in the report
   (c) Social and emotional history may provide understanding of early attachment difficulties
   (d) Employment and achievement history may be relevant to temperament applications

7. **Which of the following most thoroughly demonstrates best practices for reports?**
   (a) Include a thorough history that denotes relevant medical, social-emotional, and achievement factors
   (b) Data should be presented in concise terms that are understandable to the recipient
   (c) Providing the referral questions or evaluation purpose statements
   (d) All of the above and recommendations relevant to applying temperament data

8. **Best practices tips for verbal communication of results include:**
   (a) Employing sensitivity and cultural awareness as well as encouraging questions
   (b) Candid information with an emphasis on positive applications
   (c) a, b, and d
   (d) Ensuring adequate time for discussion and opportunity for follow-up

Answers: 1. c; 2. a; 3. d; 4. d; 5. c; 6. b; 7. d; 8. c.

Five

STRENGTHS AND LIMITATIONS OF TEMPERAMENT ASSESSMENT

TEMPERAMENT MEASUREMENT AS A STRENGTHS-BASED ASSESSMENT METHOD

As noted in the previous chapter, in addition to identifying traits that are problematic, temperament theories can also be utilized as a strengths-based assessment. From this perspective, the focus of interpretation and counseling individuals regarding their temperament is related to empowering and emphasizing the utility of traits. Existing traits are perceived as strengths that should be nurtured to help the person realize her/his potential. Epstein and Sharma (1998, p. 3) provide the following definition of strengths-based assessment, the measurement of those emotional and behavioral skills, competencies, and characteristics that create a sense of personal accomplishment; contribute to satisfying relationships with family members, peers, and adults; enhance one's ability to deal with adversity and stress; and promote one's personal, social, and academic development.

The practitioner through analysis, reports, and psychoeducational techniques acknowledges the adaptive applications of particular attributes and embraces the value of human differences. The concentration on tolerance and understanding of temperament diversity is particularly important to reciprocal interaction orientations. Applications include parent-child therapy with a goodness-of-fit model and temperament workshops for group dynamics in the workplace. Although some instruments include one or more positive categories (e.g., easy temperament pattern, resilients), others consider all of the categories to be constructive (e.g., MBTI, MMTIC, SSQ). The philosophy of interpretation is usually included in the manual as authors note their intended purpose as noted below:

"The MBTI is different from typical trait approaches to personality that measure variation along a continuum; instead, the Indicator seeks to identify a respondent's status on either one or the other of two opposite personality

DON'T FORGET

Strengths-based Assessment

Strengths-based assessments design reports and communication with a positive orientation, acknowledging competencies, positive attributes, accomplishments, and character assets that empower the individual and promote a positive outlook toward personal development.

categories, both of which are regarded as neutral in relation to emotional health, intellectual functioning, and psychological adaptation. The MBTI dichotomies are concerned with basic attitudes and mental functions that enter into almost every aspect of behavior; therefore the scope of practical applications is broad rather than narrow and includes quite varied aspects of living" (Myers et al., 1998, p. 5).

UNDERSTANDING INDIVIDUAL DIFFERENCES IN NON-PATHOLOGICAL LANGUAGE

There are a number of positive outcomes thought to be inherent in the strengths-based assessment approach especially when affirming language communication's positive regard and expectations. Strengths-based assessment strives to avoid pejorative terminology and stigmatizing labels that can be perceived as negative. It acknowledges that diversity can enrich rather than detract from interactions. A positive orientation can also have a reciprocal effect by changing how others perceive those with differing qualities, in effect teaching tolerance and maintaining positive expectations. This premise is related to the literature on self-fulfilling prophecy, also called the Pygmalion effect. Robert Merton (1968), a sociologist, coined the phrase in a collection of his essays, *Social Theory and Social Structure*. It denotes that when others are given expectations for an individual, they react in kind and the perception effects subsequent actions to the point that the expectation becomes true. It can work to facilitate positive outcomes based on positive expectations or conversely eliciting negative outcomes based on negative expectations. This was originally applied in organizational psychology and is also supported by numerous studies in the educational psychology literature related to teacher expectations of students (Rist, 2000).

Strengths-based communication can also improve motivation as it values the contribution of each person and acknowledges competencies resulting in self-esteem building. There is empirical support to suggest that merely hearing positive affirmations regarding one's own competency and value can improve self-esteem (Centers, 1999). This type of acknowledgment may also free persons to try developing opposing traits when they are perceived as an expansion of their capabilities rather than with negative connotations. To accomplish these goals clinicians may phrase goals in terms of personal enhancement or social development strategies. In vocational and rehabilitation counseling the strengths-based perspective can serve to encourage individuals who are venturing significant changes in their lives as all types of temperament are perceived to have a niche for success.

> # DON'T FORGET
>
> ## Self-fulfilling Prophecy Principle
>
> The self-fulfilling prophecy explains that individual outcomes can be influenced by the expectations of others, as those expectations result in particular actions and reactions that in turn shape the individual's behaviors.

MALLEABILITY OF TEMPERAMENT QUALITIES

As reviewed in Chapter One, temperament qualities are noted to have a biological basis. Thus, they are thought to be more resistant to change than other aspects of behavior (e.g., diet, exercise) might be. Therefore, when clinicians do think changes are advised, a more comprehensive approach to developing new traits or changing others may be warranted. McClowry (1995, 1998) provides some guidance on strategies to intervene utilizing temperament constructs. She suggests three approaches—promotion, prevention, and treatment—depending on the individual's needs and the orientation of the assessment measure.

Promotion refers to developing competency, self-esteem, and confidence. The targeted goals are to increase harmony in relationships, enhance personal or parental skills, and personal growth. Approaches can include workshops, individual counseling and discussion formats, and the clinician typically serves as a facilitator or collaborator. When promotion strategies are applied to interactions, it is recommended to acquire temperament data for each person (e.g., parent-child, work team). The promotion strategy is not deemed appropriate when there are open hostilities, mental health concerns, marital discord, or other significant negative life events, as those needs should be addressed separately. The second approach, prevention, is designed for persons who are at risk for psychological well-being. It may

> # DON'T FORGET
>
> ## Approaches to Temperament Intervention
>
> Don't forget McClowry's three approaches to temperament intervention: promotion, prevention, and treatment.

include children with emerging behavioral issues or adults who are experiencing significant stressors. The goal is to decrease risk factors and prevent negative impact. In prevention, sessions may need to be more intense, longer in duration, and individualized. As persons with high-risk factors also tend to have other life stressors (e.g., poverty, health problems), it is important to consider the individual's life context and the complex interactions of needs. McClowry's third approach is treatment, and this is intended for persons with identified maladaptive behaviors and/or mental health diagnoses. A more comprehensive approach is required in treatment including an understanding of symptoms, alignment to temperament traits, and any personal limitations (e.g., disabilities) that may impede progress.

Need for a Unified Definition of Temperament

Thus far this text has discussed a number of temperament theories illustrating the range of instruments and varied interpretation perspectives. Although this diversity in temperament provides clinicians with many options in assessment and intervention, it also provides some dilemmas for research. Unlike other psychological concepts that have narrowed over time to distill a commonly accepted set of variables, temperament has evolved to include a plethora of constructs. In addition, broad approaches to temperament vary across the age span, including which traits are measured. As an illustration, historically in intelligence research, the theoretical base started with dozens of constructs and then over time many major instruments adopted a three stratum framework (i.e., Carroll-Cattell-Horn; general "g," broad, narrow) with instruments measuring 5–7 constructs (e.g., g; Gf, Gc, Gv, Ga, Gsm, Glr, Gs). These constructs remain the same across the lifespan and some instruments can be utilized from early childhood to advanced age facilitating longitudinal research.

In contrast, temperament theory has evolved along three continuums: early childhood biobehavioral theories with an emphasis on physiologically measured arousal reactions, youth/adult survey measures based on up to 80 dimensional traits (see Rapid Reference 4.1), and categorical psychological temperament types that span from ages 8 to adulthood. In addition, there is overlap between some temperament qualities in personality theory (e.g., extroversion "super trait"). The overlap in definitions between personality and temperament, as well as the broad number of temperament traits, adds further complexity to research in this area (Strelau & Angleitner, 1991). Thus, the need for continued research with the potential to more succinctly define temperament as well as provide a unified set of constructs and empirical support for direct interventions is needed.

Psychometric Properties of Temperament Measures

In addition to wide variation in temperament definitions, varying theories regarding which traits constitute temperament, and multiple forms of interpretation, the basic psychometric properties of measures also are wide ranging. In reference to the intelligence example before, IQ measures utilize standard scores on a normal distribution curve that are all interpreted similarly. This facilitates a number of cross-comparison correlational studies including divergent and convergent validity as well as longitudinal research. Whereas longitudinal studies with temperament (e.g., Fullerton study) have required multiple temperament measures, with varying constructs at particular ages and varying types of data and scores. In addition, temperament scores are found in a variety of formats (e.g., observation codes, survey tallies, rating scale t-scores, and categorical descriptors). Each of these methods is noted to have some limitations, and the differences in measurement scores do not facilitate cross-comparisons. Therefore, as dictated by best practice in any area of assessment, it is incumbent upon the examiner to carefully review the psychometric properties of each measure utilized in assessment.

The following is a list of suggested limitations and areas for continued psychometric refinement in temperament measures.

- Categorical interpretations can be misinterpreted as discrete entities, and there are far fewer types than are represented among observed behavior patterns in the general population (Millon, 1990).
- The validity and reliability of some instruments is considered inadequate, as well as the norm samples and stratification of samples (Goldsmith & Rieser-Danner, 1990; Shapiro & Skinner, 1990).
- Some parent questionnaires provide the situation context for questions, whereas others require parents to answer based on generalized behavior over time. These two types of questionnaires should not be assumed to elicit comparable data (Goldsmith & Rieser-Danner, 1990).
- Parent interview assessments require retrospective reporting, which can be distorted by memory, subjective judgment, and parental motivation (Shapiro & Skinner, 1990).
- Questionnaires and rating scales (parent and teacher) are subject to many forms of rater bias; however, most do not have consistency, lie scales, or other validity indices to check for bias (Goldsmith & Rieser-Danner, 1990).
- There is limited respondent agreement (e.g., mother-father average .40. 60) (Bates, 1989; Goldsmith & Rieser-Danner, 1990).

- Parents have a limited norm sample reference for judging behaviors, and this impacts parent rating scores (Teglasi, 1998).
- Observational instruments are limited to situational specificity of behavior and may not represent typical parent-child interactions (Merrill, 2008).
- Few measures have extensive research across ethnicity and culture (e.g., differential item functioning, factor analysis), and constructs as well as interpretation of items may differ.
- Many cross-cultural studies have used direct translation methods rather than back-translation and/or factor analyses to verify consistency of constructs.

 TEST YOURSELF

1. **The strengths-based model focuses on communicating assessment results that:**
   - (a) Reflect high scores first and then denote low scores and deficits
   - (b) Identify pathology and maladaptive patterns for rehabilitation
   - (c) Provide a positive orientation, acknowledging competencies and positive attributes
   - (d) Denote areas of personal development that need to be strengthened

2. **McClowry's three suggested approaches to using temperament for intervention are:**
   - (a) General, broad, narrow
   - (b) Universal, supplemental, intensive
   - (c) Small group standard, small group protocol, individualized
   - (d) Promotion, prevention, and treatment

3. **Merton's term, self-fulfilling prophecy, refers to which social phenomenon?**
   - (a) Social outcomes are entirely dependent on the individual's temperament
   - (b) Repeated self-talk produces better social skills
   - (c) Perceptions create actions and reactions that facilitate the expected outcome
   - (d) Outcomes cannot be strongly influenced by others' suggestions

4. **The call for more research to further define temperament theory is based on:**
   - (a) Range of constructs, differing interpretation paradigms, lack of continuity over lifespan
   - (b) Lack of diversity in theories across ages

(continued)

(c)   Need for more assessment measures

(d)   Lack of trait constructs and flexibility in interpretation paradigms

5. **Noted limitations of parent/teacher ratings scales include all of the following except:**

(a)   Low respondent correlations

(b)   Subject to rater biases and few have validity indices for bias

(c)   Parents have a limited norm sample comparisons, other than their own children

(d)   Teachers have very limited norm sample comparisons for children's behaviors

6. **Noted limitations of categorical interpretation include which of the following:**

(a)   Categories may be misinterpreted as discrete entities

(b)   They cannot be interpreted in a strengths-based assessment model

(c)   There are far more types than are represented in the general population

(d)   They over-identify pathology and maladaptive behaviors

7. **Limitations of observational instruments include:**

(a)   May be limited to situational specificity

(b)   May not sample typical parent and child interactions

(c)   a and b

(d)   None of the above

8. **Limitations of temperament measures utilizing parent interview include:**

(a)   They under-identify pathology and adaptive behaviors

(b)   Subjective judgment, memory distortion effects, retrospective reporting

(c)   Generally reflect overly positive attributes

(d)   They underrate social skills

Answers: 1. c; 2. d; 3. c; 4. a; 5. d; 6.a; 7. c; 8, b

Six

CLINICAL APPLICATIONS OF TEMPERAMENT ASSESSMENT

Assessment can serve a number of important functions, including (1) informing knowledge of human psychological processes as discussed in Chapters One and Two, (2) providing a common nomenclature for diagnoses and differentiation of pathology as sample reports in Chapter Seven demonstrate, and (3) identifying intervention needs or enhancing personal performance, which will be discussed in this chapter. Each of these functions makes a critical contribution, and they are interdependent as research informs diagnoses and intervention, whereas diagnoses and intervention further delineate directions for research and validate its applied value to the communities that fund the research. The first section of this chapter will focus on applications of temperament interpretation to pedagogy, which primarily serves kindergarten through 12th grade students and has some implications for postsecondary as well. Psychoeducation techniques are more typically applied within a counseling context and thus are discussed in section two. Counseling therapy applications include addressing parent-child dynamics, career planning, and personal adjustment also are reviewed.

APPLICATIONS IN PEDAGOGY

In discussing applications of temperament assessment to direct educational services, strategies may be applied to instructional methods, classroom environment variables, and small group or individual strategies coaching. Personnel involved in initiating these efforts may include a wider range of professionals (e.g., administrators, teachers, counselors, curriculum specialists, social workers, behavioral analysts, school psychologists, and tutors) based on the specific goals targeted. To better understand potential opportunities for applying temperament-related strategies it is important to review common school systemic functions related to instruction and intervention development, especially for readers less familiar with school infrastructure.

Curriculum Planning

Within school districts, at both the county administrative level and each local school, there are individuals responsible for designing curriculum master plans that align with standards designated by both national and state guidelines. States typically provide very detailed academic skill goals for each grade level from pre-kindergarten through 12th grade that must be demonstrated. This process involves leadership teams often comprised of principals, assistant principals, and curriculum specialists (also called instructional coordinators) who have additional training and expertise in organizational systems management, leadership, curriculum, and instruction methods. Sometimes additional specialized personnel may also consult with the leadership team (e.g., reading specialists, school psychologists, counselors). In addition, state achievement outcome data from all schools are systematically collected, reported, and monitored for effectiveness in meeting those goals.

A greater emphasis on standardized school-wide testing to access schools' effectiveness has been prompted in part by an educational reform act in 2001 from the U.S. Congress, the No Child Left Behind (NCLB) Public Law – 107–110, 107th Congress (NCLB, 2002). The NCLB has placed a greater emphasis on accountability measurements including requirements for states to publish and disseminate their achievement progress data annually to their citizens as well as written remediation plans for poor-performing schools. The extensive provisions include directives for teacher training, enhancing parent-school involvement, a focus on empirically based teaching methods, and strong secondary education transition planning among others. In addition, the NCLB authorizes federal funding options for states that permit parents alternative school options when their child's school is not meeting performance standards. Compliance with this act is highly relevant to the work of curriculum planning teams. A full copy of the NCLB is available at http://www.ed.gov/nclb/landing.jhtml.

More specifically, leadership teams participate in textbook adoptions, personnel assignments, class size and constellation decisions, and influence resource and budget allocations that support the success of instruction. Additional responsibilities often include professional development that routinely delivers in-service continuing education or peer-mentoring opportunities for teachers. Members of the leadership team, particularly principals, may also provide observations and evaluations of teachers' skills. The topics of training change in response to emerging research in pedagogy best practices, new instructional materials, availability of advanced technologies, observed personnel needs, and team-building goals. Program evaluation is a critical component to ensuring the effectiveness of curriculum design and delivery within schools. Based on program evaluation data that may include periodic curriculum-based measures of benchmark skills, grades, reviews of portfolio products, teacher/parent feedback, retention rates, and other variables, decisions are made regarding future needs. The process is circular with standards directing target goals, research informing methods, needs analyses informing teacher supports, and student data informing effectiveness of curriculum policy and implementation. It is at this point of curriculum program evaluation that decisions may include in-service training for teachers on methods that facilitate learning for differences in temperament learning qualities. The later discussions in this chapter on matching hypothesis and repertoire enhancement are most relevant to teacher in-service discussions.

Exceptional Student Education (ESE)

The U.S. Department of Education (USDOE) in conjunction with state Departments of Education (DOE) administers programs for students with disabilities (and gifted-talented services). Access to programs is mandated by the Individuals with Disabilities Education Improvement Act (IDEIA, 2004), and state Departments of Education annually provide schools with detailed statutes and rules that delineate eligibility criteria and processes. These provisions are subject to periodic changes as placement policy and empirical support for service paradigms shift. Thus, school leadership has a complex task that requires vigilance in responding to current changes and anticipating further initiatives.

The 2004 reauthorization of IDEIA presents 13 distinct disability categories, each with differing needs, requiring a variety of teacher expertise, and differentiated instructional methods. IDEIA categories include: Specific Learning Disability, Speech or Language Impairments, Mental Retardation, Emotional Disturbance, Multiple Disabilities, Hearing Impairments, Orthopedic Impairment, Other Health Impairments, Visual Impairments, Autism, Deaf-Blindness, Traumatic Brain Injury, and Developmental Delay (see Rapid Reference 6.1). A full copy of the IDEIA legislation is available at http://www.ed.gov/index.

Based on the 28th Annual Report to Congress on the Implementation of the Individuals with Disabilities Education Act (2008), more than 7 million children receive services under IDEIA. For children ages birth through two years old, 282,733 participated in early intervention services under Part C of IDEIA (2.3 percent of the population age birth to 2). Ages 3 through 5 are entitled to intervention under IDEIA Part B, and again nearly 701,949 received services (5.9 percent). Under Part B, eligible student from ages 6 through 21 numbered nearly 6,118,437 (9.2 percent of population age 6–21) with the fastest increasing group being ages 12 to 17. Of the students ages 6 to 21 receiving services the largest category is learning disabilities (46.4%), followed by speech/language (18.8%), mental retardation (9.3%), other health impairments (8.4%), emotional disturbance (7.9%), and all other disability categories combined (9.2%). For all three groups (birth to 2, 3 to 5, 6 to 21) the total number students has steadily increased every year for 10 consecutive years (USDOE, 2008, 2009).

≡ *Rapid Reference 6. 1*

IDEIA Disability Categories Definitions

The following definitions of disability categories are found in IDEIA 2004, Part 300/A/300.8/c. State disability categories may utilize different terms and additional subdivided distinctions. However, they are required to provide services for all 13 disability areas.

(1) (i) Autism means a developmental disability significantly affecting verbal and nonverbal communication and social interaction, generally evident before age three that adversely affects a child's educational performance. Other characteristics often associated with autism are engagement in repetitive activities and stereotyped movements, resistance to environmental change or change in daily routines, and unusual responses to sensory experiences.

(ii) Autism does not apply if a child's educational performance is adversely affected primarily because the child has an emotional disturbance, as defined in paragraph (c)(4) of this section.

(iii) A child who manifests the characteristics of autism after age three could be identified as having autism if the criteria in paragraph (c)(1) (i) of this section are satisfied.

(2) Deaf-blindness means concomitant hearing and visual impairments, the combination of which causes such severe communication and other developmental and educational needs that they cannot be accommodated in special education programs solely for children with deafness or children with blindness.

(3) Deafness means a hearing impairment that is so severe that the child is impaired in processing linguistic information through hearing, with or without amplification, that adversely affects a child's educational performance.

(4) (i) Emotional disturbance means a condition exhibiting one or more of the following characteristics over a long period of time and to a marked degree that adversely affects a child's educational performance:

(A) An inability to learn that cannot be explained by intellectual, sensory, or health factors.

   (B) An inability to build or maintain satisfactory interpersonal rela-
        tionships with peers and teachers.

   (C) Inappropriate types of behavior or feelings under normal circum-
        stances.

   (D) A general pervasive mood of unhappiness or depression.

   (E) A tendency to develop physical symptoms or fears associated
        with personal or school problems.

  (ii) Emotional disturbance includes schizophrenia. The term does not
        apply to children who are socially maladjusted, unless it is determined
        that they have an emotional disturbance under paragraph (c)(4)(i) of
        this section.

(5) Hearing impairment means an impairment in hearing, whether permanent
     or fluctuating, that adversely affects a child's educational performance but
     that is not included under the definition of deafness in this section.

(6) Mental retardation means significantly subaverage general intellectual
     functioning, existing concurrently with deficits in adaptive behavior and
     manifested during the developmental period that adversely affects a child's
     educational performance.

(7) Multiple disabilities means concomitant impairments (such as mental
     retardation-blindness or mental retardation-orthopedic impairment), the
     combination of which causes such severe educational needs that they can-
     not be accommodated in special education programs solely for one of the
     impairments. Multiple disabilities does not include deaf-blindness.

(8) Orthopedic impairment means a severe orthopedic impairment that ad-
     versely affects a child's educational performance. The term includes impair-
     ments caused by a congenital anomaly, impairments caused by disease (e.g.,
     poliomyelitis, bone tuberculosis), and impairments from other causes (e.g.,
     cerebral palsy, amputations, and fractures or burns that cause contractures).

(9) Other health impairment means having limited strength, vitality, or alert-
     ness, including a heightened alertness to environmental stimuli, that results
     in limited alertness with respect to the educational environment, that—

   (i) Is due to chronic or acute health problems such as asthma, attention
        deficit disorder or attention deficit hyperactivity disorder, diabetes, epi-
        lepsy, a heart condition, hemophilia, lead poisoning, leukemia, nephritis,
        rheumatic fever, sickle cell anemia, and Tourette's syndrome; and

  (ii) Adversely affects a child's educational performance.

(10) Specific learning disability.

   (i) General. Specific learning disability means a disorder in one or more of
        the basic psychological processes involved in understanding or in using

(continued)

language, spoken or written, that may manifest itself in the imperfect ability to listen, think, speak, read, write, spell, or to do mathematical calculations, including conditions such as perceptual disabilities, brain injury, minimal brain dysfunction, dyslexia, and developmental aphasia.

(ii) Disorders not included. Specific learning disability does not include learning problems that are primarily the result of visual, hearing, or motor disabilities, of mental retardation, of emotional disturbance, or of environmental, cultural, or economic disadvantage.

(11) Speech or language impairment means a communication disorder, such as stuttering, impaired articulation, a language impairment, or a voice impairment, that adversely affects a child's educational performance.

(12) Traumatic brain injury means an acquired injury to the brain caused by an external physical force, resulting in total or partial functional disability or psychosocial impairment, or both, that adversely affects a child's educational performance. Traumatic brain injury applies to open or closed head injuries resulting in impairments in one or more areas, such as cognition; language; memory; attention; reasoning; abstract thinking; judgment; problem-solving; sensory, perceptual, and motor abilities; psychosocial behavior; physical functions; information processing; and speech. Traumatic brain injury does not apply to brain injuries that are congenital or degenerative, or to brain injuries induced by birth trauma.

(13) Visual impairment including blindness means an impairment in vision that, even with correction, adversely affects a child's educational performance. The term includes both partial sight and blindness.

Disability terms in state statutes and board of education rules may differ and include additional subcategories. Regardless of state category descriptors, they are required to provide comprehensive services across all 13 disability areas noted in IDEIA. Three disabilities that often have differing state titles include Mental Retardation (e.g., Intellectual Disabilities), Emotional Disturbance (e.g., Emotional/Behavioral Disorder, Emotional Disabilities), and Autism (e.g., Autism Spectrum Disorders). State statutes and rules typically begin with a definition of the disorder; evaluation criteria; evidence that must be documented, sometimes including outside exams (e.g., physician); exclusions (e.g., disability not due to sensory deficits); and general procedures (e.g., number of parent conferences).

The evaluation criteria portion of state regulations are particularly important to assessment as types of required evaluation methods (e.g., observations, intelligence, achievement measures, social-emotional measures) are delineated and specific evidence requirements may be noted (e.g., behavior is evident in two or more settings, length of time behavior must be exhibited). One broad application of temperament assessment data across disability categories is the implications for instructional methods and study strategies related to intervention recommendations (see Rapid Reference 6.1). An example of a more targeted application could be provided in part 4-B of the Emotional Disturbance definition which requires establishing "An inability to build or maintain satisfactory interpersonal relationships with peers and teachers." Interventions informed by temperament assessment may offer successful strategies in addressing part 4-B needs. Generally, the Departments of Education in individual states provide easy public access to all statutes and rules through their official websites, and this may be particularly helpful to private practitioners or multidisciplinary agency collaborations when professionals are not as familiar with school systems. It is important to consult local state guidelines for evaluation criteria as there are notable differences between states. School board district guidelines also can impose additional procedural guidelines related to documentation and process that may effect what types of report formats and data are expected from professionals.

In the past, the majority of referrals for special education eligibility have emerged from teacher concerns for academic, behavioral, or physical impairments. Although parent and self-referral were permitted, they do not commonly occur. Following preliminary interventions, a team decision was made to move to evaluation for ESE eligibility if deemed appropriate. Formal evaluations and individualized assessment tests were reserved for children who had been referred for eligibility consideration. At this point, the assessment process would begin. Students found eligible received services and students who did not meet criteria often continued in the previous curriculum with little change in instruction and without formal or documented interventions.

RESPONSE TO INTERVENTION MODEL (RtI)

As noted earlier, the IDEIA and NCLB are closely aligned in an effort to ensure equal access to high-quality education for all students as well as systematic outcome measures whereby national policy makers and the public can review progress. Following the reauthorization of IDEIA and the final regulations, significant changes in statutory language occurred especially related to identification of specific learning disabilities (see Rapid Reference 6.2), the largest Exceptional Student Education (ESE) category (USDOE, 2006). These changes are consistent with a response-to-intervention RtI model and due in part to initiatives by the National Institute for Child Health and Development (NICHD), the President's Commission on Excellence in Special Education, and the National Summit on

Learning Disabilities findings (NASDSE, 2005). The new IDEIA emphasizes the need for systematic early screening of all children, classroom behavioral observations in evaluations that consider ecological factors, utilization of problem-solving strategies with empirically based interventions prior to referral for ESE eligibility, and progress monitoring that informs decisions (Jimerson, Burns, & VanDerHeyden, 2007). This paradigm shift has several significant implications relevant to how many children may now be provided assessments or interventions as well as when and how frequent those services are provided. Thus, an overview of the major tenets of RtI are provided.

The initial primary focus of RtI has been addressing academic needs, specifically reading, as that is the most frequent special education need (Fletcher et al., 1994; Kovaleski, 2003; Ysseldyke et al., 2006). However, the process also is applied to behavioral and social-emotional needs. In addition, to the impetus for changes in pedagogical directives to address academic performance, the surgeon general's national agenda promulgates the need for mental health services for all children including behavioral supports delivered directly within public schools (U.S. Department of Health and Human Services, 1999; 2000). A number of critical issues have been identified for the well-being of students. The 2001–2003 National Health Interview Survey indicates 5 percent of parents reported severe or definite behavioral/emotional difficulties for their children ages 4 to 17, with twice the rate reported for impoverished families (Pastor, Reuben, & Faulkenstern, 2004). Existing child services have been noted as fragmented while a more comprehensive level of services, including prevention and intervention services, have better support for positive outcomes (U.S. Department of Health and Human Services, 1999; 2000). With its emphasis on screening, prevention, and individualized intervention, RtI has potential to meet these needs earlier.

Response to Intervention is a multitiered model that can be conceptualized within either a three- or a four-tiered framework. For the purposes of this text, the three-tiered model is provided (NASDSE, 2005; Sugai, Horner, & Gresham, 2002). Decisions for students are made at each tier by a problem-solving team. Ideally, interventions are provided early, long before special education eligibility needs are warranted. The process requires frequent review of data that is gathered systematically to make educational decisions.

The first tier (Tier I) of RtI is considered universal, serving all children in the school regardless of classification. This stage is proactive and preventative with three goals: to consistently critique curriculum; identify system-wide patterns of achievement lag that may require changes in instruction, materials, or resource allocation; and to identify at-risk students early. The leadership team and curriculum specialists as well as school psychologists discussed earlier are intricately involved in ensuring the integrity of this process. Tier I identifies children who are not acquiring academic, prosocial, and/or adaptive skills adequately, at the same pace as peers, and intervenes before deficits become large or chronic by applying interventions quickly. Determination of which children are at risk involves brief screening assessments of narrow, discrete skills (e.g., reading fluency, math calculations) rather than broad measures. The rationale for this approach is due in part to research identifying critical markers that respond well to early intervention for many students and may eliminate a need for more intensive remediation later (Fletcher et al., 1994; Kovaleski, 2003; Ysseldyke et al., 1983). As an academic example, a team may administer several short reading measures (e.g., MAZES, DIBELS, Fox-in-a-Box) for all first graders within a school several times each year. As a social-emotional example, early at-risk indicators for behavioral and social-emotional can be identified through a variety of behavioral and mental health well-being screeners that measure social skills or maladaptive behaviors (e.g., BASC-2 Behavioral and Emotional Screening System; Systematic Screening for Behavioral Disorders).

In reference to the reading screening example, if the results reveal that many children across classes have below expected scores, the data may suggest a more systematic curriculum problem requiring changing the materials or curriculum master plan sequence. It may also suggest that the group of children as a whole require more supports and thus core instruction changes are warranted. If the children's scores are low in only one classroom, instructional observations of the class including a review of teaching methods and environmental factors is most likely warranted. The leadership team may provide additional training, a mentor/coach, or consultation with the school psychologist on teaching strategies for the teacher. Teacher consultation on instructional methods may include a discussion on differing learning strengths based on temperament qualities. The concept of repertoire enhancement as it relates to temperament discussed later in this chapter may be helpful in these types of teacher consultations.

In the spirit of NCLB, it is hoped that processes such as those described in this example of data-driven and required systematic reviews several times each year will increase the accountability of school administration. These procedures prompt schools not to assume that academic lag is automatically endemic to the child. A third scenario in the aforementioned example is that the scores indicate only a few children are low in particular areas suggesting the difficulty is related to the child. The next step in these cases is to discuss Tier-II interventions through a problem-solving team process. In an RtI model, these students may be provided intervention without qualifying for special education placement. It is estimated that 80 percent of students will meet achievement goals at a Tier-I level if a high standard of curriculum and instruction are maintained. However, approximately 15 percent of students may still require additional educational supports (NADSE, 2005).

The second tier of RtI can be described as targeted, supplemental, short-term interventions. Following a problem-solving team meeting where it is important to review multiple factors contributing to achievement or behavior (e.g., attendance, health, life transition circumstances, study habits, grades), a decision is made on how to design interventions that are most likely to assist the child (McConaughy & Ritter, 2008). The interventions can begin in a matter of days rather than months as prior referral procedures required. The interventions can be multifaceted depending on needs (e.g., address academic skills and behaviors simultaneously) and either individualized or a treatment protocol. Treatment protocols are typically standardized interventions based on research that many students can benefit from, and they usually address common problems (e.g., reading fluency, social skills deficits). The choice between an individually designed intervention or use of a protocol is made by the problem-solving team and based on the type of skills that need to be addressed. It is not the intention of protocol treatments to indiscriminately assign them to all children. In reference to temperament interventions, there are a number of standard strategies that lend themselves well to protocol treatment practices. Examples may include small group counseling that targets social skills development for extremely introverted and shy children that teaches them how to utilize extroversion qualities when appropriate. As a second example, children with strong intuitive/imaginative temperament qualities can be prone to errors due to their propensity to overlook details and thus may benefit from self-monitoring interventions that prompt them to check their own work.

Progress monitoring is an integral component in ensuring success in an RtI model at Tier-II and Tier-III. Before interventions are implemented, baseline data are collected for comparison later. Typically, data is acquired regularly (e.g., weekly, bi-weekly, monthly) depending on the type of intervention, keeping the process dynamic, and permitting changes in intervention design as needed. If the intervention results in dramatic increase in skills so that intervention is no longer warranted, the supplemental instruction is withdrawn. Students can return to Tier-II later if needed. In cases where the intervention data demonstrate progress that is closing the gap between benchmarks and prior deficits, it may be decided to merely continue the same intervention with consistent monitoring to provide the student the opportunity to catch up with peers. If adequate progress is not indicated, the problem-solving team can decide to alter the intervention approach, increase the frequency and duration of intervention, or add multiple intervention strategies. When Tier II efforts are not successful in helping the student improve appropriately, the team may decide to consider the student for Tier-III services.

Tier-III RtI provides individualized interventions that are intensive, may be more frequent, and are often longer in duration. Approximately 5 percent of students are predicted to require Tier-III services. Examples of possible temperament-related interventions include individualized counseling therapy. For example, a student with very strong Thinking preferences may lack empathetic ways of relating to others or be prone to blunt interactions that are offensive; there are a variety of therapeutic approaches to addressing these behaviors. The problem-solving team may request more traditionally comprehensive assessment measures that are diagnostic in multiple areas including broad factors such as intelligence or memory (Hale, Kaufman, Naglieri, & Kavale, 2006). Students at a Tier-III stage often present with more complex, severe, and multifaceted difficulties that require a wider range of intervention. Again, interventions are progress monitored for effectiveness and decisions regarding changing methods, intensity, and frequency as dictated by the student's need. In some RtI models, Tier-III may result in classification for a special education disability program. For four-tier models, eligibility considerations occur after Tier-III interventions.

> # DON'T FORGET
> ....
>
> ## RtI Three-Tiered Model
>
> **TIER I: UNIVERSAL INTERVENTIONS**
>
> Provide for All Students, Quality Core Instruction, Preventative, Proactive, Screenings
>
> **TIER II: SUPPLEMENTAL INTERVENTIONS**
>
> Some Students (10–15%, At-Risk), Strategic, Supplemental, Often Small Group, Standard Protocol or Individual Design, Rapid Response, Short-Term, High Efficiency
>
> **TIER III: INTENSIVE INTERVENTIONS**
>
> Few Students (5%), Individualized, High Intensity, Longer Duration, Multi-faceted, If Unsuccessful Consider Special Education Eligibility

The problem-solving team process is a key factor in the success of any RtI decisions. The collaboration of these professionals each contributing their respective assessment and intervention skills can determine how well designed and appropriate services are for students. At each stage of the process assessment skills are required: screening at the universal stage, discrete skill measures at Tier II and III (e.g., curriculum-based measures, rating scales, observations) as well as comprehensive measures at Tier-III if ESE eligibility is initiated (this will depend on whether a three- or four-tier model is utilized). Objective data is a core component at each step in the process. It is the problem-solving team's responsibility to ensure the rigor of the process by maintaining best practices consistently (Upah & Tilly, 2002).

In a formal problem-solving team process, there are four steps based upon the scientific method of inquiry (Tilly, 2002). The first step is to define the problem by directly measuring it. As an example, if a child is reported to be talking too often so that it is interfering with work, observations can determine what percentage of time the student is off-task in comparison to peers and how his/her work productivity compares to others. Results may indicate the child is not atypical or that he/she is off-task more frequently and work production is low. After the problem has been defined, problem analysis, the second step, considers possible contributing factors. Data and general information are analyzed to identify discrete academic skill or social-emotional needs and consider the child within the broader context of culture and personal factors. Continuing with the prior example, record reviews may indicate good attendance and health, ruling out those factors. Interviews and temperament measures may indicate the child is highly extroversion and lacks awareness of or opportunity for appropriate conversation. A variety of assessment data including temperament measures may be warranted during problem identification depending on the presenting needs. It is important to the process, especially the ability to measure progress, that the goals be objective and measureable. The nature of the goals should guide the choices for intervention strategies, and it is critical to ensure evidence-based interventions are employed. The third step is to develop and implement the team's plan. Often a teacher, intervention specialist, or speech-language personnel are directly involved in the service delivery of academic interventions, whereas counselors, social workers, and school psychologists may provide behavioral and social-emotional interventions. Counselors, social workers, and school psychologists are more likely to also have greater knowledge regarding the implications of child temperament on intervention strategies. Therefore, these personnel should be involved and contributing to the problem-solving team process (Allison & Upah, 2006).

If temperament factors are considered to be an influence on performance, either academically or behaviorally, it will be important to bring this issue to the discussions during collaboration. In the example for this discussion, the extroversion child may benefit from

DON'T FORGET

Problem-Solving Team Process

Don't forget the four problem-solving steps: Define the Problem, Analyze the Problem, Develop and Implement the Plan, and Evaluate Plan Effectiveness instruction on appropriate times to talk as well as private teacher cues when he/she is talking out of turn and/or icon cues with a self-monitoring plan. The final step in problem solving is to evaluate how effective the intervention strategy has been. For our extroversion and highly talkative child this may consist of repeated observations of off-task chatting behavior that has decreased appropriately. By nature, the problem-solving method is cyclical, and the final step of evaluating the intervention effectiveness may close the process or begin it again based on results.

RESPONSE TO INTERVENTION—IMPLICATIONS FOR USE OF TEMPERAMENT ASSESSMENT

National shifts towards an RtI model create several changes in assessment needs, procedures, and process. Although most of the current research and implementation focus on academic applications such as reading or math remediation, RtI is also applied to behavioral and social-emotional needs. Temperament knowledge has some indirect applications to academic plans especially related to study skills, attention due to personal interactions, and curriculum presentation. There are more numerous direct applications to the behavioral and social-emotional domain. The new model places greater emphasis on screening all children, more observations of behavior, earlier narrow assessments of more students, and more short assessment measures rather than comprehensive evaluations. It is important to emphasize that RtI is a new paradigm for most states, and thus only limited national data are available for long-term implementation results. These preliminary data do indicate positive results as a result of early intervention.

Three probable changes to assessment based on the RtI model are discussed that may have implications for temperament assessment data: an increase in consideration for behavioral influences on achievement that requires observations, increase in brief assessments that may be repeated, and increase in assessment of slow learners. First the reauthorization of IDEIA coupled with the Federal Register eligibility clarifications place a strong emphasis on observations within the classroom setting that may influence academic achievement during pre-referral interventions (see Rapid Reference 6.2). If the child moves to Tier III and is considered for eligibility for special education, observations must be documented in the report with an explanation as to the influence of the behavior on academic performance. There are many circumstances through which temperament qualities can influence behavior and be noted in screenings or observations that may also prompt follow-up temperament assessment to confirm a hypothesis regarding the behavior.

At this time RtI calls for screening all students for behavioral and academic risk, however temperament measures are more commonly used as part of formal evaluations rather than as screening measures. Yet there is literature to suggest that preschool temperament traits are predictive of early school achievement and thus consideration of temperament qualities may be helpful. For preschoolers, temperament qualities associated with Thomas and Chess's three patterns: Easy, slow-to-warm, and difficult can dramatically impact behaviors and thus achievement. Easy temperament qualities increase the adaptability and likeability of a child setting into motion positive reciprocal reactions from others. The response style of slow-to-warm children may delay development of friendships and cooperative group learning potential. Difficult temperaments are at-risk for a variety of peer-neglect/peer-rejection circumstances, irritability, and low task frustration tolerance characteristics (Buss & Plomin, 1984; Thomas & Chess, 1986). As reviewed in Chapter Two, the longitudinal Fullerton study (infant to age 17) found correlations between temperament scores on the Behavioral Style Questionnaire (BSQ), Infant Characteristics Questionnaire (ICQ), Toddler Temperament Scale (TTS), Dimensions of Temperament Survey-Revised (DOTS-R), and Middle Childhood Temperament Questionnaire (MCTQ) with several academic variables:

- Parent preschool temperament ratings and teacher elementary school behavior ratings correlate significantly.
- Students with low persistence/attention were more likely to repeat grades.
- Persistence/attention, adaptability, approach/withdrawal correlated positively and negative mood correlated inversely with achievement on the Kaufman Assessment Battery for Children (K-ABC) for 5- and 6-year-olds.
- Likewise, at age six, the same temperament qualities also correlated with reading and arithmetic scores on the Wide Range Achievement Test (WRAT).
- Parent temperament ratings predicted Woodcock-Johnson reading achievement beyond intelligence variance for adolescents (Parent rating: IQ $R^2=.21$; Temperament $R^2=.39$).
- Persistence/attention correlated positively and distractibility correlated inversely with Woodcock-Johnson (WJ) reading and arithmetic scores at ages 7 to 12.
- Parent ratings of activity level correlated negatively with adolescent math achievement.
- Several cross-time measures of achievement consistently found significant correlations for persistence/attention, adaptability, distractibility, and approach/withdrawal.

- Early temperament qualities of persistence/attention, adaptability, and predictability correlated positively with high school cumulative grade point average (gpa) and distractibility, negative mood, and intensity of reactions correlated negatively with high school gpa (Guerin, Gottfried, Oliver, & Thomas, 2003).

As examples for elementary and older students, extroversion children are more likely to exhibit talking and interactions behaviors, which may be excessive. In contrast, introverted children are more likely to exhibit solitary and quiet behaviors, which can be strengths for concentrating on learning unless the child becomes withdrawn. Students who are strongly intuitive (i.e., imaginative) are more likely to overlook small but important details; this can effect carelessness in work that is evident through both observations and product reviews. For those with a sensing (i.e., practical) preference to learn based on facts, hands-on experience, and pragmatic application, theoretical approaches may increase frustration. Interaction skills can be strongly influenced by thinking and feeling attributes. Students with a thinking orientation may be perceived as blunt, critical, and argumentative in their desire for candidness and exacting truth. If inappropriately directed at others, including peers or teachers, these behaviors can have negative outcomes. On the other side of the spectrum, students with feeling qualities may be easily persuaded, lack fortitude in their desire to avoid confrontation, and place an overemphasis on pleasing behaviors. A child with high perceiving (i.e., flexible) temperament qualities may be prone to postponing deadlines, putting play before work, and lack structure in completing work. The opposite qualities are strong for judging (i.e., organized) temperament, although adaptability to change, premature foreclosure of options, and tolerance for others who are not organized can be problematic. These examples of behavioral hypotheses that might be generated by observations could be confirmed through school-age self-report temperament measures (e.g., SSQ, MMTIC, MBTI).

Research on temperament preferences and school performance has identified temperament qualities that correlate with more positive outcomes and appear to be a good match for success under current classroom instruction methods. Within Caspi's theoretical framework of temperament as overcontrollers, undercontrollers, and resilients, the latter group performed more favorably. Research found resilients demonstrated higher intelligence, academic performance, social skills, general psychological adjustment, and self-esteem (Scholte, van Lieshout, de Wit, & van Aken, 2005).

Likewise, research from psychological temperament type supports better academic outcomes for some temperament qualities. Overall dominant intuitive types (i.e., ENTP, ENFP, INTJ, INFJ) have the best academic achievement. A study of 217 seventh- and eighth-graders comparing two groups, gifted-talented and general education, found significant differences on the SSQ imaginative-practical (i.e., intuitive-sensing) scale. Gifted-talented students more often preferred the imaginative approach (Lang, 2000). A similar comparison of a larger sample (N=1554), ages 8 to 17, also found gifted students more frequently reported a preference for imaginative style, with gifted females indicating the strongest preference based on SSQ t-scores (Oakland, Joyce, Glutting, & Horton, 2000). Children not identified as gifted most frequently preferred the practical style. In their research with the MBTI, Myers and McCaulley (1962, 1980, 1985) found students with temperaments that combined intuitive and judging had among the highest grade point averages and graduation rates both for high school and college (Anchors, Robbins, & Gershman, 1989; Rigley, 1993; Waymire, 1995; Woodruff & Clarke, 1993). A study of intelligence scores and college entrance exam scores (i.e., SAT and GRE) were significantly higher for students who self-reported an intuitive temperament. A higher-than-predicted preference rate for intuitive temperament is also noted among college students.

Dominant sensing types (i.e., ESTP, ESFP, ISTJ, ISFJ) also demonstrate high grades and more frequent leadership roles in high school (especially those who are extroverts); however, they are more likely to drop out, and some research indicates they have among the lowest grades in college (Myers et al., 1998). Students with self-reported dominant thinking attributes are more likely to demonstrate leadership in schools (especially those who are extroversion). However, based on a study of school psychologists' referrals, thinking types also have higher rates of adjustment problems (especially those who are introverted). The dominant feeling temperaments (i.e., ESFJ, ENFJ, ISFP, INFP) have a propensity to excel in foreign language acquisition. Broad achievement research results are mixed with some studies reporting high persistence and retention and other studies not supporting these conclusions (Myers et al., 1998). These findings may have implications for teaching all students how to utilize learning preferences reported by intuitive-judging profiles and suggest a need

DON'T FORGET
....

Comparing SSQ and MBTI Temperament Terms

Remember when comparing research between the SSQ and MBTI, two dimensions on the SSQ have different names from the corresponding dimensions on the MBTI yet measure the same constructs. Practical-Imaginative is equivalent to Sensing-Intuitive and Flexible-Organized is equivalent to Perceiving-Judging.

for further research in this area. In considering persons with disabilities and temperament, a study of 214 students ages 10 to 17 compared two samples, vision impaired and non-impaired utilizing the SSQ. Those with visual impairments more often preferred practical, thinking, and organized styles (Oakland, Banner, & Livingston, 2000).

The second RtI assessment change is an increase in brief assessments that may be repeated. The increase in brief assessments is likely to occur as children are screened for early at-risk factors and Tier I. Again at Tier-II, there is the potential for more children to receive services through problem-solving team interventions informed by brief assessments. The component of progress monitoring in RtI behavioral applications also requires measurement; however, as temperament is considered moderately stable over time, it is unlikely that repeated measures would yield additional information. These early assessments could be considered partial or short targeted assessments when compared to the more comprehensive test batteries administered at a Tier-III level or in a traditional SLD eligibility model. Personnel may decide to assess temperament to rule out hypotheses in the define-the-problem stage of problem-solving or be asked to briefly assess the influence of temperament factors for the analyze-the-problem step in a problem-solving team process.

The third potential for increased brief assessments within RtI is related to slow learners. Under previous ESE eligibility criteria, the gateway to services was reliant on teacher referrals, often based on a sustained period of low achievement. Subsequently, comprehensive evaluations determined if criteria were met and the appropriate special education services were initiated. Nearly one-half of all disabilities are specific learning disabilities (USDOE, 2008), and the assessment was based on an aptitude-discrepancy model. Students who had achievement deficits and did not exhibit the required discrepancy were not considered eligible. Many of these students were considered slow learners.

The typical slow learner profile has an intelligence (IQ) score in the borderline to low-average range (e.g., standard IQ scores equal 70–85). The descriptions are arbitrary as IQ scores are continuous and occur on a normal distribution without distinctive cut-off points (Shaw, 2000a; 2000b). Nearly 14 percent of the students in the entire population fall in this category of slow learners, and they often struggle academically; however, under prior eligibility criteria this group did not qualify for sustained disability services. It also is interesting to note that the percentage of slow learners is higher than the percentage of all students ages 6 to 21 served under IDEIA (9.2 percent) combined across identified disabilities (U.S. Department of Education, 2008). More importantly research indicates slow learners can improve academic performance with quality core instruction and appropriate intervention (Shaw 2000a, 2000b; USDOE, 2008). This group of students typically also requires assistance with a variety of study skills and learning strategies, and temperament may play a role identifying preferred learning methods. In utilizing an RtI model, it is anticipated more of these students would receive early assessments and be more likely to progress to Tier III when academic lag is severe. Overall, the early intervention paradigm of RtI is hoped to lower the number of children and youth requiring special education, although data on outcomes are mixed and empirical support for the model is still debated (Fletcher & Vaughn, 2009; Kucera, 2008; Reynolds & Shaywitz, 2009; Torgesen, 2009).

≡ *Rapid Reference 6.2*

Select RtI-Related Statutory Language – Federal Register 2006

§300.307 SPECIFIC LEARNING DISABILITIES

(a) General. A State must adopt, consistent with §300.309, criteria for determining whether a child has a specific learning disability as defined in §300.8(c)(10). In addition, the criteria adopted by the State-

   (1) Must not require the use of a severe discrepancy between intellectual ability and achievement for determining whether a child has a specific learning disability, as defined in §300.8(c)(10);

   (2) Must permit the use of a process based on the child's response to intervention; and

   (3) May permit the use of other alternative research-based procedures for determining whether a child has a specific learning disability, as defined in §300.8(c)(10).

§309.309

(b) To ensure that underachievement in a child suspected of having a specific learning disability is not due to lack of appropriate instruction in reading or math, the group must consider, as part of the evaluation described in §300.304 through 300.306-

   (1) Data that demonstrate that prior to, or as a part of, the referral process, the child was provided appropriate instruction in regular education settings, delivered by qualified personnel; and

   (2) Data-based documentation of repeated assessment of achievement at reasonable intervals, reflecting formal assessment of student progress during instruction, which was provided to the child's parents.

§300.310 OBSERVATIONS

(a) The public agency must ensure that the child is observed in the child's learning environment (including the regular classroom setting) to document the child's academic performance and behavior in the areas of difficulty.

(b) (1) Use information for an observation in routine classroom instruction and monitoring of the child's performance that was done before the child was referred for an evaluation

§300.311 SPECIFIC DOCUMENTATION FOR THE ELIGIBILITY DETERMINATION

(a) For a child suspected of having a specific learning disability, the documentation of the determination of eligibility, as required in §300.306(a)(2), must contain a statement of –

(3) The relevant behavior, if any, noted during the observation of the child and the relationship of the behavior to the child's academic functioning;

Matching Hypothesis Application

Within the temperament literature, particularly related to learning styles, there are numerous books and articles delineating recommendations for interventions that utilize temperament-related strategies (Farris, 1991; Joyce, 2005, 2008; Kise, 2007; Lawrence, 1991, 1997; Myers et al., 1998; Oakland, Glutting, & Horton, 1996; Oakland & Joyce, 2006; Peters & Peters, 2007). The term matching hypothesis refers to one strategy of trying to match individual teacher temperament or instruction to specific students' personal learning styles. Some researchers have explored the matching hypothesis utilizing the MBTI as a measure of temperament-based learning styles without significant effects (DiTiberio, 1996). A study utilizing the SSQ as a measure of temperament and matching lesson plans based on temperament learning preferences noted significant improvement through a tutoring program for science (Al-Balhan, 2008). Others have investigated the matching hypotheses through larger samples that applied matching within classrooms. A meta-analysis of multiple learning style models in addition to the MBTI had mixed results. At least half of the studies resulted in no significant differences for improvement in academic performance (Coffield et al., 2004a, 2004b). Therefore, further research support appears to be warranted before the monumental task of trying to match teacher styles to individual students is implemented. At this time, there is limited support for matching hypothesis as well as questions regarding the feasibility of matching many differing temperaments within the same classroom.

Repertoire Enhancement Application

Repertoire enhancement is a strategy that suggests coaching teachers on how to include a broader range of learning style modalities within their classrooms, rather than relying on their own natural preferences. It is based on principles similar to Thomas and Chess's goodness of fit theory. As reviewed in Chapter One, Thomas and Chess proposed that when a person's environment requires skills the individual has, success is more likely. They noted, "stated briefly, there is a goodness of fit when the person's temperament and other characteristics such as motivation and levels of intelligence and other abilities, are adequate to master the successive demands, expectations, and opportunities of the environment (1977, p. vii)." Thomas and Chess's poorness of fit and Jung's falsification of type concepts describe the opposite circumstance. An environment that relentlessly requires and rewards traits contrary to an individual's innate preferences can be both exhausting and discouraging. By including a variety of temperament-based learning styles there are increased opportunities for all students to utilize their strengths (see Rapid Reference 6.3). Research by Cornett (1983) found support for increased student positive regard for teachers who use a range of learning styles (Cornett, 1983). Graduation rates were also noted to increase as well as students' persistence in learning new material (Schurr et al., 1997). Additional research that defines which particular strategies are most helpful including the intervention effect size and which types of temperament qualities are most malleable would be helpful in designing repertoire enhancement.

Self-Awareness and Metacognition Applications

The concept of metacognition is two-fold and refers to awareness individuals have of their own cognitive learning skills and strategies as well as the analysis process involved by the individual in utilizing their strategies. A well-developed metacognition requires the person to first know how they think and learn on a conscious level and requires self-reflection and insight. This may encompass memory strategies, attention techniques, responses to verbal versus visually presented information, preferences for sequential and factual information or holistic and theoretical approaches, time required for learning, and a host of techniques for organizing information. In addition to understanding what strategies work well or poorly for them, individuals have a process of selecting among their thinking skills and changing those as needed. This analysis stage is demonstrated when students recognize what material will require more effort, longer exposure, or multiple methods to learn. Metacognition permits the individual to adapt and change strategies that don't work well with new tasks. This set of thinking skill knowledge and applications combined can be considered the person's metacognition. Research indicates that deliberate and self-reflective selection of strategies can improve retention of information, indeed it is the meticulous self-regulation process that separates novice and expert learners (Gudbrandsen, 2006; Mitchell, 1989; Wangerin, 1988). Metacognitive strategies can be successfully taught even to children as young as five years old. Scholars have found teaching, even children in the first and second grades, metacognitive skills can improve their performance, and many of the children will apply the new strategies subsequently with enough awareness to attribute their success to the strategy choices (Best, 1993; Fabricius & Hagen, 1984; Lange & Pierce, 1992).

Often children or students who are performing poorly lack the ability to articulate their own thinking and study skills. Even when they know which methods are most helpful, they may not employ a wide range of skills or have the ability to adapt quickly. Temperament applications related to metacognition propose explicitly teaching students their own strengths so these can be readily utilized and also teaching them to recognize weaknesses. By understanding their learning profile, it is hypothesized the students can self-monitor their own learning. Several studies have found metacognition to improve learning (Naughton, 2009) among college students. In a study that instructed students to purposefully be aware of the learning strategies they were utilizing while also supplementing with additional techniques, a significant increase in student scores was indicated (Marzano, 1998).

≣ *Rapid Reference 6.3*

Classroom Applications Consistent With Temperament Preferences

Extroversion: group projects and discussions, oral presentations, brainstorming, reading aloud, public recognition and participation, frequent interaction with others. May have difficulty with independent work, lecture formats, and interrupting others.

Introverted: independent and quiet study, pursuit of in-depth knowledge, written papers, posters, allow time for introspection, privacy, silent reading, lectures, private recognition. May have difficulty with assertion, public participation, and interruptions.

Practical (Sensing): present real-world applications, hands-on activities, sequential information presentations, concrete examples, include facts/names/

(continued)

dates. May tune-out when discussing theory or abstractions or become distracted by details.

Imaginative (Intuitive): present theoretical and broad idea frameworks, discuss relationships between ideas, discuss patterns and predictions, learn by insights. May minimize the importance of details and practicality of implementing ideas.

Thinking: competitive games, debate, contrast/comparisons, direct feedback, analysis with cause-effect reasoning, objective and logical reasoning. May challenge others critically, can undervalue subjective information, can seem impersonal.

Feeling: cooperative projects, link information to people or humanitarian issues, story problems, team orientations provide sense of belonging, personalization. May placate to avoid conflicting expression of ideas, may be overly sensitive or sentimental.

Organized (Judging): explicit grading policy, structured settings, systematic schedules that permit advanced planning, and have deadlines that facilitate closure. May be rigid and lack adaptability in changing course, jump to conclusions in seeking premature closure.

Flexible (Perceiving): flexible deadlines that permit extensive time to gather information, choice in activities, pacing that permits some distractions, opportunity for movement. May have difficulty meeting deadlines, be easily distracted with other projects, unorganized.

Transition Planning for Students

High school is a pivotal educational point for many reasons: students begin to define career goals, class decisions are made for college preparation tracks, and postsecondary entrance exams are taken (Witte, 2008). High-stakes consequences are embedded at each of these junctures. In addition, students are maturing and gradually acquiring responsibility for self-advocacy. Understanding the importance of these issues, schools are structured to monitor progress, assess aptitudes and interests, as well as provide individualized guidance often through the expertise of school counselors (Trolley, Haas, & Patti, 2009). Temperament knowledge can be one important component in this process, including defining interests, increasing metacognition that facilitates personal responsibility for learning skills, and in identifying self-advocacy needs as they transition to college or technical schools.

Transition planning for most students consists of yearly discussions with the school counselor, as well as transition events open to all students (e.g., attendance at job fairs, group campus visits). For students already identified with disabilities, the Individuals with Disabilities Education Improvement Act (2004) provides regulations requiring schools to formally document ways in which they are preparing the student for transitions following high school. The transition may include preparing for a specific employment situation, military enlistment, entrance into a family business, or college (Joyce & Rossen, 2006; Levinson, 2008; Stroebel, Krieg, & Christian, 2008). The goals are based on a collaboration between the student, his or her family, and school personnel. As early as the age of 16, transition steps toward facilitating the goal have to be written within student's Individualized Education Plan (IEP). Additional skills that will be required by the student to successfully transition must also be included with a sequential plan to acquire those skills with measureable goals, and some of the targeted skills may be temperament-related.

The importance of transition planning, especially to students with disabilities, is reflected in the steady increase over the past decade of college enrollment among this group. Based on 2003–2004 data, 11.3 percent of students enrolled in undergraduate institutions have a disability (USDOE, 2006). Among those with disabilities, the most common are orthopedic impairments (25.3 percent) followed by mental illness/depression (21.9 percent, majority females), health impairments (17.4 percent), attention deficit disorder (10.9 percent, mostly male), other (7.9 percent), specific learning disability (7.4 percent, majority males), hearing (4.9 percent), vision (3.8 percent), and speech (.4 percent). Temperament-related learning strategies may be the most relevant to college students with specific learning disabilities and attention deficit disorders. Whereas temperament-related counseling techniques may be more important to students with mental illness/depression, and implications are discussed later in this chapter.

Continued study skills and learning strategies support remains a need for students even after entering college as many require remedial coursework during their first two years. Among all students 43 percent of those attending two-year colleges and 35 percent of those attending four-year institutions required remediation courses. Math remediation is reported to be the greatest need (76.4 percent no disability, 79.8 percent with disabilities), followed by writing (35.3 percent no disability, 30.3 percent with disabilities), and reading (27.4 percent no disability, 31.1 percent with disability). Many of the students also require remedial classes dedicated solely to teaching study skills (11.8 percent no disability, 15.5 percent with disability).

Another important aspect of transition planning is teaching students the self-monitoring and advocacy skills necessary to advocate for themselves in a postsecondary environment. For students who are highly organized (i.e., judging temperament) timely progress on long-term projects and allotting adequate time for test preparation is noted to be a better developed skill. Those with flexible (i.e., perceiving temperament) propensities may lack some structure in study habits. For students with extroversion and/or thinking temperament qualities advocacy may be more comfortable. However, for introverted students and those with feeling temperaments that avoid confrontation, voicing their needs may require more coaching and practice. The importance of self-advocacy, especially for students with disabilities, in postsecondary can be best understood by briefly reviewing how college accommodations differ from those in high schools.

The Individuals with Disabilities Education Improvement Act (IDEIA, 2004) provides a multitude of identification, remediation, and accommodation safeguards for students with disabilities. Its systematic procedures give schools responsibility for proactively seeking out children with special needs and a formal documentation system mandates periodic review as well as family involvement in the process. Progress monitoring through re-evaluations and updated Individual Education Plans (IEPs) has rigorous guidelines as well. However, IDEIA does not extend to postsecondary education, and thus most of the responsibility for acquiring assistance falls to the individual student. In addition, most postsecondary students are of adult age and privacy laws prevent parent access to information without the student's consent. Therefore, it is important to foster self-advocacy well in advance of the first day of college (ADA Compliance Office, 2002).

At the postsecondary level, the Rehabilitation Act of 1973 and the Americans with Disabilities Act assure provisions of services for college students with disabilities (U.S. Department of Justice, 2004). The Rehabilitation Act of 1973 (Public Law 102–569, Section 504) states that persons with disabilities cannot be denied equal access or benefits from any federally funded program or activity. This provision includes public institutions such as colleges, and to avoid discrimination against persons with disabilities (including learning disabilities), educational institutions must provide reasonable changes in their policies, practices, and procedures to accommodate students with disabilities. This does not guarantee entrance as each individual still must meet core requirements.

What students can expect as "reasonable" accommodations include such provisions as extra time on entrance exams, assistive technology devices if warranted, opportunity to take exams in a quiet and non-distracting setting, as well as some course substitutions. It is up to the individual student to contact the institution, provide assessment verification from a professional of the disability, register with the disabilities office, and ensure that accommodations are discussed. The student does not have to disclose a disability and can attend without accommodations if desired. Many institutions also require that the student individually notify each instructor of his/her needs, which can be a particularly intimidating process for someone who is highly introverted. In addition, the student must self-monitor their own accommodation needs as the institution does not collect or review progress monitoring data for the student. When instructors are resistant to providing accommodations that the disabilities office has approved, there is typically a complaint process, which also must be initiated by the student.

When advising high school students regarding transition or assessing students with disabilities in a college setting, there are a number of study skill measures that can compliment temperament assessment. For example, the Learning and Study Strategies Inventory (LASSI; Weinstein, 2002) as well as the Motivated Strategies for Learning Questionnaire (MSLQ; Pintrich et al., 1991) can provide confirmatory support for learning preference dimensions on temperament instruments such as the SSQ, MMTIC, or MBTI.

There are numerous accommodation services available through colleges, and the structure for ADA support varies by institution (see Rapid Reference 6.4). Some will provide advisors to counselor students on needs, tutors, organize study groups, provide assistive technology labs, study skills workshops, mental health and motivation clinics, and maintain private testing space for student use. Others may not have the resources, and in those circumstances, self-initiated strategies become more important for the individual. Many of the accommodations assumed in K-12 educational institutions are no longer available in postsecondary (e.g., curriculum changes, special education classes, slower instructional pacing, use of notes for exams, streamlined exams). Although course substitutions may be available, there is a caveat in that the course cannot be a core content area for the degree sought. For example, a highly introverted student may not be approved to take a substitute for a class in public dance performance if the professional degree sought is performing arts. The Americans with Disabilities Act (1990) regulations (§240.153) regarding reasonable substitutions for graduation requirements is only for courses that do not constitute fundamental knowledge in the degree area. Coupled with knowledge of college accommodation guidelines and self-advocacy skills, students with disabilities are better assured success.

≡ *Rapid Reference 6.4*

Advocating for College Accommodations

Exams/Instruction: extra time on tests, alternate answer formats (e.g., scantron), test breaks, separate test setting, lecture copies if impaired writing, large print handouts for vision disabilities, assistant for required fine motor tasks (e.g., science lab experiments), tutors, study groups, study skills workshops

Classroom: priority seating, equipment (e.g., handicap accessible desk), note taker if physically impaired, scribe, sign-language interpreter, flexible attendance for documented and required medical treatments, extra course drops and re-takes with approved petitions, course substitutions, permission to tape record lectures, assistive technologies (e.g., listening devices), large print textbooks

APPLICATIONS IN COUNSELING

Temperament research regardless of the theoretical orientation, from infant studies to adult psychological types, has documented social and emotional outcomes correlating with temperament qualities. Some qualities such as Thomas and Chess's easy temperament pattern, Caspi's resilients, or Kagan's unhibited children are associated with positive achievement and psychological well-being factors. Others, as noted by the difficult temperament pattern, undercontrollers, overcontrollers, and inhibited, are associated with risk for a variety of poor outcomes. Within the adult psychological temperament paradigm for Jung, pathology risk was perceived as correlating with very extreme qualities that left deficits in the opposing dimension.

Myers and Briggs generally perceived psychological temperament qualities as profiles of personal strengths and lesser-developed attributes. Murphy, Meisgeier, and Oakland expanded type theory applications to the learning and personal interaction styles of children. All of these theoretical approaches can serve to inform counselors and therapists as they intervene. The choice of assessment instruments and methods will reflect the intended age group as well as the training and orientation of the practitioner (e.g., counselor, psychologist, school psychologist).

Parent-Child Interactions

Parent-child counseling services may be provided in a variety of settings and formats by a wide range of professionals. Therefore, service models will differ as well as the types of assessment data utilized. As examples, hospitals, especially those associated with universities, may offer multiple parent-child clinics for children with early risk factors. In hospital clinics referrals are often generated by neurologists and pediatricians who provide services for high-risk infants, toddlers, and young children. These children may have physical health as well as psychiatric diagnoses and can present complex needs. Some clinics also accept parent and agency referrals for inclusion in their programs. General public access programs are often at least partially supported by research or public and private grants with specific missions to advance knowledge and also provide direct services. Clinics also may accept insurance and offer sliding scale rates as their purpose is to assist at-risk children and families, and they may also have limited financial resources. The orientation of these types of clinics tends to be behavioral healthcare, and they are often associated with clinical psychology, child psychology, counseling psychology, pediatric medicine, or psychiatry departments. The length of participation in the clinic programs may be short or long-term depending on the type of assistance and mission of the program.

Although hospital-based outpatient clinics can be designed to accept a variety of general behavioral needs, they also may be designed as specialized clinics, limited to patients with particular physical or mental health challenges. Specialized clinics may be limited to a specific age range; however, they also can be designed to serve both children and adolescents depending on the syndrome. In these types of clinics, the counseling therapy may be targeted at treatment compliance, behavioral management of symptoms, and/or family stress and coping mechanisms. Examples of clinics providing a combination of physical health care with psychological and behavioral services for parent-child dynamics include:

- Child/adolescent behavioral clinics for oppositional, defiant, aggressive, rapid mood changes, attachment issues, depression, anxiety, adjustment reactions to trauma or dramatic life events, or self-injurious behaviors. Clinics may require a mental health diagnosis based on the Diagnostic and Statistical Manual of Mental Disorders, Fourth Edition, Text Revision (DSM-IV-TR) for inclusion (American Psychiatric Association, 2000). Common diagnoses include depression, bipolar, general anxiety, separation anxiety disorder, oppositional defiant disorder, conduct disorder, post-traumatic stress disorder, and adjustment disorders (see Rapid Reference 6.5). Some programs also accept children without a diagnoses that present with subclinical symptoms that are deteriorating family functioning and thus warrant treatment. Treatment modalities include psychoeducational, behavioral, cognitive-behavioral, and medication regimens as well as parent-child interaction therapy.

- Child/Adolescent units for severe and chronic illnesses that may be incurable or physically limiting (e.g., degenerative genetic disorders or chromosomal abnormalities) monitor long-term treatment regimens that may be particularly stressful to children and families; counseling focuses on pain management, building coping and stress management skills, decreasing child/parent conflicts, increasing medical compliance factors, fostering nurturing parental instincts, connecting families with agencies of financial or social services, as well as parent support groups.

- Child/adolescent diabetes treatment compliance clinics focus on teaching diet management and self-monitoring of blood glucose utilizing psychoeducational and behavioral approaches for difficult-to-manage cases coupled with parent counseling for enabling escape behaviors, poor diet monitoring or family nutrition habits, and poor medication adherence.

- Child/adolescent morbid obesity units, combining in-patient and out-patient services for determination of best candidacy for bypass surgery and post-surgical diet management combined with parent counseling for enabling behaviors related to poor family nutrition habits, utilizing a cognitive-behavioral approach.

- Child/adolescent obsessive-compulsive disorder clinics providing short-term, out-patient therapy often with follow-up booster sessions, utilizing cognitive-behavioral, exposure and response prevention approaches, and addressing parent interaction behaviors that reinforce or facilitate maladaptive behaviors (e.g., accommodating repeated hand washing or just right rituals, reinforcing escape from anxiety-invoking circumstances or prompting fear obsessions).

- Adolescent substance abuse programs may provide short-term out-patient therapy or continuum services from in-patient to out-patient for intensive treatment of refractory substance abuse, including family therapy for enabling or denial behaviors, polysubstance abusers, and addiction patterns across multiple family members.

Within clinical settings, assessment begins with the initial intake interview and includes health/psychiatric history and establishing level of impairment. When

≡ Rapid Reference 6.5

DSM-IV-TR Disorder Symptoms

In considering temperament qualities that may be applicable to mental health disorders, it is important to be familiar with the symptoms and characteristics that constitute some common childhood diagnoses.

Adjustment Disorders: Symptoms include clinically significant distress in excess of typical stressor responses; significant social, academic or occupational functioning impairment; subtypes include depressed mood, anxiety, and emotional and conduct disturbances. The temperament qualities of adaptability, threshold of responsiveness, intensity of reaction, quality of mood, inhibited, over- or under-controllers, and introversion or extroversion may be relevant to how individuals cope with major life stressors.

Bipolar: Symptoms include manic episodes, depression, and significant impairment in social, academic or occupational performance. Specifiers may include psychotic features, seasonal patterns or rapid cycling. Relevant temperament qualities may include intensity of reaction, quality of mood, threshold of response, under-controllers, and social impairment or manic behaviors may be relevant to feeling, or introversion and extroversion.

Conduct Disorder (CD): Symptoms may include repetitive and persistent patterns of bullying, threatening or intimidating, physical aggression toward others, cruelty to animals or people, destruction of property, fire-setting, theft, lying, running away, and truancy. If aspects of the conduct disorder behaviors are thought to be related to anger management, frustration, or tolerance for others, the following temperament qualities may be relevant: adaptability, threshold of responsiveness, intensity of reaction, quality of mood, under-controllers, thinking, and extroversion expressions.

Depressive Disorders: Symptoms may include depressed mood such as feelings of emptiness or sadness (irritability in children), decreased interest or pleasure in activities, significant weight change (loss or gain), sleep disturbance (insomnia or hypersomnia), psychomotor agitation or hyperactivity, fatigue, decreased concentration, difficulty with decision making, and preoccupation with thoughts of death or suicidal ideation. Activity level, rhythmicity, approach/withdrawal, adaptability, threshold of responsiveness, intensity of reaction, quality of mood, inhibited, over-controllers, and feeling temperament qualities may be topics of discussion in parent-child therapy for children with depression.

General Anxiety (including Overanxious Disorder of Childhood): Symptoms may include anxiety, worry, apprehension, restlessness, fatigue, difficulty concentrating, irritability, tense muscles, and sleep disturbances. These

(continued)

symptoms are accompanied by significant impairment in social, school, or occupational performance. Related temperament qualities include approach/withdrawal, adaptability, threshold of responsiveness, intensity of reaction, inhibited, over-controllers, and perhaps feeling or organized (i.e., judging) characteristics.

Oppositional Defiant Disorder (ODD): Symptoms include a long-term pattern of hostile, negative, and defiant behaviors with significant impairment in social, academic, and/or occupational success. Specific behavioral manifestations include temper outbursts, arguing, defiance, noncompliance, deliberate agitation of others, blaming, being easily annoyed, resentfulness, vindictiveness, spitefulness, and anger. Adaptability, threshold of responsiveness, intensity of reaction, attention span/persistence, and under-controller temperament traits may be related to the low tolerance and highly reactive nature of ODD symptoms. If ODD behaviors are thought to be a result of rigid concrete-thinking patterns, misinterpretation of verbal intercourse, or lack of empathy, sensing (i.e., practical), and thinking temperament qualities may also be important topics for counseling therapy.

Post-traumatic Stress Disorder (PTSD): Symptoms include exposure to a traumatic event that is re-experienced through intrusive thoughts, dreams, hallucinations, or flashbacks; intense response with fear, helplessness, or horror (agitation or disorganization in children); avoidance of trauma-related stimuli; and/or persistently increased arousal states. Related temperament vulnerabilities may include early childhood approach/withdrawal, adaptability, threshold of responsiveness, intensity of reaction, inhibition, over-controllers, and a feeling orientation. In all mental health disorders, it is important to discuss temperament in lieu of points of personal vulnerability or coping mechanisms to strengthen. This caution is especially true of PTSD to avoid victim-blaming, misinterpretations, and counter-therapeutic consequences.

Separation Anxiety Disorder (SAD): Symptoms must be developmentally inappropriate for the child's age and include excessive anxiousness in regards to separation from the home or attachment figures (e.g., caregivers). Features include distress when away from home or family, worry about losing others, unwarranted anticipation of troublesome events (e.g., kidnappings, accidents, muggings), fear of being alone or separated from attachment figures, persistent nightmares, refusal or resistance to sleeping away from home/individuals they are attached to, and somatic complaints (e.g., stomachaches, headaches, nausea). In very young children fears many include animals, the dark, and imaginative figures such as monsters. Temperaments that include problematic approach/withdrawal, adaptability, threshold of responsiveness, intensity of reaction, inhibited, over-controller, feeling, and introversion qualities may present notable vulnerabilities.

temperament data are acquired to inform counseling, this can utilize both rating scales (e.g., parent, self) as well as direct clinical observations of parent-child interaction. Evaluation results may guide planning for specific topics in individual therapy sessions or guide assignment of families to small groups protocol units that routinely address common parenting issues, or emotional disorders depending on the clinic's program design. For example, Barlow has recommended a protocol that persons with anxiety, depression, and phobias are responsive to as a first line of treatment based on his research (DeAngelis, 2008). In addition, to hospital-based treatment facilities, hybrid clinics exist that combine hospital-affiliated treatment with direct services through public agencies or the home. These collaborative units may be government sponsored and often serve distinct needs that require multi-agency professional expertise. Examples of multidisciplinary and multi-agency clinics include:

- Child/adolescent diagnostic centers for complex learning disabilities, co-morbid learning and physical disabilities (e.g., SLD with seizure disorder) that provide clinical assessments, family counseling, in-school classroom teacher consultations, and participation in intervention planning for response-to-intervention or exceptional student education services.
- Child/adolescent long-term rehabilitation units (e.g., traumatic brain injury requiring retraining of speech, ambulatory mobility aids or prosthesis) provide family counseling for pain management, coping with body image changes, and reengaging in social functions.
- Homebound Liaisons are professionals who may work for school boards or hospitals; they ensure communication between the hospital and school on continuing academic instruction for children in long-term in-patient care, establish homebound school services as the patient is recuperating and assist parents with study at home behaviors. They again provide parent to school advocacy and preparation for reentry into the school and peer interactions once the student is ready to return. Depending on the illness or injury this process may extend for weeks or months and thus require greater responsibility for monitoring instruction at home on the part of the parents.
- Forensic Services may include child abuse or neglect protection units that assign case managers to support in-patient intake treatment followed by collaboration with criminal prosecution and witness preparation, support for custody hearing, foster care transitions or adoption matches. Child/adolescent forensic evaluations can also be a community outreach function of university law programs in defending families

requiring support services for special education in public schools and/ or manifestation determinations or threat evaluation circumstances.

In considering parent-child therapy temperament applications, it is important to acknowledge several underlying premises. First, temperament traits have biological underpinnings and can be identifiable early, even from infancy. As noted by Rothbart, Chew, and Garstein (2001), some temperament qualities are evident from the first month after birth. Therefore, temperament assessment and parent counseling, especially regarding behavioral modification strategies, is possible even from the toddler stage of development. Secondly, although considered innate, scholars also emphasize the interactive and reciprocal nature of early development including temperament traits. Thus, therapy should consider the interaction of the caregiver, teacher, environment, and child's response patterns. Thomas and Chess (1977) describe the goodness-of-fit principle as:

> This formulation stems from the conviction that normal or pathologic psychological development does not depend on temperament alone. Rather, it is the nature of the interaction between temperament and the individual's other characteristics with specific features of the environment, which provides the basic dynamic influence for the process of development. If there is a goodness of fit between children and environment, the foundation for a healthy self-concept and stable self-esteem is laid down. If there is a poorness of fit, a negative, denigrated self-evaluation begins to crystallize. If, in latter childhood or even in adult life, a poorness of fit can be altered, such as by the emergence of new positive capacities or a favorable change in the environment, then a negative self-image may be transformed into a positive one (p. 15–16).

This approach requires sensitivity on the part of practitioners that acknowledges temperament differences while respecting opposing needs of parents and children without interpreting them in a derogatory manner. The third premise is the conceptualization of early temperament as a predictive factor of risk for later psychopathology and/or achievement outcomes. Goodness of fit and risk predictive approaches are not mutually exclusive and a counselor will often combine these concepts to develop hypotheses about the child's functioning and devise counseling strategies.

Adolescent/Adult Mental Health

Mental health counseling can be provided in traditional hospital settings through residential, inpatient, and outpatient care. It is also common to receive counseling through public agencies (e.g., community mental health centers, substance abuse treatment centers, domestic violence programs, homeless rehabilitation support programs) and individual therapy in private practice clinics. In regards to individual therapy, it is the one area for temperament theory where the matching hypotheses that was discussed earlier has direct effects. In a study that trained counselors to match the patient's temperament style (MBTI) in therapy, lower therapy dropout rates, and attendance at more sessions was noted (Newman, 1979).

Within the school settings, intensive and long-term counseling services are usually provided through alternative education programs for students with emotional disturbance, and the providers may be school employees or contracted community mental health providers. The juvenile justice system also provides graduated levels of treatment for sex offenders, adjudicated youth, and incarcerated youth. The relevance of temperament to counseling in these settings will be based on the issue being addressed. Discussion of temperament in reference to general personal adjustment and coping skills is most common as they represent vulnerabilities. Regardless of temperament patterns, pathology is the result of a more complex constellation of factors. The list below provides a number of highlights from research utilizing adolescent and adult temperament assessment (Myers et al., 1998).

- Individuals with dominant sensing type (ESTP, ESFP, ISTJ, ISFJ) are overrepresented in problem behaviors in college (Provost, 1985).
- In the areas of work, finance, children, intimate relationships, school, health, care-giving for elderly parents, and balancing home and work, introverts report the highest perceived stress, suggesting extroversion may serve to insulate individuals somewhat from the effects of stress.
- Intuitive types report they are more likely to talk to a professional, try to think of options, and exercise in response to stress.
- Sensing/feeling types report they are likely to try to avoid stressful situations.
- Extroverts report they are more likely to confront problems (especially if also thinking type) when dealing with stress.
- Feeling types more often note they handle stress by avoiding the situation, talking to someone close, relying on religious beliefs (especially if also judging), and developing physical symptoms in response to stress.
- Introverts indicate watching television and getting upset without showing it more frequently as coping strategies.
- Emotional exhaustion is self-reported as highest among ISFP, ISFJ, ESTJ, and INTJ.

- Positive affect is highest for ESTP, ENTJ, ENFJ, and ESTJ.
- The majority of students with a diagnoses of Oppositional Defiant Disorder and Conduct Disorder indicate a preference for thinking style (Joyce & Oakland, 2005).
- A preference of practical (e.g., sensing) learning qualities is noted by students with Oppositional Defiant Disorder (Joyce & Oakland, 2005).

A select list of DSM-IV-TR adolescent/adult mental health disorders relevant to temperament characteristics is noted in Rapid Reference 6.6. It should also be acknowledged that some professionals, especially those in hospital settings, utilize the International Classification of Diseases (ICD) for diagnostic labels and symptom severity terminology consistent with the International Classification of Functioning, Disability, and Health (ICF) when diagnosing mental health disorders (Joyce & Dempsey, 2009; Joyce & Rossen, 2008). These systems are expected to better align when the ICD and DSM revisions are published in 2011.

☰ Rapid Reference 6.6

DSM-IV-TR Adolescent/Adult Disorder Symptoms

Avoidant Personality Disorder: Symptoms appear by early adulthood and may include social inhibition, feelings of inadequacy, hypersensitivity to negative evaluation, avoiding school and work activities with high interpersonal interactions, fear of disapproval or criticism, hesitancy in initiating involvement with others, fearing shame or ridicule in intimate relationships, distracted with thoughts of social rejection, inhibited due to inadequacy feelings, feeling socially inept or unappealing, and fear of embarrassment. These symptoms are particularly relevant to introverted and feeling temperament traits.

Dependent Personality Disorder: Symptoms begin in early adulthood and include a pervasive desire to be taken care of, fearfulness in separation, clinging, submissiveness, seeking reassurance often, feeling helpless when alone, and lacking self-confidence to initiate interactions. Weaknesses for extreme introversion and feeling qualities may align with this syndrome.

Schizoid Personality Disorder: Symptoms begin in early adulthood and include a notable pattern of social detachment, limited emotional expression, lack of close friends, indifference to criticism or praise, and a strong preference for solitary activities. Adult temperament qualities may align with the weaknesses of thinking and introversion characteristics.

CAREER COUNSELING AND BUSINESS

There are a number of career guides that assist novices with preliminary steps in identifying work interests based on analyzing the task components required for particular jobs. These guides then provide extensive lists based on research with a temperament measure (e.g., Kiersey Temperament Sorter, MBTI) that denote which specific job titles are most common and fulfilling among persons of specific temperaments (Martin, 1995). Utilizing the lists can help individuals consider options they may not have thought of before. Similar services are available online providing computer assessment and quickly generated structured reports in nontechnical language than explains temperament scores. Supplemental statistical data on job requirements, education, training, salaries, future employment patterns, and satisfaction are updated yearly and available to the public through the U.S. Bureau of Labor Statistics Occupational Outlook Handbook, found at: http://www.bls.gov/OCO/.

For more extensive and personalized career guidance, an individual may wish to consult a professional career counselor. A consultant who is trained in temperament and personality assessment as well as career applications can assist beyond just identifying good vocational choices. They can provide coaching that optimizes work performance and resolves any lesser-developed skills that are interfering with professional growth. They provide multi-facet assessments that include formal measures of interests (e.g., Campbell Interest and Skills Survey, Strong Interest Inventory) as well as measures of discrete skills (e.g., writing sample). In addition, career options are discussed in depth with consideration for their relevance to finding self-actualization based on assessment of the individual's personality and temperament (Lowman, 1991). Aptitudes may be assessed with intelligence tests (IQ) and processing measures (e.g., verbal reasoning, perceptual speed). Clinical career consultants provide formal reports and recommendations to clients. They also have knowledge of business networking and infrastructure that can facilitate career advancement planning. On a larger scale, consultants offer on-site training to small groups or entire corporations. Services may include workshops, team-building exercises, leadership development, and organizational analyses.

LIMITATIONS

Research has identified a number of long-term outcomes, both positive and negative, related to measures of temperament. These outcomes include PreK–12 academic achievement, college success, psychological well-being factors, and some forms of pathology. Interventions applied to learning styles, behavioral modification, counseling therapies, and business consulting are numerous. However, interventions, counseling, and treatment are based on limited research across a number of theoretical approaches. Treatment effect sizes of results often are not reported. In addition, much of the intervention literature does not provide information on efficacy of implementation or details on sample stratification that may consider gender, ethnicity, or cultural differences in treatment response. In fact, it appears the assessment literature is better developed than the intervention literature.

This dilemma is not unique to temperament, as multiple national organizations have called for more extensive and better designed intervention research and training. In the early 1990s medicine began calling physicians to move away from clinical judgment and rationales based on professional experience for treatment decisions and toward a more evidenced-based approach (Montori & Guyatt, 2008). Psychiatry through the National Institute of Mental Health called for expanding the national research portfolio to include a greater emphasis on public health outcomes from pharmacological and psychotherapeutic treatments (Norquist, Lebowitz, & Hyman, 1999). As the field of school psychology has moved to a response-to-intervention model many scholars have noted that training programs have not kept pace with national policy shifts (Dawson, Cummings, Harrison, Short, & Palomares, 2004; Ehrhardt-Padgett, Hatzichristou, Kitson, & Meyers, 2004). They call for more training in evidence-based intervention and instructional strategies (Elliot, Witt, Kratochwill, & Stoiber, 2002; Ysseldyke et al., 2006). The field of teacher education programs also has been encouraged by the American Psychological Association to rethink their college curriculum in response to limited teacher knowledge on interventions (Belar & Nelson, 2002). Therefore, directions in future research should include a significant emphasis on better delineation of treatment effects.

🏹 TEST YOURSELF 🏹

....

1. **In a three-tiered Response to Intervention (RtI) model, Tier II interventions are:**
   (a) Proactive, screening measures, universal
   (b) Intensive, individualized, longer duration
   (c) Supportive, universal, graduated in intensity
   (d) Supplemental, targeted, short-term, rapid response

2. **The steps in the Response to Intervention Problem Solving Process are:**

   (a) Explore the Issue, Analyze the Factors, Evaluate Behaviors, Set Goals

   (b) Define the Problem, Analyze the Problem, Develop and Implement the Plan, Evaluate Plan Effectiveness

   (c) Analyze the Program, Set Goals, Implement Plan, Refine the Intervention

   (d) Review Factors, Measure Behaviors, Analyze Behaviors, Set Goals

3. **For temperament interventions, the Matching Hypothesis refers to:**

   (a) Aligning curriculum sequence to benchmarks

   (b) Pairing children with similar learning styles together in cooperative groups

   (c) Coaching teachers to match their teaching styles to the student's learning style

   (d) Matching progress monitoring data sources to initial assessment data

4. **Repertoire Enhancement as related to temperament strategies includes:**

   (a) Providing more in-depth detail on a subject

   (b) Encouraging creativity in learning such as incorporating art and music themes

   (c) Expanding learning modalities within classrooms so there are a variety of methods in which students may acquire new information and provide answers or work products

   (d) Increasing the number of learning materials in classrooms such as books

5. **The definition of metacognition includes:**

   (a) Awareness, analysis, and reflection of one's own learning processes

   (b) Cognitive dissonance

   (c) Remediation of cognitive deficits

   (d) Cognitive congruence

6. **Which answer best encompasses major areas career counselors can assess?**

   (a) Career interests, personal satisfaction factors

   (b) Technical skills, job references, resume-writing skills

   (c) Intelligence, reading/math/writing achievement

   (d) Cognitive processes, interests surveys, aptitude tests, temperament measures

7. **Mental health forensic evaluations for children refer to:**

   (a) Multidisciplinary team arena assessments

   (b) Abuse/neglect case management, foster care transitions, legal proceedings

(*continued*)

(c) Learning styles teacher consultations

(d) Comorbid learning and mental health disabilities evaluations

8. Applications of temperament to rehabilitation for children include:

   (a) RtI universal screening assessment

   (b) Math and reading remediation

   (c) Restructuring memory strategies

   (d) Pain management, body image, transition to school

Answers: 1. d; 2. b; 3. c; 4. c; 5. a; 6. d; 7. b; 8.d

Seven

ILLUSTRATIVE CASE REPORTS

This chapter provides several sample psychological, psychoeducational, and counseling reports utilizing temperament measures. Temperament data are utilized by a wide range of professionals from the medical, mental health, educational, and career development communities. The reports illustrate integration of temperament data as a component of comprehensive evaluations for a variety of referral concerns, including family therapy, learning disabilities, threat assessment, behavioral concerns, rehabilitation planning, and counseling. The cases also provide application perspectives from a variety of settings, ages, and circumstances for which temperament information can be informative in understanding the individual's functioning. It should be noted, these samples are not all inclusive. There are many other widely utilized functions for temperament data including personality assessment, career planning, and corporate business team-building interpretations that are not represented in these select samples. Each section offers a brief case scenario that describes the context of the assessment and then a full report or summary including intervention or treatment recommendations as warranted.

DON'T FORGET

Multi-faceted Approach to Assessment

As noted in Chapter Four, best practices standards for educational and psychological assessment requires a multi-faceted approach rather than reliance on one data measure (AERA, 1999).

EVALUATION REPORTS—EARLY CHILDHOOD SAMPLES

Parent-Child Interaction Therapy Sample Utilizing the TABS

The first sample report in this chapter provides an example of behavioral concerns related to interactions between parents and their preschool child. The setting is a private clinic that specializes in family-child interaction support services. A variety of resources including parenting workshops, individual or family counseling, tutoring, social skills training, anger management techniques, stress management strategies, and parent support groups are provided. Referrals are generated from other medical or mental health professionals, as well as schools, youth agencies, and parents. The treatment or counseling plan is customized to each family's needs based on information from prior reports, intake interview, and in-clinic observations. Once services are implemented, participation in periodic follow-up visits are required to assess the effectiveness and adjust services as needed. In addition, the clinic offers collaboration with other agencies including public school systems.

≡ Rapid Reference 7.1

Thomas and Chess's Goodness of Fit Principle

Goodness-of-fit and poorness-of-fit are key considerations in parent-child interaction assessments utilizing temperament data. Parent and child temperaments do not have to be the same to foster good relationships. It is the understanding and tolerance of differences or lack thereof that determines if differences become sources of conflict and stress.

Child & Adolescent Family Clinic 982 Morris Avenue, Waterford, CT 18895

Intake and Counseling Plan Summary

Client Name: Mr. Robert and Mrs. Amanda Fuyu	Child's Name: Rebecca Fuyu
Intake Interview Date: 3–8–09	Case Number: 654321
Child's Age: 5 years, 5 months	Therapist: Dr. Emilia Rogers
Insurance Provider: Blue Cross/Blue Shield 56–56–876	

Rebecca Fuyu is a healthy five-year-old female who was first seen in clinic on March 8th, 2009, accompanied by her mother and father. Her parents indicate concerns for her excitability and sometimes disagreeable behaviors. The family is seeking guidance on parenting strategies.

Developmental History
Based on parent report and medical records, Rebecca was born full term without complications, and Ms. Fuyu had good prenatal care. No injuries or illnesses

are indicated, and Rebecca receives regular physical wellness exams from her pediatrician, Dr. Patricia Nelson. A developmental history indicates all major milestones were achieved on time and Rebecca began speaking somewhat earlier than typical.

Rebecca is an only child and resides with both parents. Her family is of Japanese descent, and both of her parents were born and educated in the United States. Ms. Fuyu has a master's degree in horticulture and stayed home to care for Rebecca till this year when she started preschool. She is currently teaching at Vanderson Community College. Mr. Fuyu is a chemist and employed at Alcon Products.

Her parents describe Rebecca as a lively child who is smart and asks questions all the time. They note she is loving and considerate most of the time. She has many friends at preschool, enjoys ballet class, and plays well with others. She has a good sleep routine, appears rested in the mornings, and the family is diligent in maintaining a healthy diet at home. Rebecca is usually provided fruits, nuts, or popcorn for snacks. Her appetite is described as hardy. Her parents enjoy a number of peaceful activities at home including reading and board games. They note Rebecca seems to prefer active hobbies like jumping on the trampoline or her bed, running in the yard, and she likes to have the television on all the time. The family enjoys bike riding, swimming, hiking, and attending movies together. As Rebecca is an only child, they often invite one of her friends along for recreational activities.

Most of the time, Rebecca is noted to be happy; however, her parents indicated as a toddler she had a propensity to whine and tantrum on occasion if she was prevented from engaging in a preferred activity. They thought she would grow out of this stage, and this did decrease with age. However, at the ages of three and four, Rebecca's behaviors appeared to shift to talking back and defiantly saying "No-No" to her parents' requests when she did not wish to comply. It was also difficult to get Rebecca to sit calming for any length of time. They have noted since entering preschool Rebecca is becoming more skilled at negotiating requests and arguing; she is also increasingly running off to play and just ignoring their directions. This has resulted in more parent-child disagreements and tension. Her parents are also embarrassed when these behaviors occur in public.

At preschool, her teachers describe Rebecca as a lovely child who is craving the attention of other children. They noted she has many friends and enjoys almost any activity. She learned to write numbers, letters, and her name quickly and has memorized all the words to their rhyming songs. They describe her as very bright. They note she can sit and contently chat with friends but becomes impulsive, silly, and teases others if left alone. The school recommended her parents discuss these characteristics with her pediatrician. Rebecca's parents followed up on the request and have provided this clinic with a copy of the evaluation. Based on parent/teacher ratings and examination, the findings ruled out Attention-Deficit/Hyperactivity Disorder at this time.

Parent/Child Temperament

Observation and interview of the parents' interaction style appears to indicate both are highly introverted, prefer quiet activities, and present a demur demeanor. They have strong expectations that Rebecca will also be content in solitary and quiet activities. In addition, they expect her to be less active than is developmental typically for five-year-old children. This difference in temperament qualities appears to be creating stress for the family. The parents were asked to complete the Temperament and Atypical Behavior Scale (TABS), a 55-item measure that assesses early childhood indicators of developmental dysfunction. Results indicate no significant concerns for Detached (t-score = 52), Underreactive (t-score = 51), or Dysregulated scales (t-score = 52). However, Hyper-sensitive/Active (t-score = 37) was in the delayed range.

> Detached: Rebecca reportedly does not stare, makes good eye contact, plays with toys appropriately, and does not wander inappropriately.

> Underactive: She is noted to smile and enjoy humor, play well, and has appropriate reaction to surprises and noises.

> Dysregulated: Her sleep hygiene is good, and she does not experience nightmares.

> Hyper-sensitive/Active: Rebecca is described as easily upset or frustrated, quick to anger, bossy, and demanding of attention.

Observation

Prior to the intake interview, the family was observed by an intern in the play area for 45 minutes. It was noted that both Mr. and Mrs. Fuyu presented a caring and respectful interaction style with Rebecca. They answered her repeated questions, kept a protective and watchful observance of her activities, offered to play a board game, which she was not interested in, and encouraged her to play with other children. When asked for a soda from the hallway snack area, her mother initially said no and suggested fruit juice, but acquiesced after several more requests. When Rebecca was left in the care of the intern as her parents were interviewed, she presented a very engaging and charming demeanor. She appeared genuinely interested in talking to the intern and wanted to share stories she appeared to be playfully making up. She was very interested in playing a toss game with two other children and followed the intern's directions well. She was able to take turns appropriately and share. Rebecca did have some difficulty disengaging from the game when her parents returned and it was time for her to leave. It was noted she at first argued, then pouted and dragged her feet as her parents escorted her out.

Family Counseling Plan

Based on initial interview and observations parent/child dynamics suggest very differing parent-child temperament qualities and some emerging oppositional behaviors that may be ameliorated with parent discipline skills training. Therefore, participating in the clinic's 10-session Positive Parenting Workshops is highly recommended. The workshops are based on Russell Barkley's Ten Steps program as noted below (Barkley, 1997). In addition, follow-up clinic visits and parent/child interaction observations will be provided at weeks five and eight to discuss progress and assess needs.

> Week One: Understanding Why Children Act Out. This session includes a discussion of how child-parent temperament differences may be recognized and perceived to lessen conflicts. The reasons and precursors to misbehavior are also reviewed.

> Week Two: Positive Attention. Session two teaches observation techniques and when it is important to ignore innocuous behaviors.

> Week Three: Fostering Compliance. Session three provides parents with strategies to build rapport with their children, as well as recognizing and complimenting appropriate behaviors.

> Week Four: Token Economies. Contingency management, setting clear rules, and the power of rewards and privileges are incorporated into session four.

> Week Five: Time Out and Other Tricks. Information on age-appropriate use of the time out strategy is provided.

> Week Six: When Time Out Doesn't Work. This session reviews the efficacy of parents' practice with timeout and enhances applications.

> Week Seven: Showtime — Kids and Public Events. Techniques for planning public trips and materials to bring so children are engaged is reviewed. In addition, parents participate in planning one specific event for the following week.

Week Eight: A+ Kids at School. Homework plans and skills for collaboration with school personnel are reviewed and practiced.

Week Nine: Staying a Step Ahead. Principles of behavior change plans are introduced.

Week 14: Booster Session & Celebration (Final session is one month after week nine to review progress).

Collaboration

The Child and Adolescent Family Clinic is committed to successful parent/child outcomes. Copies of reports and collaboration with other health care professionals and students' schools are available by parent request and written consent.

Dr. Emilia Rogers, LMHC 12345

Clinical-setting Learning Disability Sample Utilizing the SSQ

This psychological evaluation sample is based on a referral for an elementary-age child who was referred to a pediatric clinic specializing in cases comorbid for both mental health and physical disabilities. Children with chronic health needs are often at risk for poor academic achievement for a variety of reasons. They incur more absences due to treatment needs often they are prescribed multiple medications that require change and trial adjustments as they mature. In addition, they may experience medication side effects that impact learning and sometimes have physical disabilities that impede academic performance depending on the health concern. Outpatient clinics of this type typically serve children with more complex needs that require the expertise of multiple healthcare professionals (e.g., pediatricians, physical therapists, neurologists), monitoring for long-term medication compliance, and children who most likely already receive in-school intervention services yet learning difficulties persist despite these efforts. Cases of this type often require multifaceted interventions that address medical, mental health, learning disabilities, personality factors, and personal motivation to help children best adjust to their challenges. Temperament data can enhance a holistic view of the individual.

> **DON'T FORGET**
> ....
>
> **Dimension Term Differences for SSQ and MBTI**
>
> Remember two dimensions on the SSQ differ from the MBTI. Practical-Imaginative is equivalent to Sensing-Intuitive and Flexible-Organized is equivalent to Perceiving-Judging.

Glover West Children's Clinic Department of Pediatrics
2929 Hilltop Road Glover, MO 12345

Psychological Evaluation		
Name: Penelope Gonzalez	Age: 10	Date of Birth: 1–2–99
Evaluation Date: 1–21–09	Sex: Female	Grade: 3rd

This report contains privileged/confidential information protected under provision of HIPAA and may only be released with written patient or legal guardian consent, except as provided by law.

I. REASON FOR REFERRAL

Penelope was referred to Glover West Children's Clinic by her mother because of long-standing medical concerns that may negatively impact her education. She is a 10-year-old female who is repeating the third grade at Glencove Elementary School. The student has not made adequate progress for two years in reading. Her teachers note difficulty with frequent chatting, lack of attention to instruction, difficulty remembering new information, and a lack of attention to details including careless errors. She has a history of idiopathic seizures. The goal of this evaluation is to better understand her cognitive profile, achievement needs, and to consult with the school and parents on learning strategies.

II. HISTORY AND OBSERVATIONS

Family and Medical History. A review of medical records indicates that Penelope was born full term without complications, weighing eight pounds and two ounces. At six months of age, she experienced several idiopathic seizures and was diagnosed with epilepsy. She was prescribed divalproex sodium (Depakote) to treat her seizures. At the age of five she was diagnosed with Attention Deficit/Hyperactivity Disorder, combined type and prescribed Adderall. This was recently changed to methylphenidate (Ritalin). Penelope reached all her developmental milestones within normal limits and no other illness or injuries are reported.

During an interview with her mother, she noted Penelope has always been rambunctious and full of energy. She also mentioned that Penelope is good-hearted, kind, and fun. Penelope has many friends, enjoys a variety of activities (e.g., playing tag ball, swimming, drawing, dancing), and treats others with respect. She is compliant with most requests, although she sometimes is inattentive, forgets direction, and can be impulsive. Penelope lives with her mother, grandmother, and sister (Angela, age 8). They reportedly share a room, have a very close relationship, and both are very neat in organizing their personal things.

The family heritage is Hispanic-American as Penelope's paternal grandparents immigrated to the United States 42 years ago from Cuba. The only language spoken in the home has been English, and the family has not maintained contact with extended family in Cuba for two generations. Both of Penelope's parents and her sister were born and attended school only in the United States. Her parents are divorced, and Penelope and her sister spend every other weekend, some holidays, and part of the summer with their father. The parents have positive communication, share custody, both attend the same Catholic church, and participate in family/school conferences to ensure that their daughters have cohesive family support.

Educational History. A review of school records indicates a lack of work completion often due to chatting, or out-of-seat visiting behaviors, and poor early reading skills in kindergarten. In first grade, Penelope's Dynamic Indicators of Basic Literacy Skills (DIBELS) scores were below benchmark levels for several areas (i.e., initial sound fluency, phoneme segmentation, and nonsense word fluency). Subsequently, she began receiving small group, Tier II supplemental instruction for an additional 30 minutes each day and made initial improvement. In addition, she was provided a Section 504 plan for testing and work accommodations based on her epilepsy and ADHD diagnoses. During second grade, she started the year meeting benchmarks, but small group intervention was again required for the spring semester. Mrs. Gonzalez reports that Penelope experienced a significant increase in seizures at that time and there were several medication trials to adjust her treatment through the spring term. Although her attendance is usually good, she missed 21 days of schools that semester due to illness and medical appointments. In consultation between the parent and school, it was thought that these factors were contributing to her academic difficulties, especially given that Penelope often could not recall recently learned information following more severe seizures. At the end of the year, it was decided that Penelope would repeat second grade. During the second year of second grade her seizures decreased dramatically and performance improved. However, at the beginning of her current third grade fall term, she again has low DIBELS, MAZE, Fox-in-a-Box, and curriculum-based measurement scores in reading fluency and comprehension. So far this year she has been provided 10 weeks of Tier III intensive reading remediation support (total 150 minutes per day) in a group of three children by the school reading specialist. If her scores do not improve by spring, she will be considered for eligibility for Tier IV, Exceptional Student Education (ESE) placement.

III. EVALUATION MEASURES

Behavior Rating Inventory of Executive Function, Teacher Form (BRIEF-T)

Behavior Assessment System for Children, Second Edition (BASC-2)

Children's Memory Scale (CMS)

Comprehensive Test of Phonological Processing (CTOPP)

Conners' Teacher Rating Scale–Revised, Long Version

NEPSY-II, Second Edition

Student Styles Questionnaire (SSQ)

Woodcock Johnson Test of Cognitive Abilities, Third Edition (WJ-III-Cog)

Woodcock Johnson Test of Achievement, Third Edition (WJ-III-Ach)

IV. EVALUATION

Behavior Observation. Penelope's psychological evaluation was conducted in the mornings on two different occasions, lasting approximately three hours each session and breaks were provided every hour. On each day, she had taken her medications prior to evaluation. She presented an effervescent, outgoing demeanor, eagerly greeting clinic staff and often attempting to engage the examiner in conversation. Rapport was easily established, and Penelope seemed eager to participate in most tasks. It was noted that she utilized sub-vocalizations when pondering answers, often quietly talking to herself. On math items, she would count on her fingers and draw numbers in the air with dramatic gestures using her fingers. She looked to the examiner frequently and appeared to thrive on attention with noticeable increase in work energy. She exhibited good attention with occasional fidgeting but was easily redirected. Penelope sometimes gave quick answers with little deliberation. On items she found more complex, she would persist in trying to think of an answer and then shrug her shoulders. Overall, her effort and concentration appeared good.

Memory. On the Children's Memory Scale (CMS), her General Memory score is in the lower extreme range (63, 1st percentile). She had the most difficulty remembering complex information, on subtests requiring sustained attention, and mental manipulation of information. Her ability to recall verbal information (both immediately and after a short delay) was better when it was personally meaningful (e.g., placed within a story). In contrast, she had difficulty with isolated verbal information such as lists. She did not appear to utilize any explicit memory strategies (e.g., verbal rehearsal, categorizing, grouping). Working memory—the ability to temporarily store information, reorder, and then recall the information—was particularly difficult for Penelope. She received a score well below average.

Attention and Concentration. Attention and Concentration skills were assessed with the CMS, BASC-2, and sustained attention work samples. It was noted that Penelope's attention was variable and subject to distractions from innocuous stimuli (e.g., AC, quiet footsteps in the hallway). On CMS tasks that required sustained attention to recall numbers and information sequences, it was difficult for her to recall more than 4 items. On the BASC-2, both teacher and parent ratings indicated at-risk concerns for attention problems. More specifically, they endorsed questions suggesting a short attention span, distractibility, propensity to interrupt others, and careless errors.

Executive Functioning. The Behavior Rating Inventory of Executive Function (BRIEF) was completed by Ms. Gonzalez. Her responses indicate difficulties with self-regulating behavior and metacognitive skills (e.g., ability to inhibit impulsive responses, use of problem-solving strategies, and self-monitoring of behavior). In addition, select tests were administered from the NEPSY-II that measure ability to quickly change tasks, attend to information, and inhibit impulsiveness. Her responses include many omissions and errors suggesting difficulty with attention and inhibiting impulses. She performed well on tasks requiring conceptual categorization of objects. She experienced the most difficulty with tasks requiring her to plan, visually organize, and integrate visual information to solve problems. She also found visual matching of patterns and visual discrimination difficult. When asked to analyze and reproduce simple two-dimensional spatial designs, she was able to follow directions but became easily frustrated with complex samples.

Processing Speed. Penelope's processing speed was assessed with select tasks from the Woodcock Johnson Test of Cognitive Abilities, Third Edition (WJ-III-Cog) that required her to quickly identify patterns under time-limited circumstances. She found this detail-oriented task laborious, worked slowly, and became frustrated towards the end of the task.

V. ACHIEVEMENT ASSESSMENT

The Woodcock Johnson Test of Achievement, Third Edition (WJ-III-Ach) and the Comprehensive Test of Phonological Processing (CTOPP) were administered to measure achievement and grade-level norms are provided as she was retained. On the WJ-III-Ach, her broad reading score was well below average (SS = 69). She had difficulty reading short sentences, identifying 3–6 letter words and comprehending short sentences. On the Comprehensive Test of Phonological Processing (CTOPP), her scores were below average on tasks requiring her to analyze and synthesize oral language as well as recall phonological information. Her broad ability to solve math problems and apply math concepts was in the low-average range (SS = 88, WJ-III-Ach). Calculation skills requiring addition and subtraction under timed conditions was average.

VI. SOCIAL-EMOTIONAL FUNCTIONING

Parent ratings on the BASC-2 indicate at-risk range concerns for externalization characteristics such as oppositional and defiant behaviors (e.g., arguing, disobedience). In contrast, the teacher rating notes these areas as in the average or normal range. Parental ratings also indicate at-risk range concerns for internalizing symptomology including anxiety, depression, and somatization (e.g., worrying, quick mood changes, crying, and vague sickness complaints).

School and Peer Relationships. Teacher ratings for school and learning problems are in the at-risk to clinically significant range. Both her mother and teacher note several positive qualities for Penelope (i.e., makes friends, shows good judgment, shows respect, helpfulness to others).

Temperament. Penelope was administered the Student Styles Questionnaire (SSQ) as a measure of temperament. Results indicate a very strong preference for extroversion as she endorsed items noting she prefers to work in groups, utilize verbal expression, indicated she has lots of friends, and likes to talk. Her enthusiasm for interacting with others and her desire for personal attention were also evident throughout her visits to the clinic and during testing as well as items on the BASC-2. On items related to her learning preferences, she endorsed a moderate desire for imaginative traits including enjoying ideas over facts and made-up stories. She prefers a moderate feeling orientation to making decisions, noting she likes to help others and is prone to sensitive responses when others are upset or she perceives she is being teased. Her desire to interact with others in a helpful manner was also noted in parent/teacher BASC-2 data. Lastly, Penelope's scores indicate a mild propensity toward organized temperament qualities in organizing her daily life activities. She prefers structure and order. Her mother also mentioned this quality in noting how organized Penelope keeps her bedroom.

VII. SUMMARY

Penelope is a ten-year old girl who is repeating the third grade. She was referred by her mother because despite numerous school interventions, she is still struggling in reading. In addition, there are concerns for attention and off-task behaviors. Penelope has a history of epilepsy and a prior diagnosis of ADHD Combined Type. She is currently taking medications for both and reportedly her seizures have decreased significantly in frequency.

Assessment indicates she has difficulty remembering complex patterns of visual information, verbal memory tasks, and working memory. Both her teacher and mother report attention problems and risk for hyperactivity despite current medication for ADHD. Executive functioning measures indicate difficulty inhibiting impulses, planning and problem-solving strategies, as well as the ability to self-monitor her own behavior. She demonstrated difficulty discriminating between visual stimuli, perceiving spatial location, and integrating visual information. Reading skills are significantly below average including fluency and synthesizing sounds. Penelope's math skills were in the low average range for problem solving, arithmetic, and math reasoning. Behavioral ratings indicate at-risk concerns for hyperactivity, oppositional/defiant behavior, anxiety, depression, and somatization characteristics. She endorses an extroversion-imaginative-feeling-organized temperament profile.

VIII. DIFFERENTIAL DIAGNOSIS

Axis I: Attention Deficit Hyperactivity Disorder, Combined Type (314.01)

Axis II: None (V71.09)

Axis III: Epilepsy, Grand Mal (345.10)

Axis IV: Academic Problems (V62.3)

Axis V: GAF = 60

IX. RECOMMENDATIONS

- Penelope has a diagnosis of ADHD combined type, and despite medication, ratings of hyperactive behaviors remain high. Therefore, it may be important to discuss this evaluation with her pediatrician. Children with ADHD benefit from structured environments and work space that is free of unnecessary distracting objects. They may need assistance in organizing their work (e.g., iconic schedule, reminders, color coded notebooks or folders, frequent homework checks, and close monitoring) as well as in-class proximity control and cueing techniques to ensure they are on task. In addition, teaching Penelope self-monitoring strategies to remind her to stay on task, checking work for careless errors, and delaying impulsive actions may be helpful. Teacher cueing reminders to return to task may also be helpful. Tracking strategies, such as a creating a cut-out window in an index card that she can utilize as she reads, also may help her focus. In addition, organizing work into smaller segments with frequent breaks may improve attention.

- To address parental concern for emerging oppositional behaviors, resources on strategies for positive commands, redirection, and positive reinforcement have been provided.
- Increase reading instruction support and consider individual rather than group remediation instruction. Explicit instruction in phoneme segmentation (e.g., deleting and adding individual phonemes for words) and phoneme blending may be helpful.
- Penelope needs additional practice with applied math problems and calculations to increase her speed/fluency. Therefore, she may benefit from step-by-step cue cards for problem solving as well as timed games for building math speed.
- To improve memory, Penelope would benefit from explicit instruction in memory strategies (e.g., chucking, elaborative rehearsal, mnemonic strategies).
- Penelope indicates an extroversion-imaginative-feeling-organized temperament profile. As her endorsement of extroversion is very strong, she has significant strengths in this area that should be encouraged. For example, despite her occasional public seizures she is not easily embarrassed, has good social skills, and does not shrink away from engaging in activities with others. Instructional techniques that incorporate high-energy opportunities for participation, discussions, and cooperative group methods can be particularly engaging. Public recognition also can be highly motivating to extroverts and thus a potent reinforcer in modifying behavior. In contrast, listening to teacher lectures and independent or solitary tasks (e.g., reading silently) are more difficult and skills Penelope will need encouragement to foster. Her moderate propensity for imaginative learning methods is consistent with conceptual learning strategies that focus on ideas utilizing words, metaphors, and symbols. The opposing practical qualities are lesser developed as noted by her parent/teacher indication that she overlooks details and makes

minor errors. Establishing an icon or nonverbal teacher reminder cue to check her work may reduce these types of errors. Instruction that is presented in the context of connection to people is of particular importance to children with feeling qualities. By all reports, Penelope is very interested in the well-being of others and thus elaboration memory strategies that link new information to its human relevance may improve her recall ability. She also expresses a mild preference for organization qualities that can be capitalized on in structuring her assignments.

Janelle Roberts, PhD
Psychologist, License # 1234–5Q

IV. PSYCHOMETRIC DATA SUMMARY
Behavior Assessment System for Children (BASC-2)

	Teacher		Parent	
	T-Score	Percentile	T-Score	Percentile
Externalizing Behaviors	48	49	67	94
Hyperactivity	58	82	72	96
Aggression	43	24	60	85
Conduct Problems	42	20	65	92
Internalizing Behaviors	46	42	65	92
Anxiety	45	37	64	92
Depression	53	73	59	84
Somatization	43	21	64	90
School Problems	68	95	—	—
Attention Problems	68	95	69	96
Learning Problems	66	91	—	—
Behavioral Symptoms Index	55	75	69	95
Atypicality	53	75	65	92
Withdrawal	49	58	62	88
Adaptive Skills Composite	38	11	40	17
Adaptability	52	56	41	20
Social Skills	42	22	54	64
Leadership	35	5	38	12

	Teacher		Parent	
	T-Score	Percentile	T-Score	Percentile
Activities of Daily Living	—	—	39	15
Study Skills	34	8	—	—
Functional Communication	32	6	37	11

Behavior Rating Inventory of Executive Functioning (BRIEF)

	T-Score	Percentile
Behavioral Regulation Index	64	93
Inhibit	77	96
Shift	49	65
Emotional Control	61	90
Metacognitive Index	81	98
Initiate	85	>99
Working Memory	99	>99
Plan/Organize	61	87
Organization of Materials	46	60
Monitor	84	>99
Global Executive Composite	77	96

Children's Memory Scale (CMS)	Standard Score	Percentile
Visual Memory – Immediate	75	5
Visual Memory – Delayed	78	7
Verbal Memory – Immediate	63	1
Verbal Memory – Delayed	78	7
General Memory	63	1
Attention/Concentration	63	1
Learning	72	3
Delayed Recognition	63	1

Comprehensive Test of Phonological Processing (CTOPP)

	Standard Score	Percentile
Phonological Awareness	73	4
Phonological Memory	61	<1
Rapid Naming	70	2
Alternate Phonological Awareness	73	4

NEPSY II

	Scaled Score	Percentile
Animal Sorting – Correct Sorts	9	37
Animal Sorting – Combined	8	25
Auditory Attention – Total Correct	5	5
Auditory Attention – Combined	6	9
Response Set – Total Correct	1	1
Response Set – Combined	9	37
Clocks	2	4
Inhibition – Naming Total Time	3	1
Inhibition – Naming Combined	1	1
Inhibition – Total Time	5	5
Inhibition – Combined	6	9
Switching Total Time	11	63
Switching Combined	5	5
Inhibition Total Errors	1	.1
Arrows	2	.4
Design Copying Total Score	9	37
Design Copying Motor Score	6	9
Design Copying Global Score	8	25
Design Copying Local Score	15	95
Geometric Puzzles	1	.1
Picture Puzzles	2	.4

Student Styles Questionnaire (SSQ)

	T-Scores
Extroversion	80
Imaginative	64
Feeling	56
Organized	54

Woodcock-Johnson Tests of Academic Achievement, Third Edition (WJ-III ACH)

(Norms based on grade)	Standard Score	Percentile	95% Band
Broad Reading	69	2	(63–75)
Basic Reading Skills	77	6	(72–82)
Letter-Word Identification	75	5	(63–75)
Reading Fluency	—	—	—
Passage Comprehension	81	16	(78–92)
	Standard Score	Percentile	95% Band
Word Attack	89	23	(83–95)
Broad Math	88	21	(83–93)
Math Calculation Skills	93	33	(86–100)
Calculations	97	42	(89–105)
Math Fluency	80	9	(72–87)
Applied Problems	85	16	(78–92)

Woodcock-Johnson Tests of Academic Achievement, Third Edition (WJ-III ACH)

(Norms Based on Age)	Standard Score	Percentile	95% Band
Broad Reading	52	<0.1	(47–58)
Basic Reading Skills	69	2	(66–73)
Letter-Word Identification	60	.4	(56–65)
Reading Fluency	—	—	—
Passage Comprehension	66	1	(60–73)

Word Attack	82	7	(77–87)
Broad Math	74	4	(69–78)
Math Calculation Skills	74	4	(68–81)
Calculations	79	8	(70–88)
Math Fluency	63	1	(57–69)
Applied Problems	72	3	(66–79)

Woodcock-Johnson Tests of Cognitive Abilities, Third Edition (WJ-III Cog)

	Standard Score	Percentile	95% Band
Processing Speed	74	4	(69–79)
Decision Speed	97	43	(90–104)
Visual Matching	59	.3	(53–64)

EVALUATION REPORTS: ADOLESCENTS

School-based Threat Assessment Sample Utilizing the SSQ

This case report provides a sample psychoeducational report illustrating integration of the Student Styles Questionnaire as a measure of temperament for a school-based evaluation that was thought to possibly include pathology. The evaluation required a social-emotional focused assessment and was initiated by a perceived written threat against other students at the school. The student had a history of early speech delays and fatigue when writing. These difficulties had resulted in early identification for Exceptional Student Education (ESE) services for speech-language impairment and occupational therapy. The student met remediation goals and was eventually dismissed from services; however, a Section 504 plan was recommended and continued to provide accommodations including extra time on tests and modified curriculum. During interviews reports of multiple subclinical symptoms including sensitivity to noise, tactile sensory aversions, attention difficulties, and staring episodes were noted. The evaluator also was asked to address concerns for compliance with work assignments, difficulties with social isolation and peer relationships, poor organization skills, and recommendations on well-being supports that may be needed when the student returned to school. Therefore, the approach to the evaluation included interviews, threat assessment measures, broad omnibus measures of social-emotional constructs followed up with narrow measures in the areas of concern, as well as personality and temperament assessment. In addition, a simultaneous psychiatric evaluation through a hospital clinic was required by the school board before the student could be permitted back on campus.

Victory High School 123 Martin Lane, Copperville, GA
Psychoeducational Evaluation

This report contains privileged and confidential information for a minor and may only be released with written parental consent except as provided by law.

Identifying Information	
Student's Name: Jimmy Smith	**Parent/Guardian:** Ms. Anna Smith
Date of Birth (DOB): 1–2–1989	**Chronological Age:** 14–0
Sex: Male	**Grade:** 9th
Examiner: Rex Kendall, Ph.D., NCSP	**Dates of Evaluation(s):** 1–2–03, 1–3–03, 1–5–03

Reason for Referral

Jimmy is a 14-year-old student at Victory High School who was referred for a social-emotional evaluation. The evaluation was prompted by a 10-day suspension for a note suggesting a threat on the safety of other students. In addition, his grades have also recently fallen and concern was noted for processing speed. A Manifestation Determination hearing was conducted on 1–2–03 and parental consent was provided for an evaluation. In addition, authorization was signed to share information with a psychiatrist (Dr. West at Clairmont Hospital Adolescent Psychiatric Unit) and Ms. Arthur, a school district social worker. A simultaneous psychiatric evaluation was initiated in conjunction with this psychoeducational assessment as required by the school board before Jimmy is permitted to reenter the school while classes are in session and other students are on campus.

Background Information

Medical/Social Emotional History. School records indicate a health examination prior to attending Victory High School (8–15–02) with all health factors in the normal range. There are no indications in school records of current medications or health needs. Jimmy's mother, Ms. Smith, provided the following information through an interview and completion of the Behavior

Assessment System for Children, 2nd Edition, Structured Developmental History on 1–2–03. Both parents are college graduates with long-term, stable careers. Ms. Smith indicated she is currently self-employed as a floral designer (5 years) and has recently started a second job as a nurse. Her husband, Mr. Jackson Smith Sr., has been employed in the textile industry (18 years). Jimmy resides with both parents and four siblings. English is the only language spoken in the home. Jimmy's relationship with his siblings is described as mostly good with typical sibling teasing, fussing, and occasional bickering. The family is also close to both sets of grandparents. Paternal grandparents reside in Idaho and visit annually. Maternal grandparents also live in Copperville and visit weekly, interacting with both Jimmy and his siblings on a consistent basis. The family enjoys frequent activities together (e.g., camping, snorkeling, racing, deep sea diving) and has recently returned from a two-week vacation in Europe.

Ms. Smith related a number of Jimmy's positive qualities including his honesty, work ethic, ability to see things fairly, and mentioned he is a "real sportsman." As he matures, her aspirations for him include being fulfilled, self-sufficient, self-reliant, and securely employed. She would also like to see improvement in his academics and completion of homework to help him achieve his desire to attend college. Discipline methods include talking about issues, taking Jimmy's computer away for a short time period, and grounding that is contingent on behaviors. For example, he may go to the movies if homework is completed but is prohibited from one movie each week if the homework is unfinished. Ms. Smith did note that removing his computer is effective; however, this is very stressful for Jimmy, and he will "shut down" communication, sometimes not speaking to the family for days.

Jimmy was born one-month premature (6lbs, 2oz) following an induced labor, and his mother reports good prenatal care. Both mother and child were released in two days from the hospital and Jimmy was considered healthy. Early development was noted as delayed for speech and all motor skills. Ms. Smith also indicated one daughter had delayed speech as well. Toilet training was described as difficult with continued soiling accidents through second grade. These occurrences were thought to be the result of reduced sensory prompts and only two additional incidents had occurred in second grade. No social or emotional concerns during early development were noted, and Jimmy was described as a very quiet, contented, and undemanding child. It was noted that he had a very calm demeanor, and no hyperactivity, impulsivity, or attention-related issues were indicated. He has had only one injury, a broken toe as the result of a bicycle fall at the age of four.

He receives yearly well-check visits through his pediatrician, Dr. Stanley with Vista Medical, and is not prescribed any medications at this time. Ms. Smith reports he was provided a two-week medication trial in third or fourth grade for attention difficulties. However, she does not recall an actual diagnosis, and Jimmy had a severe negative emotional reaction, so the medication was discontinued promptly. Hypersensitivity to loud, repeated, or sudden noises as well as aversion to some tastes/food textures have been noted since he was young. He also finds some fuzzy fabric textures "creepy" and too uncomfortable to wear (e.g., corduroy, flannel) and until recently only wore nylon shorts and T-shirts to school. Mr. Smith noted this year, as Jimmy is maturing, he is now able to wear long pants made of soft cotton and is less sensitive to textures. His pediatrician ruled out autism spectrum diagnoses and sensory integration concerns at the age of three (see attached report dated 2–5–92). No family history of major illness, learning difficulties, mental health diagnoses, or allergies were indicated.

Jimmy's personality was described as easy-going and fun-loving by his parents. He is noted to have good friends (both male and female of differing ethnicities and ages) and no drug or alcohol use was indicated. His interests include video games, playing the saxophone in the school band since fourth grade, and his strong attachments to some of the band student members. Ms. Smith indicated the things that make Jimmy angry are people not believing him, repeated teasing, and a sense that others are impolite. In regards to academic work, she noted he is able to perform well on tests as a result of his intellect; however, he has great difficulty completing homework. She thinks this is because he feels he already knows the material, that homework assignments are stupid, and he considers the work to be mundane. Jimmy did not attend preschool or daycare as his mother stayed home to provide care and was concerned he would become ill if in daycare with other children.

Educational History. Records indicate Jimmy enrolled in kindergarten at Emery Elementary, and all evaluation categories were noted as demonstrated consistently (e.g., listening, independent work, responsible behavior, communication). Similarly, during first and second grades most benchmarks were at or above grade level with satisfactory effort and social-emotional growth goals. During third grade, his achievement in reading and language arts was noted as needing improvement and inconsistent work habits were documented. Difficulties staying on task were also recorded. In fourth grade, letter grades were assigned for the first time (Reading – C, Writing – D, Math – C, Science – B, Social Studies – C). In addition, a request for a parent conference to discuss attention and work completion concerns was noted. During fifth grade, most course grades were an A or B. During sixth and seventh grades, most of Jimmy's scores were Bs and Cs with at least one D each year. Last year (eighth grade) his grades were somewhat lower (3-Ds, 1-C, 1-B, 1-A in Music). His teachers this year note a continued trend toward lower grades and several incomplete class and homework assignments. Attendance has generally been good. Jimmy's Georgia State Comprehensive Assessment (GSAT) scores are noted below. As originally mentioned by his third-grade teacher, although he struggles to complete homework and some class assignments, his state comprehensive scores remain notably above the mean.

	Reading	Math
3rd Grade	85%	79%
4th Grade	66%	96%
5th Grade	74%	92%
6th Grade	74%	78%
7th Grade	67%	97%
8th Grade	82%	94%

Prior Interventions

Records indicate an initial speech/language evaluation in third grade because Jimmy had failed his annual speech/language screening. He was subsequently found eligible for services based on speech/language impaired classification. The report indicated low oral motor functioning, compromised tongue/lips movement, significant hyperactive gag reflex, and a tongue thrust swallow pattern. He was noted to have moderate oral motor difficulties and concomitant articulation deficits (5th percentile compared to others his age). He received speech/language therapy twice a week for 30 minutes over two years. In fifth grade, an Individual Educational Plan (IEP) record indicates he met his goals and was dismissed from speech/language services.

In fifth grade, an occupational therapy (OT) evaluation was conducted by the school occupational therapist. Teacher concerns were noted for difficulty with writing. Results indicated left hand dominance with a grasp in a "hook" appearance. It was also noted that he did not tilt his paper when writing. Hypotonic gross motor tone and trunk posture were indicated. Specifically, he was slumping when sitting, wrapping his legs around the chair, and occasionally falling out of his seat. Visual perceptions noted difficulty with scanning the printed line and letter placement/sizing. Records indicated Jimmy had some intermittent complaints regarding difficulty with handwriting and pain. Several school-based recommendations were noted including using lined paper with dotting lines, desk height adjustment, a therapy ball for muscle tone development, pencil grips, and utilization of a tilt board. Therapy was provided weekly at 45 minutes per week for one academic school year. He met his goals by the middle of sixth grade and was dismissed from OT services.

Based on concerns for academic difficulties, a psychoeducational evaluation was also conducted in fifth grade. Classroom observations indicate approximately 66 percent off-task behaviors, primarily staring into space. During an interview at that time, Jimmy expressed some difficulty staying focused in his classroom whenever there was elevated noise. In addition, he noted some difficulty with organization and completing homework, but mentioned school was going "okay" for him. His intellectual functioning was in the high average range (SB-V, FSIQ 119) with Reading (WJ-III, SS = 98) and Math (WJ-III, SS = 103) in the average range. Short-Term Memory was high-average (WJ-III, SS = 116) and Cognitive Efficiency was average (WJ-III, SS = 100). His Processing Speed was in the low-average range (SS = 85). Recommendations were made for extra time on tests and a physician consultation regarding mental alertness and attention. The examiner and Jimmy's mother also noted the possibility that he was watching video games late into the night as a possible reason for his lack of alertness in school. His mother indicated she would remove the computer from his bedroom to the family room.

The family pediatrician indicated a diagnosis of Attention Deficit Disorder was not indicated but requested a Section 504 plan based on OT concerns. Subsequently, a Section 504 plan was implemented to provide accommodations including seating near the teacher, avoiding distracting stimuli (e.g., AC unit, high traffic area), extended time on tests and work products, supplemental support in beginning the assignment, breaking tasks into smaller segments, permitting gum chewing for additional stimulation when testing, nonverbal signal cueing for on-task reminders, use of organizational supports, and small-group testing situations as needed.

Assessment Instruments

Adolescent and Child Urgent Threat Evaluation (ACUTE)

Behavior Assessment System for Children, 2nd Ed: Parent Rating Scales (BASC-2 PRS)

Behavior Assessment System for Children, 2nd Ed: Self-Report Adolescent (BASC-2 SRP-A)

Behavior Assessment System for Children, 2nd Ed: Structured
Developmental History (SDH)

Behavior Assessment System for Children, 2nd Ed: Teacher Rating
Scales (BASC-2 TRS-A)

Children's Depression Inventory: Parent Version (CDI)

Conners' Parent Rating Scale Revised: Long Version (CPRS-R:L)

Conners' Teacher Rating Scale Revised: Long Version (CPTS-R:L)

Learning and Study Strategies Inventory: High School Version
(LASSI)

Minnesota Multiphasic Personality Inventory-Adolescent (MMPI-A)

Psychosocial Evaluation and Threat Risk Assessment (PETRA)

Social Skills Rating Scale (SSRS)

Student Styles Questionnaire (SSQ)

Wechsler Intelligence Scale for Children – Fourth Edition (WISC-IV)

Woodcock-Johnson: Third Edition Tests of Cognitive Abilities
(WJ-III Cog)

Suspension Incident

At this time, Jimmy is serving a 10-day out-of-school suspension for a threatening
note he had left at a friend's house scribbled on a magazine (per Manifestation
Determination form 1–01–03) that suggested bringing a weapon to school and
made reference to injury of three victims. The note was noticed by the friend
several days later, school officials were contacted, and then the local police
department. Police Public Records (LIQ12345) indicate a report that Jimmy
had recently broken up with a girlfriend at the school although this was not
one of the students mentioned in the note. During police interview, Jimmy
acknowledged he had written the statement after playing Halo with a friend, but
considered, "it was a joke." He noted being upset when the note was written over
fellow students they had discussed whom he considers sometimes disruptive in
class, making it difficult for him to think. He mentioned they "tick him off" and
he "does not like their attitudes." When asked if he had "recurring thoughts of
hurting people, he replied yes." According to police records, when questioned
regarding any thoughts of harming himself, Jimmy began to cry, but regained
his composure with soothing from his mother. His father indicated to police that

there are guns in the house; however, they are kept in a locked display cabinet, and no one else has the key. The police decided not to press charges or require psychiatric intervention. The content of the message was "I have a cool idea. When I snap, I could bring a gun to school and (three students' names) could be gone-gone-gone."

Behavioral Observations
This evaluation was conducted during a 10-day out-of-school suspension; therefore, the opportunity for classroom observations was not available. However, during this timeframe, Jimmy was permitted on campus when school was not in session to complete his mid-term exams. Exams were administered and observed by the behavior specialist, and the following behaviors were mentioned during interview. Jimmy was described as very cooperative, he followed directions well, responded to light-hearted comments from school staff appropriately, and occasionally smiled during social interactions. It was also noted that he was not prepared (e.g., forgetting his pencils/pens and water) and he took a very long time to complete tests, even given his extended time accommodations. For example, some tests required double the typical time limit, and on one he was noted to sit very quietly with almost no movement staring at the paper without writing for nearly 35 minutes. He indicated he understood the directions.

Following an initial discussion of confidentiality limits, Jimmy assented to assessment. He was polite, cooperative, well-mannered, and followed directions well. His demeanor was quiet, respectful, and somewhat timid. He appeared alert, engaged, and smiled several times. Breaks were taken every hour including snacks and short walks. He appeared to make a diligent effort and results are considered to be valid at this time. It was noted that at one point, his hand appeared fatigued from marking true/false questions and additional rest time was provided. In addition, he stared into space several times, appearing to be concentrating and deliberating his answers. Most of the measures were self-rating scales, rather than typical testing. Jimmy also chewed gum and ate snacks when he felt the need for stimulation to remain alert.

Cognitive Processing
Jimmy was administered select subtests from the Wechsler Intelligence Scale for Children – Fourth Edition (WISC-IV) as a measure of Processing Speed. Processing Speed measures the ability to rapidly discriminate between visual shapes and visual-motor coordination. The tasks required him to distinguish between and reproduce symbols under timed conditions. The subtests included Coding and Symbol Search. His performance was in the extremely low

range (1st percentile). The tasks presented are similar to classroom demands for copying written letters or quickly scanning symbols. As an additional measure of Processing Speed, select subtests from the Woodcock-Johnson Tests of Cognitive Abilities were administered. The WJ-III presents timed Processing Speed tasks in a different manner from the WISC-IV. Items are presented with numeric or pictorial representations and require the ability to recognize and match similar items. Thus, it is not necessary to reproduce small symbols. Under these circumstances, his performance falls in the average range (45th percentile). Based on his complaints about the distracting nature of classroom noise, the Auditory Processing subtests (Sound Blending, Auditory Attention) were also administered. His score falls in the low-average range (22nd percentile). During this subtest, Jimmy indicated the background noise was much like his classroom and very distracting to him, making it difficult to think.

Social-Emotional Functioning

Psychiatric Consultation. As a condition of Jimmy's return to campus, the school board required an emergency psychiatric evaluation in conjunction with this psychoeducational evaluation (Dr. West at Clairmont Hospital Adolescent Psychiatric Unit). Data from this report were shared through a consultation meeting with Dr. West and this examiner. It was agreed that criteria for Autism-spectrum disorders, anxiety, depression, and ADHD/Inattentive Type were not met at this time although continued monitoring for depressive-type symptoms was indicated. It was also noted that Jimmy is not considered an immediate threat to himself or others at this time (see Dr. West report dated 1–3–09). A general recommendation to return to school if extensive supports are in place and the family pursues counseling was noted; however, no specific interventions were indicated.

Parent Ratings/Interviews. Mr. and Ms. Smith both completed the Behavior Assessment System for Children (BASC), 2nd Edition, Parent Rating Scale. The BASC is a system of ratings for emotional and behavioral characteristics that integrates teacher, parent, and student perceptions of behaviors to inform educational and emotional needs. The measure provides information on several clinical scales (i.e., Hyperactivity, Aggression, Conduct Problems, Anxiety, Depression, Somatization, Atypicality, Withdrawal, and Attention Problems). In addition, several Adaptive skills scales (i.e., Adaptability, Social Skills, Leadership, Daily Living, Functional Communication) are included. Both parent ratings had acceptable F scale, Response Pattern, and Consistency indices and no significant clinical scales. Positive ratings included his ability to adjust well to changes in routine, his creativity, encouragement to others, and problem-solving suggestions. On the Adaptive Scales, Social Skills and Activities of Daily Living were noted as in the at-risk range by Ms. Smith but not Mr. Smith. Ratings indicated concern that Jimmy sometimes eats too little, is easily annoyed, never attends to personal safety, and sometimes does not attend to personal hygiene. An additional parental rating of depression characteristics (Children's Depression Inventory) was not significant. The Conners' Parent Rating Scales (CPRS) was administered as an additional measure of attention. Results indicated mildly atypical Cognitive Problems/Inattention, ADHD Index, and DSM-IV Inattentive symptoms.

In interview, both parents indicated they did not think Jimmy had any intention of following through on the scribbled note. They describe him as a caring, gentle, and kind person who has been experiencing increasing frustration in school. His mother noted he has mentioned the students who sometimes disrupt class before and how he tells them they waste time and make it difficult for him to concentrate. They also noted difficulty at home with completing homework but mentioned he stays focused much better with individual assistance. When upset, they describe him as reacting by remaining very quiet and being non-communicative rather than acting out. Jimmy's father mentioned he had purchased a gun for his son two years ago and they had gone hunting a few times. However, Jimmy found the noise of the gun aversive and did not want to continue hunting. He has not recently been interested in or used the family guns.

Teacher Ratings/Interviews. The Behavior Assessment System for Children (BASC), 2nd Edition, Teacher Rating Scale was administered to five teachers. All of the teachers have recently taught Jimmy and some have known him for several years. Similar to parent ratings, the teacher also noted positive ratings for his ability to change plans, manners in saying thank you and please, problem-solving suggestions, and willingness to help others. The predominant pattern among teacher ratings indicated at-risk to clinically significant concerns for characteristics of Depression, Withdrawal, Attention Problems, Learning Problems, and Atypicality (see table below). All of the teachers noted that Jimmy appears to be easily annoyed by others. Depression and Withdrawal concerns included seeming sad, lonely, negative, pessimistic, sometimes refusing to talk, and easily crying. Additionally, complaints about being teased were noted. Attention Problems included difficulty listening to directions, being distracted easily, and a short attention span. Atypicality concerns were noted for seeming out of touch with reality and seeming unaware of others at times.

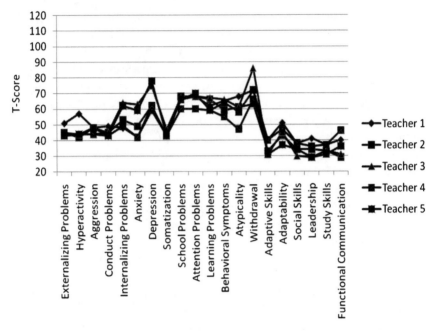

Figure 7.1 T-Score

A teacher measure of specific social interactions (Social Skills Rating System) indicated low assertion skills, specifically the ability to initiate conversations and introduce himself, ability to express feelings, ability to give compliments, confidence in social interactions, skills in inviting others to join activities, the ability to standup for others, and the ability to politely refuse requests. Two additional teacher measures of narrow attention skills were also administered (Conners' Teacher Rating Scale) indicating atypical scores for anxious-shy behaviors, inattention, and social problems.

Five of Jimmy's teachers and the school resource officer were interviewed, and each noted positive qualities mentioning he always complies with requests, is never disruptive, has insightful answers when he participates, and he responds but only when others initiate an interest in him. Jimmy was described as a good, extremely quiet student, who is very capable. All of the teachers expressed concern for his self-initiated social isolation, his difficulty with work completion, his occasionally sad affect, and the tremendous effort that work completion appears to take for him. It was noted he does have a few very close friends but will often sit at the edge of the room alone and may not speak during the entire class. Each teacher mentioned he has long staring episodes in class, on a regular basis, and usually appears tired. On some occasions, he has begun drooling during the staring episodes and almost appeared asleep. The teachers also indicated he often appears timid, sometimes even fearful, and he is sensitive, sometimes crying during parent/teacher conferences. Interviews with the school counselors indicated he has not been referred for social or emotional issues prior to this evaluation. They also noted there are only occasional disruptions in their classrooms with students talking out and considered this typical of teenagers and those who speak out are not the students named in his threat.

Self-Reported Ratings/Interviews. Jimmy completed the Behavioral Assessment System for Children, 2nd Edition, Self-Report of Personality. The clinical and adaptive scales were not significant with most falling in the average range. He did indicate on one item that he sometimes feels no one understands him. On a personality measure (Minnesota Multiphasic Personality Inventory – Adolescent) the Depression scale was clinically significant and Paranoia and Social Introversion were moderately elevated. On the Psychosocial Evaluation and Threat Risk Assessment (PETRA) scale, his self-ratings indicate normal range scores for Psychological Domain, Ecological Domain, and Resiliency Problems. The Egocentrism Cluster was somewhat high. A measure of personal study skills (LASSI-HS) indicated higher than typical test anxiety (70th percentile); specifically this scale measures worry about grades and negative impact on performing on tests. He rated his own attitude toward school including the importance of school to his own goals, motivation (i.e., willingness to work hard), and time management skills as somewhat lower than typical.

During interview with Jimmy, he mentioned he likes attending school and especially enjoys music. He reports having about three good friends, the kind he "can hang out and be silly with." His hobbies include bowling and video games (e.g., PG, Racing, Role Playing). He also likes a speed bike his father bought for him. He hopes to eventually attend the local community college and perhaps study digital music. Jimmy indicated he is "wild about" war games and other cartoons. He noted he owns a copy of the video game Halo, and although some of the cartoons he watches are violent, most are not. Jimmy mentioned he does not go to bed at regular times but rather prefers to fall asleep watching his shows and sleep with the noise of the TV in his room on all night. He also mentioned he had broken up with his girlfriend just before the winter break but they are still friends, and she is "alright," but he was bored with her.

When asked about the scribbled note, Jimmy said he wrote it during his break when he was at a friend's house just hanging out because he was dreading going back to school and having to deal with "mouthy loud jerks." He noted he scribbled the note quick and then forgot about it and he never actually thought people would read it. He noted he dislikes it when students make lots of comments in class and others cannot learn. When asked to describe what he meant in his message about the "snap" point, Jimmy indicated it is the "place when someone just acts with no more thinking about it." He said he was "not really serious about it" and he has "never really been serious about that." When asked how close he has been to the "snap" point that he mentions in his message, he noted he has felt it before but so does everyone else and he is sure he would not do that even though some people might think so. When asked if he was likely to write another similar message if he were frustrated again, Jimmy indicated, "probably not since everyone overreacted or at least I'd throw it away." An assessment utilizing the Adolescent and Child Urgent Threat Evaluation (ACUTE), suggests low clinical range level. Significant factors include identification of classmates, recent loss of a girlfriend, and the anticipation that he will return to the same classroom dynamic/environment situation.

Temperament. The Student Styles Questionnaire was administered as a measure of temperament. Jimmy's temperament profile is introverted-practical-thinking-flexible. His responses indicated a strong preference for introversion. Students with a preference for an introverted style generally are introspective and derive their energy from within. Jimmy endorsed items indicating, in school, he prefers quiet seatwork and listening rather than group discussions. He notes a preference to watch others before interacting and a slow pace in making new friends. These items are consistent with teacher observations of his propensity to self-isolate in the classroom and rarely engage in conversation. He also notes preferring to keep his thoughts secret and to himself, has a few close friends, a few well-developed interests, and enjoys a variety of solitary activities. Introverts are inclined to be hesitant to share their ideas with others and learn best by having time to think about and reflect upon what they have learned. They have a strong need for personal space and privacy. When extreme, introverted students can have underdeveloped social skills and find extended exposure to groups tiring, which may account for some of Jimmy's frustration with the classroom context.

On test items addressing his preferred learning style, Jimmy indicated a strong preference for a practical style. Students with this preference focus their attention on what is seen, heard, or experienced through their senses. They often base their decisions on facts and personal experience, learning best using step-by-step sequential approaches and hands-on activities. They value learning most when they perceive it has direct application to their lives. This is illustrated in reports of Jimmy's keen dislike for homework based on his opinion that it is unneeded and irrelevant. Students with a practical preference can become discouraged when work seems complex or esoteric.

He also noted a strong inclination toward thinking qualities in making decisions. Students with a preference for a thinking style rely on objective and logical standards when making decisions. Their strengths include a keen sense of what is fair and a desire for truth to be expressed accurately. Further, because they highly value the truth, they may tell others unpleasant things in a blunt fashion and may hurt others' feelings in the process. As noted by his mother, Jimmy does become quickly impatient with others who do not remain on task in class and has been known to make direct comments. Consistent with his father's description, Jimmy endorsed items indicating his discomfort with openly expressing emotions or feelings. These students tend to enjoy competitive activities and learn best when information presented is logically organized.

His scores indicate moderate flexible temperament qualities. Students who prefer a flexible style delay decision making as long as possible and feel that they never have sufficient information to make decisions. They prefer a flexible and open schedule as indicated in Jim's item responses. They may not respond well to externally imposed rules and regulations and often need assistance with organization skills.

Summary and Recommendations

Jimmy is a 14-year-old student at Victory High School who was referred for a social-emotional evaluation. The evaluation was prompted by a 10-day suspension for a note that was thought to suggest a threat. In addition, his grades have also recently fallen. He was born one month premature, and significant delays in speech and all motor skills were noted. Academic records indicate good progress from kindergarten through second grade. However, in third grade he began having difficulty with reading and language arts as well as attention and work completion. He received services as speech/language impaired for two years due to poor oral-motor tone and articulation difficulties. He has also received occupational therapy for difficulty with writing, motor tone, posture, and visual perception difficulties. Speech/language and OT remediation goals were met, and he was dismissed from services. His grades have declined for the past three years as well as his completion of homework. However, Jimmy continues to perform well above average on the yearly state comprehensive exams in both reading and math. A prior psycho-educational evaluation indicated high-average intelligence with average Reading and Math and low-average Processing Speed. Subsequently, Jimmy has received accommodations with a Section 504 plan which is still in place.

Teacher and parent behavioral ratings indicate Jimmy adjusts well to changes in routine, is creative, encourages others, and sometimes offers good problem-solving suggestions. The predominant pattern among teacher ratings indicated at-risk to clinically significant concerns for characteristics of Depression, Withdrawal, Attention Problems, Learning Problems, and Atypicality. All of the teachers noted that Jimmy appears to be easily annoyed by others. Depression and Withdrawal concerns included seeming sad, loneliness, negative outlook, pessimistic, sometimes refusing to talk, and easily crying. Attention Problems included difficulty listening to directions, being distracted easily, and a short attention span. Atypicality concerns were noted for seeming unawareness of others at times.

Jimmy also rated his feelings of depression as significant on one measure but not the other. He reports enjoying attending school, particularly participating in music. He hopes to eventually attend community college and perhaps study music. He indicated he is "wild" about video games and enjoys playing some that are violent, although mostly with cartoon characters. He also noted he does not go to bed at regular times but rather prefers to fall asleep watching his cartoons on TV each night, and this may be part of the reason he is not alert at school. He mentioned he had broken up with his girlfriend just before the break but they are still friends, and it was his choice to break up. In reference to the note, Jimmy indicated he gets frustrated by arrogant students who make too many comments in class and that type of behavior makes it very difficult for him to learn. He mentioned he understands when some people cannot take something any longer and react to it; however, he does not think he would ever do this. When asked about coping skills, he only mentioned he just becomes quiet when upset and quits talking. His father also confirms this behavior, noting Jimmy becomes very quiet and keeps his feelings inside. Consultation regarding a concurrent psychiatric exam indicates criteria for Autism-spectrum disorders, anxiety, depression, and ADHD/Inattentive Type were not met at this time, although continued monitoring for depressive-type symptoms was indicated. It was also noted that Jimmy is not considered an immediate threat to himself or others at this time (see Dr. West report dated 1–3–09). A recommendation to return to school if supports are in place and the family pursues counseling was indicated. Facilitating factors for Jimmy's success include his intelligence level, his desire to attend college, his passion for music study, and his bonds with friends and family.

1. Processing/Auditory: At this time, Jimmy is requiring nearly double the time to complete in-class assignments and expresses frustration with classroom noise. Auditory Processing and Processing Speed are in the low-average range suggesting he may benefit from continued testing accommodations and seating away from high traffic or noise areas as well as equipment (e.g., AC unit).

2. Inattention: Rating scales and interview indicate significant concerns for inattention including staring sometimes up to 35 minutes, not following through on directions, and difficulty remembering assignments. These behaviors have been noted in school records since third grade and follow-up discussion with a pediatrician is recommended. In addition, Jimmy may benefit from explicit instruction on organization skills (e.g., planner, color coded assignments, visual reminders, home-school daily planner signed) as well as private cueing to return to task and the opportunity for movement to increase alertness.

3. Tiredness: Coupled with inattention concerns, Jimmy is reported to often appear tired or lack alertness. It is unclear if this may be a result of late-night video games/television or a general mood. Therefore, discussion of this issue with his pediatrician is also recommended in addition to establishing a good sleep hygiene and monitoring his sleep schedule at home.

4. Social Skills: Ratings and interview suggest Jimmy may benefit from instruction on positive assertion skills as well as coping and general social interaction skills. The following specific skill deficits were noted: the ability to initiate conversations and introduce himself, ability to express feelings, ability to give compliments, confidence in social interactions, skills in inviting others to join activities, the ability to stand-up for others, and the ability to politely refuse requests. The school offers social skills groups.

5. Temperament: Jimmy self-reports an introverted-practical-thinking-flexible temperament type. He reports enjoying time alone, requires privacy, prefers learning in a linear manner based on facts, and likes flexibility in deadlines and assignments. Based on his profile, his ability to engage in solitary tasks, appreciate practical solutions, process information logically, and be flexible with deadlines are strengths. However, social interactions, conceptual approaches to learning, expression of feelings, and organization skills are lesser developed. Therefore, he may benefit from assistance with social skills training, hands-on and applied learning techniques, explicit instruction on appropriate self-expression of emotional needs, and organization skills. In addition, Jimmy's school offers some web-based, online course options next year for 10th grade (at home or in the school library with adult monitoring). Given his introverted preference to work alone, his slow pace, and his desire for flexibility, he may benefit from exploring

this online, self-paced option. As a note of caution, Jimmy is not highly structured and does not demonstrate good self-initiation of homework; thus it is recommended that any initial trail of web-based curriculum be monitored through the school library option first.

6. Homework/Coursework: He expresses difficulty organizing and remembering homework. Therefore, it is important to set aside a study space away from his video games and bedroom that is well organized with supplies and quiet to ensure homework completion.

7. Depression/Withdrawal: Characteristics of depression and withdrawal were noted by several raters and Jimmy reports these symptoms on one self-rating scale. In addition, he appears to have a pattern of becoming non-communicative when under stress, both at school and home. He was unable to articulate any positive coping strategies or give voice to his feelings. Therefore, a consultation for family and/or individual counseling therapy is highly recommended. In addition, the school counselor and school psychologist are important resources for counseling services at school.

8. At this time, Jimmy indicates he would not act on the threat; however, he also has not expressed remorse, cannot articulate alternative coping strategies for frustration, and continues to anticipate stressful reactions in a typical classroom. Therefore, comprehensive supports, as noted earlier are recommended immediately when he returns.

9. The school psychologist is available to consult with parents on designing a positive reinforcement plan for homework and study techniques, as well as a sleep hygiene behavioral plan for the home. In addition, the examiner is available to consult individually with teachers on instructional and classroom behavioral strategies.

Rex Kendall, Ph.D., NCSP

School Psychologist, License # 12–3456–7

DON'T FORGET

Temperament Recommendation Resources

Test manuals are a ready source of recommendations for report writing relevant to particular temperament characteristics. The perspective (e.g., academic, behavioral, counseling, career planning) typically depends on the age range assessed by the instrument.

EVALUATION RESULTS

Adolescent and Child Urgent Threat Evaluation (ACUTE)

Risk Category	
Threat Cluster	Low Clinical Risk Factors
Precipitating Factors	Low Clinical Risk Factors
Early Precipitating Factors	Low Clinical Risk Factors
Late Precipitating Factors	Low Clinical Risk Factors
Predisposing Factors	Low Clinical Risk Factors
Impulsivity Cluster	Low Clinical Risk Factors
ACUTE Total	Low Clinical Risk Factors

Behavior Assessment System for Children, 2nd Edition – Parent Rating Form

	T-Score—Father	(%)	T-Score – Mother	(%)
Externalizing Problems	39	9	37	3
Hyperactivity	38	7	7	1
Aggression	42	23	38	2
Conduct Problems	41	16	41	16
Internalizing Problems	45	33	34	2
Anxiety	47	40	32	2
Depression	52	65	41	18
Somatization	38	4	38	4
Behavioral Symptoms	47	45	43	25
Atypicality	57	81	51	65
Withdrawal	46	41	46	41
	T-Score—Father	(%)	T-Score – Mother	(%)
Attention Problems	53	62	55	70
Adaptive Skills	57	74	44	25
Adaptability	57	72	63	93
Social Skills	56	69	35	7
Leadership	58	79	51	55
Activities Daily Living	50	45	31	4
Functional Communication	58	75	43	25

Behavior Assessment System for Children, 2nd Edition (BASC-2)–Teacher Rating Form

	Teacher 1	Teacher 2	Teacher 3	Teacher 4	Teacher 5
	T-Score (%)	T-Score (%)	T-Score (%)	T-Score (%)	T-Score (%)
Externalizing Problems	51 (66)	45 (34)	44 (30)	43 (26)	45 (34)
Hyperactivity	57 (81)	42 (17)	44 (35)	44 (35)	44 (35)
Aggression	48 (61)	48 (61)	44 (27)	44 (27)	48 (61)
Conduct Problems	49 (64)	45 (44)	45 (44)	43 (25)	43 (25)
Internalizing Problems	48 (49)	53 (66)	64 (91)	49 (54)	62 (89)
Anxiety	42 (24)	49 (55)	63 (89)	42 (24)	59 (84)
Depression	59 (85)	62 (89)	75 (97)	62 (89)	78 (97)
Somatization	43 (21)	43 (21)	47 (54)	43 (21)	43 (21)
School Problems	66 (93)	68 (95)	67 (94)	60 (85)	66 (93)
Attention Problems	68 (94)	68 (94)	68 (94)	60 (82)	70 (96)
Learning Problems	62 (86)	66 (91)	67 (94)	59 (83)	59 (83)
	Teacher 1	Teacher 2	Teacher 3	Teacher 4	Teacher 5
	T-Score (%)	T-Score (%)	T-Score (%)	T-Score (%)	T-Score (%)
Behavioral Symptoms	65 (92)	59 (84)	66 (93)	55 (75)	64 (92)
Atypicality	68 (93)	61 (88)	61 (88)	47 (60)	58 (85)
Withdrawal	72 (96)	63 (90)	86 (99)	66 (93)	72 (96)
Adaptive Skills	40 (17)	33 (4)	31 (4)	40 (15)	31 (3)
Adaptability	51 (52)	43 (25)	45 (31)	47 (37)	37 (11)
Social Skills	38 (12)	34 (6)	30 (2)	38 (12)	34 (6)
Leadership	41 (21)	34 (5)	29 (1)	36 (9)	29 (1)
Study Skills	37 (13)	33 (5)	33 (5)	37 (13)	31 (2)
Functional Communication	40 (17)	29 (2)	31 (4)	46 (35)	36 (9)

Behavior Assessment System for Children, 2nd Edition: Self-Report of Personality

	T-Scores	Percentile
School Problems	43	24
Attitude to School	41	22
Attitude to Teachers	47	45
Sensation Seeking	45	34
Internalizing Problems	44	31
Atypicality	43	28
Locus of Control	42	26
Social Stress	49	50
Anxiety	48	49
Depression	45	42
	T-Scores	Percentile
Sense of Inadequacy	48	50
Somatization	43	31
Inattention/Hyperactivity	47	42
Attention Problems	54	67
Hyperactivity	41	18
Emotional Symptoms	49	51
Personal Adjustment	48	39
Relations with Parents	47	35
Interpersonal Relations	53	54
Self-Esteem	52	47
Self-Reliance	43	23

Children's Depression Inventory (CDI) (Mother)

	T-Score
CDI Total	42
Emotional	40
Functional	45

Conners' Parent Rating Scale Revised – Long Form (Father)

	T-Score
Conners' ADHD Index	61
Conners' Global Index: Restlessness-Impulsive	51
Conners' Global Index: Emotional Lability	49
Conners' Global Index: Total	51
	T-Score
DSM-IV: Inattentive	64
DSM-IV: Hyperactive-Impulsive	50
DSM-IV: Total	59
Oppositional	44
Cognitive Problems/Inattention	65
Hyperactivity	54
Anxious/Shy	54
Perfectionism	50
Social Problems	45
Psychosomatic	48

Conners' Parent Rating Scale Revised – Long Form (Teachers)

	Teacher 3	Teacher 2
	T-Score	T-Score
Conners' ADHD Index	59	61
Conners' Global Index: Restlessness-Impulsive	56	58
Conners' Global Index: Emotional Lability	51	57
Conners' Global Index: Total	54	58
DSM-IV: Inattentive	66	73
DSM-IV: Hyperactive-Impulsive	43	43
DSM-IV: Total	56	61
Oppositional	45	48
Cognitive Problems/Inattention	72	62
	Teacher 3	**Teacher 2**
	T-Score	T-Score
Hyperactivity	44	44
Anxious/Shy	87	79
Perfectionism	42	49
Social Problems	90	59

Learning and Study Strategies Inventory: High School Version

	Percentile
Attitude	25
Motivation	20
Time Management	25
Anxiety	70
Concentration	50
Information Processing	30
Selecting Main Ideas	45
Study Aids	35
Self-Testing	40
Test Strategies	60

Minnesota Multiphasic Personality Inventory – Adolescent (MMPI-A)

	T-Score
Validity Indicators	
VRIN	38
TRIN	50
	T-Score
Infrequency	
F1	48
F2	44
F	44
L	59
K – Defensiveness	58
Clinical Scales	
Hypochondriasis	38
Depression	66
Hysteria	40
Psychopathic Deviate	51
Masculinity-Femininity	51
Paranoia	60

Psychasthenia	60
Schizophrenia	50
Hypomania	45
Social Introversion	61
($\geq$ 65 = Clinically Significant; 60–64 = Moderately Elevated)	

Psychosocial Evaluation and Threat Risk Assessment (PETRA)

	T-Score	Percentile
Psychological Domain	49	45
Ecological Domain	47	41
	T-Score	**Percentile**
Resiliency Problems Domain	50	54
Total Domain	40	47

	Descriptive Category
Depressed Mood	Average
Alienation	Average
Egocentricism	High
Aggression	Low
Family/Home	Average
School	Low
Stress	Average
Coping Problems	Average

Social Skills Rating System (SSRS)

	Teacher 1		Teacher 4	
	Standard Score	**%**	**Standard Score**	**%**
Social Skills	90	25	70	2
Problem Behaviors	113	81	117	87
Academic Competence	84	14	–	–

Student Styles Questionnaire (SSQ)

	T-Score		T-Score
Introversion	75	Thinking	74
Practical	72	Flexible	63

Wechsler Intelligence Scale for Children: Fourth Edition (WISC-IV)

Scaled Score	Standard Score	(Confidence Interval)	Percentile
Processing Speed	65	(60–78)	1
Coding	1		
Symbol Search	6		

Woodcock-Johnson III Tests of Cognitive Abilities (WJ-III

	Standard Score	(Confidence Interval)	Percentile
Auditory Processing	88	(83–94)	22
Sound Blending	87	(81–93)	19
Auditory Attention	96	(89–102)	39
Processing Speed	98	(95–102)	45
Visual Matching	94	(89–98)	34
Decision Speed	104	(99–108)	60

Postsecondary Transition Sample Utilizing the MMTIC

Temperament data can serve a unique role in high-school evaluations, especially for students with disabilities as documentation of written transition planning is required. In addition to updating instructional and remediation needs, high school reports at age 16 begin discussing study strategies, accommodations needs, and self-advocacy techniques that are applicable to college goals. Research with the SSQ has indicated children as young and eight years old show predictable vocation preference corresponding to temperament qualities. For example, feeling types express frequent interest in counseling and introverted types express a desire to be writers. Differences also were noted within temperament types for gender and racial/ethnicity (Oakland, Stafford, Horton, & Glutting, 2001).

A variety of work interest surveys, aptitude questionnaires, and temperament measures may be available online through the school guidance office to assist students in career decisions. The Murphy-Meisgeier is one example of a self- administered high-school age temperament measure with quick online scoring. The program will provide a general temperament type based on the 16 Jungian-Myers-Briggs theory types.

Career implications, teacher instructional tips, and personal study suggestions are included in the reports, which are written for easy interpretation by teens.

This case sample addresses a supplemental psychoeducational evaluation that is designed to add additional information on successful study skills for a college-bound student. The report is intended to be strength-based acknowledging the positive qualities the student already possesses that are important to college success. There are no implications for pathology or extensive remediation. Rather mild areas of underdeveloped attributes are approached as factors to be aware of and apply compensatory strategies. In many cases merely making individuals cognizant of their personal profile pattern and providing reminders of opposing qualities they tend to overlook can serve to enhance performance.

> # DON'T FORGET
> ....
> ### MMTIC and MBTI
>
> The MMTIC for children is based on the same theoretical constructs at the MBTI.

Williamsburg High School Griffenville, IL 12345

Psychoeducational Re-evaluation Report

This report contains privileged and confidential information and may only be released with written parental consent except as provided by law.

Student's Name: Aakar Comare   Parent/Guardian: Ms. Tina Comare

Date of Birth (DOB): 2–1–1990   Date of Evaluation: 2–1–07, 2–2–07

Chronological Age (CA): 17year, 0 months   Sex: Male

School: P. K. Yonge   Grade: 12th

Evaluator(s): Ms. Anna Roberto, Ph.D., NCSP

Reason for Referral:
Aakar was referred for triennial re-evaluation and college transition planning. His Individual Education Plan (IEP), 4–12–06, indicates a primary exceptionality of Language Impaired; therefore, this evaluation serves as supplementary information to his primary re-evaluation for speech/language services, which is currently pending. Parental consent for re-evaluation was signed on 1–12–06, and Aakar passed his vision and hearing screenings on 1–13–06.

Background Information:
Developmental History. Aakar was born full-term without complications, and his mother reports good prenatal care. No early injuries or illness are noted, although

his mother notes his speech was somewhat delayed and words were sometimes difficult to understand. He is an only child living with both his biological mother and father who own a small sports equipment store. The family heritage is Indian-American as Aakar's paternal grandparents immigrated to the United States from India when Aakar's father was one year old. Only English is spoken in the home. Both Aakar's paternal and maternal grandparents are deceased, and the family does not live near extended family relatives. However, Aakar is noted to have close friendships with other boys his age in the neighborhood, teens at the health club, and their families. Ms. Comare describes Aakar as a very polite, considerate, and responsible son. She noted he has always been somewhat soft-spoken, perhaps because of his speech difficulties. However, he is not shy and is friendly with customers in the store. His mother is happy with Aakar's academic achievement thus far, and her primary interest is in ensuring that speech/language accommodations will remain in place as Aakar transitions to college in the fall. She would also like any suggestions to assist with study strategies.

Educational History. Aakar's academic records indicate multiple IEP's beginning in first grade for Language Impaired services. His original scores on the Clinical Evaluation of Language Fundamentals-Preschool, administered 9–26–95, indicated Receptive Language in the low-average range (SS = 80, 9th percentile), Expressive Language below average (SS = 70, 2nd percentile), and Total Language Score below average (SS = 73, 2nd percentile). IEP goals for Aakar included learning to discriminate rhyming words, following 3–4 part commands, increasing awareness of syllables in spoken words, ability to correctly articulate some sounds (e.g., t, f, th, s, double vowels) and increased ability to use sound awareness and letter knowledge in reading and writing. During elementary school, Aakar was provided speech-language pull-out services on a bi-weekly basis. Middle and high school IEP's reflect speech/language services on a consultative basis. Notes indicate early improvement in rhyming, phoneme awareness, and letter sound knowledge. However, his last recent re-evaluation continues to note difficulty with articulation of some sounds, a slight lisp, and low-average expressive vocabulary (see speech/language report dated 1–10–2004).

His IEP, dated 4–11–05, notes Aakar's strengths include being polite, eager-ness to please, good effort, participation in class, helping out, and math skills. An IEP, dated 4–12–06, notes goals included checking his planner for assignments, studying ahead of tests, and attending after-school tutoring as needed. His priority educational goal was to develop reading strategies to improve text comprehension. It was reported his disability affects his ease in acquiring new vocabulary through listening and reading, as well as information presented orally. Parental concerns were noted that Aakar perform better in science and

English. Recent State Comprehensive Exam scores and current grades are noted below:

YEAR	READING	MATH
2002	35nd percentile	29th percentile
2003	35th percentile	50th percentile
2004	36th percentile	71st percentile
2005	45th percentile	88th percentile
12th Grade	**1st Quarter, 1–9–07**	**2nd Quarter, 2–9–07**
Env Science	C	C
American Government	B	B
Applied Math	B	B
Beginning Weight Training	B	A
Keyboard	A	A
English IV	C	C
Teacher Interviews		

Aakar's teachers indicate he is a likeable, respectful, and a cooperative student who is a pleasure to have in class. He appears to have close friends and be involved in several extracurricular activities (e.g., chess club, performance back-stage tech team). They noted he will voluntarily participate in small-group class discussions but does not like to be called on for answers. They think this is due to his occasional lisp and difficulty pronouncing some words as he is friendly in individual conversations. Two teachers mentioned he occasionally turns work in late and this appears to be because he has genuinely forgotten the deadline rather than his ability to complete the assignments. The other teacher noted she reminds him often when assignments are due and how they should be structured. If he has questions in math, he is good about attending the after-school tutoring help sessions. The late work results in lost points. They also mentioned he has tried two dual-enrolled classes at the local community college this year (i.e., English IV and Environmental Science). His grades in the dual-enrolled classes were lower than his general grades, and this may be a result of adjusting to the new setting and greater independence.

Interview and Testing Observations. Aakar presented a confident, poised, well-mannered, and mature demeanor. He indicated he likes the school and the friends he has there, but he is ready for the freedom of college. His long-term goal is to either study criminology or something that involves government. Aakar mentioned participation in a summer internship that involved the advocacy in the judicial system had sparked his interest in criminology. His interest in government has evolved from his curiosity about how policy occurs, although he is not interested in being a lawyer. He also noted he could work in the family business when he needs to and plans to do this, especially through college. He also mentioned he enjoys his current part-time job at the family store because he can afford a car. Aakar indicated he takes his achievement seriously and desires to perform well. He noted he could probably put in more time studying and not wait till the last minute before exams.

During evaluation he demonstrated excellent attention, concentration, and effort. Aakar assented to testing and followed directions easily. He was notably persistent even on items he found difficult. A slight lisp was noted occasionally however his vocabulary was readily understandable. Based on his excellent effort and concentration, results of intellectual and achievement assessment are considered valid at this time.

Assessment Instruments:

Kaufman Assessment Battery for Children: Second Edition (KABC-II)

Murphy-Meisgeier Type Indicator for Children (MMTIC)

Woodcock-Johnson Tests of Achievement (WJ-III Ach)

Intellectual Functioning:
Aakar was administered the Kaufman Assessment Battery for Children: Second Edition. For students his age, this instrument includes five indices with two subtests in each scale. Based on his Language Impaired exceptionality, he also was administered additional subtests from the Nonverbal Index for comparison with a measure of full-scale intelligence (IQ). His overall Fluid-Crystallized Index (FCI) score was in the average range (SS = 94, 34th percentile). Aakar's Nonverbal Index was also in the average range (SS = 97, 41st percentile).

His Short-Term Memory skills, the ability to acquire and hold information in immediate memory for use within a few seconds, were in the average range. Short-Term Memory tasks were presented verbally, and Aakar was asked to repeat the information verbatim. His Visual-Processing skills, the ability to perceive, manipulate, and think with visual patterns, was in the average range. These tasks required him to apply reasoning skills to manipulate objects in re-creating complex patterns. His

Long-Term Storage and Retrieval was in the average range. Aakar's Fluid Reasoning was in the average range, and these tasks require novel problem solving that incorporates both inductive and deductive reasoning skills. Crystallized Ability, specific accumulated knowledge including words and facts, was in the low-average range.

Academic Achievement:

The Woodcock-Johnson Tests of Achievement were administered to provide a national norm-reference measure of achievement. Broad Reading was in the average range (SS = 99, 47th percentile). He demonstrated good Letter-Word Identification skills including strategies to sounding-out unfamiliar vocabulary. His ability to read simple sentences under timed conditions (Reading Fluency) and his comprehension of sentences and short passages also were in the average range. Broad Math ability was in the low-average range (SS = 89, 23rd percentile). His ability to complete single-digit addition, subtraction, and multiplication problems under timed conditions was average with few errors (Math Fluency). Aakar was also able to complete applied math problems presented verbally. The area of math he found most difficult was calculations, especially division and problems with fractions. He mentioned he was unsure of how to perform double-digit division problems and knew he needed to review those skills. He also made some careless errors. Broad Written Language was in the average range (SS = 96, 39th percentile) including Spelling and Writing Fluency (i.e., writing short sentences under timed conditions with key vocabulary words provided). His ability to create descriptive sentences in an untimed condition, including embedded phrases and logical sequence of events, was in the average range.

Temperament:

Aakar completed the Murphy-Meisgeier Type Indicator for Children online through the school counselor's office as a measure of temperament. Results indicated his preferences are extroversion, intuition, feeling, and perceiving (ENFP). Students with this combination of temperament qualities are often outgoing, friendly, enjoy working with others, and are energized by groups. They can be innovative in their thinking, easily embracing ideas and concepts. Their strengths include trust, sensitivity, a willingness to help others, and decision-making based on their feelings. They prefer to keep options open, are not particularly concerned with rules, enjoy multitasking, and may postpone studying to the last minute. Careers that foster creativity and communication with others are especially compatible with this temperament (e.g., counseling, teaching, arts). Balancing their need for extroversion and freedom with solitary study tasks and rigid deadlines may be more difficult. In addition, this temperament type may avoid confrontation, seek harmony over debate, and overlook important practical details.

Summary and Recommendations:

Aakar is a 12th-grade student at Williamsburg High School who is preparing for graduation and has taken two dual-enrollment courses this year at the local community college. He was referred for re-evaluation based on Language Impaired exceptionality. Therefore, this evaluation serves as supplementary information to his primary language needs evaluation. Current assessment indicates both full-scale IQ and nonverbal intelligence in the average range. Broad Reading and Broad Written Language skills were average. His Broad Math score was in the low-average range. Within the math skills assessed, Aakar had the most difficulty with division and addition/subtraction of fractions. He mentioned he is aware he needs to review these particular skills and that he also makes some careless errors. Facilitating factors for Aakar's achievement success include his intelligence, positive regard for educational achievement, and his notably strong concentration and effort.

1. Math: Aakar's Broad Math scores, particularly calculations with fractions and division are low-average. He expresses awareness of a need to review these skills. As his IEP already includes access to tutoring it may be convenient and most efficient to target these specific skills in those tutoring sessions. He also acknowledges careless errors and thus a self-reminder cue would be helpful.

2. Temperament/ Study Strategies: Study strategies that utilize Aakar's temperament strengths include group discussions or cooperative projects, theory, metaphors, recognition of patterns in information, relating material to human values, and flexibility. The community college offers small study groups for some courses, and these can also be initiated by students. Teaching Aakar elaboration memory techniques that incorporate a human context or personal relevance to new information may also be helpful. Given his feeling type attributes, which often includes avoidance of conflict, it will be helpful to coach Aakar on self-assertion skills as he will have to approach professors in college to request and advocate for accommodations. In high school, Aakar has been somewhat reliant on teachers to provide him with reminders of assignment deadlines. However, this will not be facilitated in college and given his temperamental propensity to overlook details and postpone deadlines, it will be important to consider the following strategies:
   • Use of a daily planner or tracking diagrams for long-term projects and exams.
   • Calendar alarms can also be set in advance of deadlines on his cell phone and computer outlook program.

- Self-reminders to check his work for details (this can be as simple as an icon on a book or notebook, etc.).

3. College Transition: Aakar plans to attend community college next year, and rules for accessing accommodations differ at the college level. Unlike K-12 schools, college-level accommodations are self-initiated, and at the student's age of 18 parents are not privy to educational records or decisions. Therefore, information on how to contact the college ADA disabilities office and self-advocate have been provided to Aakar. College accommodations can include course substitutions and waivers (e.g., foreign language courses) under certain disability circumstances, which may be beneficial to Aakar. Therefore, it will be important, pending the outcome of his Language Impaired evaluation, to discuss transition planning strategies with the college office and provide copies of both reports. A list of possible accommodations is posted on the college website.

Ms. Anna Roberto, PhD NCSP
Licensed Psychologist, # 12345-a

Evaluation Results:

Kaufman Assessment Battery for Children: Second Edition (KABC-II)

Area Subtest	Scaled Score	Standard Score (95% Band)
Short-Term Memory (Gsm)	91	(82–100)
Number Recall	8	
Word Order	9	
Visual Processing (Gv)	100	(90–110)
Rover	13	
Block Counting	7	
Long-Term Storage & Retrieval (Glr)	94	(86–102)
Atlantis	9	
Rebus	9	
Fluid Reasoning (Gf)	108	(95–119)
Story Completion	11	
Pattern Reasoning	12	
Crystallized Ability (Ga)	87	(79–95)

Area Subtest	Scaled Score	Standard Score (95% Band)
Verbal Knowledge	7	
Riddles	8	
Fluid-Crystallized Index	94	(89–99)
Nonverbal Index	97	(89–105)
Story Completion	11	
Triangles	8	
Block Counting	7	
Pattern Reasoning	12	
Hand Movements	10	

Woodcock-Johnson III Tests of Achievement (WJ-III Ach)

Standard Score	Percentile	
Broad Reading	99	47
Letter-Word Identification	98	44
Passage Comprehension	90	25
Reading Fluency	104	59
Broad Math	89	23
Mathematics Calculation Skills	87	20
Calculation	76	5
Math Fluency	107	67
Applied Problems	90	24
Broad Written Language	96	39
Written Expression	97	41
Spelling	93	32
Writing Fluency	93	32
Writing Samples	113	80

EVALUATION REPORT — ADULT SAMPLE

Rehabilitation Counseling Sample Utilizing the MBTI

This report differs from prior reports in this section as the interpretation emphasis is on career implications rather than interpersonal or learning factors. The illustrative case incorporates use of the Myer-Briggs Type Indicator in a Rehabilitation

Counseling model. Career counseling serves a critical role for persons who are recovering from traumatic injury. These types of injuries typically have life-altering consequences that can effect cognitive as well as physical capabilities. They may occur at any age and often prematurely end a highly productive and fulfilling career trajectory.

The role of rehabilitation counselors is multi-faceted. They must be able to conduct vocational assessments including job skill analyses to identify discrete components that comprise a position, recognize which skills are transferrable to other career choices that are feasible for the client, and help this individual transition to a new set of opportunities. For some individuals, training in assistive technologies (e.g., voice recognition software) may be required.

In many cases, job-seeking skills including resume writing, current technological methods of searching for postings, and even interview skills must be developed for the patient. The emotional impact of losing or changing a career also cannot be underestimated as an individual's identity and self-esteem are often significantly entwined with their chosen work. In addition, the counselor will assess the degree of employability when full-employment or similar employment is no longer feasible. Therefore, a number of assessment tools including measures of personality and temperament may be employed to transition clients.

Monroe County Hospital Rehabilitation Counseling Center
5672 Sadler Street, Monroe, CA, 34571

Patient Case Progress Notes		
Client: Mr. Randall Cooper	Age: 49	Record # 798–380
Initial Intake Date: 12–12–08	Code: AQ-136	Current Date: 2–3–09

Client History:

Mr. Cooper is a single 49-year-old male who was admitted to Monroe Emergency Room care on 11–28–08 with severe laceration and fracture of his right knee. The injury was a result of an on-the-job saw accident while demonstrating a carpentry technique in remodeling at the Hilton Hotel lobby. As reported by his co-workers, the accident occurred when Mr. Cooper slipped on scaffolding, falling approximately five feet and was hit by a small electric saw. He does not remember the details of the accident when it happened, and he was initially stunned when he fell. It was unclear if he monetarily lost consciousness. He was wearing protective equipment including chaps, leggings, and protective pants as required by code standard ASTM F 1897–08 and had current safety training certifications.

Following surgical repair for a compound fractured tibia and quad tendon laceration he was released from the hospital on 12–5–08. Mr. Cooper indicated some difficulty with clarity of thinking; however, his physician noted this is a common side effect from pain medication (Demerol) he was prescribed at that time. He began daily outpatient physical therapy at Physician's Physical Therapy Center on 12–8–08. Mr. Cooper was referred to the Rehabilitation Counseling Center for assessment of his strengths and weaknesses, personality orientation, and vocational interests to inform appropriate vocational goals.

Clinic Visits:

12–12–08: During Mr. Cooper's initial intake visit to the center, he presented a positive, out-going and friendly demeanor and noted a desire to return to work quickly. He indicated he has 21 years experience in the building industry and specializes in custom decorative wood carpentry installations such as ceiling moldings, column sculptures, and vaulted insets. He takes pride in the creativity involved in these projects as they are large, unique projects typically found in public buildings and a testament to the skills of him and his crews. At the time of the accident, he was transitioning to a dual role as project foreman, which included training and supervising other carpenters as well as managing and inspecting project completion. He was excited about this new opportunity as he enjoys teaching and interacting with others. He also finds the attention to detail required for inspection rewarding. In addition, the new responsibilities had included a salary supplement.

Mr. Cooper was administered a measure of intelligence by Dr. William Bradford, due to his report of difficulty with memory. His cognitive abilities as measured by the Woodcock-Johnson: Third Edition were noted in the average range (IQ = 116), and both short- and long-term memory also were in the average range (STM = 113, LTM = 115). Counseling focused on pain management, coping strategies for adjustment to the rigors of physical therapy, and his apprehension regarding returning to work quickly. He has worker's compensation and job injury insurance benefits that are adequate to cover his financial obligations at this time and did not express any need for social services supports.

1–18–09: Mr. Cooper has completed five weeks of physical therapy with good progress. He is no longer prescribed medication for pain and indicates soaking his knee as well as Ibuprofen following therapy are adequate. His physical therapist notes a positive outlook during most sessions despite initial pain and remains optimistic that Mr. Cooper will regain significant range of movement. Conversations with his employer reveal they are very pleased with his past work, as noted by annual job evaluations, and they would like for him to return if he can meet the same obligations following therapy. However, as his prior position required climbing scaffolding and ladders as well as crawling into small access spaces for inspection of work, this may no longer be possible. The employer has communicated this information to Mr. Cooper in a formal letter. An analysis of Mr. Cooper's recent job abilities and expertise was conducted, and he was counseled on transferrable skills. His current resume was reviewed with editing suggestions, job search skills including use of the center's online resources, and career life planning strategies were provided. Although Mr. Cooper was at first resistant in discussing the need to consider alternative employment, he agreed that as long as he could stay in the building industry with a similar pay level, he could probably be content. In addition, Mr. Cooper completed the Strong's Interest Inventory and the Myers-Briggs Type Indicator®.

2–3–09: Following eight weeks of physical therapy, good progress was noted with current 80 percent range of movement. Mr. Cooper can walk with a steady gait however, he reports difficulty keeping his knee bent or placing his full weight on it for any length of time. His physician, Dr. Walter Martin, indicates Mr. Cooper is unlikely to regain complete range of motion due to the severity of his injury. He has been dismissed from therapy, and a home exercise regiment has been provided. He is scheduled for a follow-up office visit with Dr. Walter Martin in three months. Mr. Cooper has updated his resume based on counsel from the last session and begun exploring job postings.

This session focused on interpretation of the Strong's Interest Inventory and the MBTI for vocational implications. On the Strong's Profile his two highest themes were Enterprising (e.g., managing, selling) and Realistic (i.e., building, repairing). His MBTI results indicate an ESTP (Extroversion, Sensing, Thinking, Perceiving) profile. Extroverts typically enjoy variety, an action-oriented pace, and the opportunity to frequently interact with others in their work. This is consistent with Mr. Cooper's observed outgoing demeanor. Sensing types are pragmatic, attentive to details, enjoy precision work, and have realistic expectations. Individuals with Thinking preferences like logical order, reason, and are analytically oriented. Perceiving refers to the ability to adapt to change well, preferring to leave options open, flexibility, and a propensity to postpone deadlines. Mr. Cooper agreed the Extroversion, Sensing, and Thinking qualities were consistent with his self-perceptions. However, he indicated the Perceiving dimension was only partially applicable as he does prefer flexibility but also desires to meet deadlines promptly (Judging quality). Research on careers persons with an ESTP or ESTJ temperament often find rewarding and pursue were noted (i.e., marketing, skilled trades, business, law enforcement, technology, management). Mr. Cooper indicated he had always noticed the project administrators who provided cost bids and meet with clients during the design stage of a project.

He thought this type of job could blend his expertise on installations, materials and his detail orientation with his outgoing personality. In collaboration, a plan to explore this option as well as other similar building industry administrative roles was initiated.

Ms. Rebecca Walters, M.A., Rehabilitation Counselor

Appendix
Definitions of Temperament Terms

Activity Level. This term is one of nine dimensions in Thomas and Chess's early temperament theory. It refers to assessment of the typical level of movement by calculating a ratio of active to inactive time.

Adaptability. This term is one of nine dimensions in Thomas and Chess's early temperament theory. It refers to assessment of how easily a baby's first response to a stimulus is modified or how quickly the infant adjusts and habituates.

Approach/Withdrawal. This term is one of nine dimensions in Thomas and Chess's early temperament theory. It refers to assessment of infants' initial responses to new stimuli (e.g., meeting a new person, a new object, or first seeing a jack-in-the box toy). Observers determine if the responses are fearful or exploratory.

Artisan. The Artisan temperament type is a descriptor provided in the Keirsey Temperament Sorter model of interpretation. It includes persons who share both Sensing and Perceiving orientations (i.e., ESTP, ESFP, ISTP, ISFP) regardless of whether the person is introverted-extroversion or thinking-feeling. Broad characteristics of the Artisan include audacity, spontaneity, creativity, and a pragmatic perspective.

Asthenic. The term asthenic was designated by Ernst Kretschmer, in his book *Physique and Character* to persons with tall, frail, thin and weak body types. His theory postulated that some mental health disorders and associated temperament attributes were most common to particular body types. He associated introverted and timid attributes with this type and thought schizophrenia, especially the negative symptoms, was more common for asthenic types.

Asthenic/Leptosomic. The term asthenic/leptosomic was designated by Ernest Kretschmer as a combined group of persons with thin, lanky body type (i.e., asthenic) and those with an athletic, muscular body type. His theory postulated that some mental health disorders and associated temperament attributes were most common to particular body types. He asserted that schizophrenia was more common among patients he observed with thin or athletic body types and thin persons exhibited the greatest frequency of schizophrenia when compared to athletic body types.

Attention Span/Persistence. This attribute measures how long an infant can sustain attention once a stimulus or activity is initiated. It is one of the nine original temperament qualities from the Thomas and Chess theory.

Choleric. Following the early work of Hippocrates, Galen hypothesized four humors or temperaments based on physical and emotional characteristics. The choleric temperament was denoted as shrewd, quick tempered, and ambitious. Physical characteristics included being hairy and having a yellow tone skin. The other three temperaments were phlegmatic, melancholic, and sanguine.

Difficult Temperament. In their research on infants and toddlers, Thomas and Chess identified three temperament behavioral patterns, easy, slow-to-warm, and difficult. Each is associated with differing long-term outcomes. The difficult temperament exhibited negative responses when new stimuli was introduced (e.g., crying, tantruming) and had more irregularity in their physiological cycles (e.g., eating, sleeping, elimination). In addition, children in this category have the poorest long-term adjustment outcomes.

Distractibility. This term assesses how easily a child is distracted or redirected when a new stimulus such as a toy is introduced. Distractibility is one of nine original temperament dimensions from the Thomas and Chess theory.

Easy Temperament. In their research on infants and toddlers, Thomas and Chess identified three temperament behavioral patterns, easy, slow-to-warm, and difficult. Each is associated with differing long-term outcomes. The easy child temperament is described as adaptable to change with good frustration tolerance, exhibiting regular physiological cycles (e.g., sleeping, eating) and having a cheerful disposition. Long-term adjustment outcomes for these children were typically positive.

Ectomorphy. This term originates from William Sheldon's theory identifying three body somatotypes: endomorphy, mesophorphy, and ectomorphy. Each type was related to a particular layer of embryonic cells that later contributed to major bodily functions. Ectomorphy was related to the ectoderm or outer layer and associated with nervous system development and some outer skin formations (e.g., fingernails). The features of this body type included a tall, slender frame. These individuals were thought to possess Cerbrotonia temperament qualities including creative, artistic qualities as well as an introverted and sensitive demeanor.

Endomorphy. One of three body types postulated by William Sheldon's theory, the endomorph was described as a stout, more rotund body shape with little muscle tone. Each of the three types (endomorphy, mesophorphy, and ectomorphy) were considered related to three early tissue development layers (e.g., endomorphy associated with inner layer) that later supports development of a major body system as an embryo matures. The endoderm is associated with gastrointestinal/

digestive system development. A viscerotonia temperament was thought to be most prevalent for this body type and was characterized as extroversion, outgoing, and comfort seeking with a propensity to seek luxury.

Extroversion. This term originates from Carl Jung's temperament theory and describes persons who renew their energy from the external environment or outer world of people and objects. Extroverts tend to be outgoing, form attachments quickly, seek many friends, and share ideas readily. The term is also found in other instruments such as the Myers-Briggs Type Indicator® (MBTI), the Murphy-Meisgeier Type Indicator for Children (MMTIC), and the Student Styles Questionnaire (SSQ). The opposing temperament quality is Introversion.

Falsification-of-Type. Carl Jung designated falsification-of-type as a term to describe circumstances whereby individuals may be required to persistently present qualities that are contrary to their own innate temperament attributes. These opposing characteristics would be lesser developed and thus present more dissonance and be more straining for the individual to maintain over long periods of time. This phenomenon may occur in home environments, work situations, social demands, or personal relationships. Jung suggested that persons functioning in situations that value their own temperament strengths benefit from repeated reinforcement as well as opportunities to further enhance these qualities that promote good psychological adjustment. See Thomas and Chess's later goodness-of-fit and poorness-of-fit concepts to review applications of this tenet to children.

Feeling. This term originates with Carl Jung's temperament theory. However, it is also found in other instruments such as the Myers-Briggs Type Indicator® (MBTI), the Murphy-Meisgeier Type Indicator for Children (MMTIC), and the Student Styles Questionnaire (SSQ). It refers to how individuals prefer to make decisions. Persons with this temperament quality prefer an emphasis on subjective values such as empathy and well-being of others in their decisions. They seek harmony and can be charming and diplomatic in their interactions. The opposing temperament quality is Thinking.

Flexible. This term originated with the Student Styles Questionnaire (SSQ) and is consistent with the term Perceiving from Myers-Briggs temperament theory. Flexible refers to how an individual prefers to structure his or her daily life. Persons with this preference approach the outer world in a spontaneous and adaptive manner. They are tolerant, willing to change readily, and like to multitask, keeping options open. On the Myers-Briggs Type Indicator® (MBTI) and the Murphy-Meisgeier Type Indicator for Children (MMTIC) the equivalent term is Perceiving. The opposing temperament quality is Organized (Judging on the MBTI and MMTIC).

Goodness-of-Fit. In their seminal work on early childhood temperament Thomas and Chess coined the term goodness-of-fit to describe situations where the child's temperament qualities and the environmental demands are most compatible. This circumstance can occur in one of two ways. If the child and parents share common characteristics (e.g., introversion), there is a natural alignment in expectations, needs, and understanding. When a perfect match is not indicated, parents who are able to understand and appreciate the child's differences may also create an environment that remains nurturing and supportive. In addition, if a child's temperament qualities are well-suited to the demands of the environment (e.g., a calm, compliant demeanor in school), the child automatically receives positive feedback and can succeed more readily. The opposing situation was termed poorness-of-fit.

Guardian. The Guardian temperament type is a descriptor provided in the Keirsey Temperament Sorter model of interpretation. It includes persons who share both Sensing and Judging orientations (i.e., ESFJ, ISFJ, ESTJ, ISTJ) regardless of whether the person is introverted-extroversion or thinking-feeling. Broad characteristics of the guardian include trust-worthiness, dependability, humility, and an appreciation for rules.

Idealist. The Idealist temperament type is a descriptor provided in the Keirsey Temperament Sorter model of interpretation. It includes persons who share both Intuition and Feeling orientations (i.e., ENFJ, INFJ, ENFP, INFP) regardless of whether the person is introverted-extroversion or judging-perceiving. Broad characteristics of the Idealist include being cooperative, caring, trusting, and they tend to value personal intuition and ideas.

Imaginative. This term originates with the Student Styles Questionnaire (SSQ) and refers to Carl Jung's original temperament quality of Intuition as found on the Myer's-Briggs Type Indicator (MBTI) and the Murphy-Meisgeier Type Indicator for Children (MMTIC). Persons with this quality prefer learning concepts through ideas and theories first, adding details later. They are interested in the big picture or patterns with lesser attention to detail. The opposing temperament quality is Practical (or Sensing on the MBTI and MMTIC).

Inhibition. In temperament research and theory this term usually refers to behavioral inhibition often in early childhood studies. Strelau, Eysenck, Kagan, Reznick, Clark, Snidman, Eaton and others have utilized a number of observational and rating scale measures to assess behavioral inhibition. Measures are based on arousal states as noted by activity level, emotional tone, and initial responsiveness to new stimuli. Studies often compare twins and adopted siblings and investigate possible genetic contributions.

Intensity of Reaction. This term is one of nine temperament qualities for infants identified by Chess. It refers to the energy level evident in a response (e.g., does the child grin or robustly laugh if he or she is pleased?).

Introversion. This term originates from Carl Jung's temperament theory and describes persons who renew their energy from their inner world of thoughts and introspection. Introverts prefer solitude or small groups, self-reflection, acquire a few close friends, and often have a few in-depth interests. The term is also found in other instruments such as the Myers-Briggs Type Indicator® (MBTI), the Murphy-Meisgeier Type Indicator for Children (MMTIC), and the Student Styles Questionnaire (SSQ).

Intuitive. This term originates from Carl Jung's temperament theory and describes a style of learning that assimilates new information holistically often with spontaneous insight. Persons with this quality prefer learning concepts through ideas and theories first, adding details later. They are interested in the big picture or patterns with lesser attention to detail. The term is also found in other instruments such as the Myers-Briggs Type Indicator® (MBTI) and the Murphy-Meisgeier Type Indicator for Children (MMTIC). It is called Imaginative on the Student Styles Questionnaire (SSQ). The opposing temperament quality is Sensing (or Practical on the SSQ).

Judging. This term originated from Myers-Briggs temperament theory and is also found on the Murphy-Meisgeier Type Indicator for Children (MMTIC). It refers to how an individual structures his or her daily life. Persons with this temperament quality prefer structure in daily interactions with the outer world. They like routines, organization, schedules, and planning ahead. They are prone to seeking closure on projects and prefer to finish one task at a time. On the Student Styles Questionnaire this term is called Organized. The opposing temperament quality is Perceiving (Flexible on the SSQ).

Melancholic. In his writings, Galen wrote about four humors with distinct physical and emotional characteristics that he based on the early work of Hippocrates. The melancholic temperament was prone to dramatic mood changes and could be blissfully happy, sad, or depressed. The other three temperaments were choleric, phlegmatic, and sanguine.

Mesophorphy. This term originates from William Sheldon's theory identifying three body somatotypes: endomorphy, mesophorphy, and ectomorphy. Each type was hypothesized to be related to particular cell layers that the emerging science of his day perceived as responsible for developing into specific bodily functions. Mesophorphy was related to the mesoderm (i.e., middle layer of cell tissue) that eventually develops into the body's circulation system and muscle structure. The features of this body type included an athletic or muscular physique. A somatonia temperament was associated with mesophorphy and described as having an active, assertive, and competitive persona prone to risk taking.

Organized. This term originated from Student Styles Questionnaire (SSQ) and refers to Myers-Briggs original temperament quality of Judging found on the Myers-Briggs Type Indicator® (MBTI) and the Murphy-Meisgeier Type Indicator for Children (MMTIC). It refers to how an individual structures his or her daily life. Persons with this temperament quality prefer structure in daily interactions with the outer world. They like routines, organization, schedules, and planning ahead. They are prone to seeking closure on projects and prefer to finish one task at a time. The opposing temperament quality is Flexible (Perceiving on the MBTI and MMTIC).

Overcontrollers. Caspi and others proposed a theoretical framework for three temperament descriptions (overcontrollers, undercontrollers, and resilients) based on the earlier work of Block and Block related to ego-control and ego-resiliency attributes. Overcontrollers present strong self-control in their ability to regulate emotional impulses that can result in rigidity. On measures of the Big Five personality model they present with lower extroversion and emotional stability, high conscientiousness, moderate agreeableness and openness scores. Achievement measures are high, whereas social skills and long-term psychological well-being are lower.

Perceiving. This term originated from Myers-Briggs temperament theory and is also found on the Murphy-Meisgeier Type Indicator for Children (MMTIC). It refers to how an individual prefers to structure his or her daily life. Persons with this preference approach the outer world in a spontaneous and flexible manner. They are tolerant, adaptive, and like to multitask, keeping options open. On the Student Styles Questionnaire (SSQ) this term is called Flexible. The opposing temperament quality is Judging (Organized on the SSQ).

Personality. Personality refers to a wide variety of personal qualities; demeanor characteristics, including social appeal and expressive energy; traits; cognitive attributions; emotional response patterns; behaviors; and temperament that together form a unique constellation recognized by others as the individual's persona. However, any of these factors separately also can be identified as personality variables common to many persons. It is the unique combination and degree of expression of personality traits that is specific to the individual rather than the actual traits.

Phlegmatic. In his theory of temperament, Galen noted four humors: choleric, phlegmatic, melancholic, and sanguine. Individuals with a phlegmatic temperament were considered self-content, relaxed, mild-mannered, and prone to fantasy as well as somatic complaints.

Poorness of Fit. This term was proposed by Thomas and Chess to describe circumstances where a child's temperament qualities may be inconsistent with environmental demands. For example, poorness-of-fit can occur if parent-child temperaments are dramatically different and there is a lack of tolerance for those differences, resulting in competing needs and a conflictual relationship. Poorness of fit also may exist in environments outside the home, such as school, if the child's characteristics are counterproductive to expectations resulting in higher frustration and more negative feedback. Goodness-of-fit describes a consistent match between temperament and environment expectations that is associated with better outcomes.

Practical. This term originates with the Student Styles Questionnaire (SSQ) and refers to Carl Jung's original temperament quality of Sensing as found on the Myers-Briggs Type Indicator® (MBTI) and the Murphy-Meisgeier Type Indicator for Children (MMTIC). It refers to how an individual prefers to acquire new information. Persons who are practical rely on tangible evidence, utilizing their five senses to acquire new information. They prefer real-life, concrete experiences, practical applications, realistic goals, and are pragmatic and detail oriented. The opposing temperament quality is Imaginative (Intuitive on the MBTI and MMTIC).

Pyknic. The term pyknic was designated by Ernst Kretschmer, in his book *Physique and Character* to persons with round, obese, or overweight body types. His theory postulated that some mental health disorders and associated temperament attributes were most common to particular body types. He associated sociability and expansive expression attributes with this type and thought manic depression was more common for pyknic types.

Quality of Mood. In early Thomas and Chess temperament theory, quality of mood was one of nine infant attributes assessed. It refers to the comparison of the ratio of positive responses an infant gives such as giggles, to negative responses such as frowning.

Rational. The Rational temperament type is a descriptor provided in the Keirsey Temperament Sorter model of interpretation. It includes persons who share both Intuition and Thinking orientations (i.e., ENTJ, INTJ, ENTP, INTPJ) regardless of whether the person is introverted-extroversion or judging-perceiving. Broad characteristics of the Rational include being quizzical and skeptical, valuing logical reasoning, independence, and a strong work ethic.

Resilients. Resilients are one of three temperament profiles mentioned by Caspi and others. Persons in this category are noted to have the ability to adapt readily as a result of their flexibility in impulse control. In self-report studies utilizing the Big Five personality scales, resilients are high on each of the five factors: Extroversion,

Emotional Stability, Conscientiousness, Agreeableness, and Openness. Studies also indicate higher IQ, achievement, social skills, and self-esteem.

Rhythmicity. This term is one of nine dimensions in Thomas and Chess's early temperament theory. It refers to assessment of predictability and regularity of daily biological activities (e.g., sleeping, feeding, and elimination). Observers note if a routine or schedule is naturally established by the infant.

Sanguine. Choleric, phlegmatic, melancholic, and sanguine are the terms for four temperament humors identified by Galen. Sanguine temperament was described as having quick and impulsive qualities as well as a loving personality.

Sensing. This term originates with Carl Jung's temperament theory. However, it is also found in other instruments such as the Myers-Briggs Type Indicator® (MBTI) and the Murphy-Meisgeier Type Indicator for Children (MMTIC). It refers to how an individual prefers to acquire new information. Persons who are sensing rely on tangible evidence, utilizing their five senses to acquire new information. They prefer real-life, concrete experiences, practical applications, realistic goals, and are pragmatic and detail oriented. This term is equivalent to the term practical on the Student Styles Questionnaire (SSQ). The opposing temperament quality is Intuitive (Imaginative on the SSQ).

Slow-to-Warm Temperament. Thomas and Chess identified and investigated nine early childhood temperament qualities. From these data they identified three temperament behavioral patterns, easy, slow-to-warm, and difficult. Each is associated with differing long-term outcomes. The slow-to-warm temperament exhibited a cautious demeanor when approaching new stimuli although this hesitancy subsided with repeated exposures of the same stimuli. Their physiological cycles were regular including eating and sleeping patterns. For this group of children, longitudinal research indicates mixed results depending upon the child's characteristics; however, in general, difficulties with anxiety-related factors are more prevalent.

Temperament. Temperament refers to core personality components that are considered predispositions with a stronger biological basis than personality traits. They are developmentally evident earlier and are less mediated by environmental influences. A relationship is acknowledged between biological and environmental influences that can shift temperament qualities over time. Temperament may be conceptualized as a foundational substrate for the subsequent development of personality through its effect on response instincts and thus the self-selection of environmental experiences (e.g., personal interactions, activities) that will further strengthen or diminish predispositions.

Threshold of Responsiveness. This term is one of nine dimensions in Thomas and Chess's early temperament theory. It refers to assessment of the intensity required to elicit a response, such as a startle or cry, from an infant given a stimulus (e.g., wet diaper).

Thinking. This term originates with Carl Jung's temperament theory. However, it is also found in other instruments such as the Myers-Briggs Type Indicator® (MBTI), the Murphy-Meisgeier Type Indicator for Children (MMTIC), and the Student Styles Questionnaire (SSQ). It refers to how individuals prefer to make decisions. Persons with a thinking temperament quality prefer to deliberate decisions based on facts, impartial logic, objective data, and analysis. They emphasize principles of justice and truth in decision-making and seek fairness. The opposing temperament term is Feeling.

Undercontrollers. Within the Caspi framework of temperament, undercontrollers describes individuals who lack strong impulse and motivational control. Research utilizing Big Five model personality measures found undercontrollers had higher scores on extroversion and lower scores for agreeableness and conscientiousness. Correlational studies indicate lower academic achievement, peer approval, and higher behavioral problems and delinquency among teenagers in this group.

References

ADA Compliance Office. (2002). *Providing services and access to students and employees with disabilities in higher education: Effective and reasonable accommodations.* Gainesville, FL: University of Florida.

Akiskal, H. S., & Akiskal, K. K. (2007). In search of Aristotle: Temperament, human nature, melancholia, creativity and eminence. *Journal of Affective Disorders 100,* 1–6.

Al-Balhan, E. M. (2008). The Student Styles Questionnaire in relation to improved academic scores in Kuwaiti middle-school science classes. *Social Behavior and Personality, 36*(2), 217–228.

Allison, R., & Upah, K. (2006). The danger of response-to-intervention to school psychology: Why we shouldn't be afraid. *Communiqué 34*(5).

Allport, G. W. (1961). *Pattern and growth in personality.* New York: Holt, Rinehart, & Winston.

American Educational Research Association. (1999). *Standards for educational and psychological testing.* Washington DC: American Educational Research Association.

American Psychiatric Association. (2000). *Diagnostic and statistical manual of mental disorders* (4th ed., text revision). Washington, DC: Author.

Americans with Disabilities Act of 1990, 42 U.S.C.A. § 12101 et seq. (1993).

Anchors, S., Robbins, M. A., & Greshman, E. S. (1989). The relationship between Jungian type and persistence to graduation among college students. *Journal of Psychological Type, 17,* 20–25.

Archer, R. P., & Krishnamurthy, R. (2001). *Essentials of MMPI-A assessment.* Hoboken, NJ: John Wiley and Sons.

Athanasou, J. A. (2003). *The New York Longitudinal Scales Adult Temperament Questionnaire.* Scottsdale, AZ: Behavioral-Developmental Initiatives.

Auerbach, J., Geller, V., Lezer, S., Shinwell, E., Belmaker, R. H., Levine, J., et al. (1999). Dopamine D4 receptor (D4DR) and serotonin transporter promoter (5-HTTLPR) polymorphisms in the determination of temperament in 2-month-old infants. *Molecular Psychiatry, 4*(4), 369–373.

Auerbach, J. G., Benjamin, J., Faroy, M., Geller, V., & Ebstein, R. (2001). DRD4 related to infant attention and information processing: A developmental link to ADHD? *Psychiatric Genetics, 11*(1), 31–35.

Barkley, R. A. (1997). *Defiant children: A clinician's manual for assessment and parent training.* New York: Guilford Press.

Bassett, K. D. (2004). *Nature, nurture, and temperament: Comparisons of temperament styles displayed by U. S. students.* Unpublished doctoral dissertation, University of Florida, Gainesville, FL.

Bates, J. E. (1989). Concepts and measures of temperament. In G. A. Kohnstamm, J. E. Bates, & M. K. Rothbart (Eds.), *Temperament in childhood* (pp. 1–58). New York: John Wiley and Sons.

Bates, J., Freeland, C.A.B., & Lounsbury, M. L. (1979). Measurement of infant difficultness. *Child Development, 50,* 794–803.

Bates, J. E., Wachs, T. D., & Emde, R. N. (1994). Toward practical uses of biological concepts of temperament. In J. E. Bates & Y. D. Wachs (Eds.), *Temperament: Individual differences at the interface of biology and behavior* (pp. 275–306). Washington, DC: American Psychology Association.

Batsche, G. M., Castillo, J. M., Dixon, D. N., & Forde, S. (2008). Best practices in linking assessment to intervention. In A. Thomas, & J. Grimes (Eds.), *Best Practices in School Psychology V* (pp. 177–194). Bethesda, MD: National Association of School Psychologists.

Belar, C. D., & Nelson, P. D. (2002). *Rethinking education in psychology and psychology in education: Education leadership conference.* Washington, DC: American Psychological Association.

Benson, N., Oakland, T., & Shermis, M. (2008). Cross-national invariance of children's temperament. *Journal of Psychoeducational Assessment, 20*(10), 1–14.

Berden, L. E., Keane, S. P., & Calkins, S. D. (2008). Temperament and externalizing behavior: Social preference and perceived acceptance as protective factors. *Developmental Psychology, 44*(4), 957–068.

Best, D. (1993). Inducing children to generated mnemonic organizational strategies: An examination of long-term retention and materials. *Developmental Psychology, 29,* 324–336.

Beutler, L. E., & Groth-Marnat, G. (2003). *Integrative assessment of adult personality* (2nd ed.). New York: Guilford Press.

Block, J. (1977). The Eysencks and psychoticism. *Journal of Abnormal Psychology, 86,* 431–434.

Block, J. H., & Block, J. (1980). The role of ego-control and ego-resiliency in the organization of behavior. In W. A. Collins (Ed.), *Minnesota symposium on child psychology:* (Vol. 13, pp. 39–101). Hillsdale, NJ: Erlbaum.

Bohlin, G., Hagekull, B., & Lindhagen, K. (1981). Dimensions of infant behavior. *Infant Behavior and Development, 4,* 83–96.

Bouchard, T. J., Jr. (1984). Twins reared together and apart: What they tell us about human diversity. In S. W. Fox (Ed.), *Individuality and determinism: Chemical and biological bases* (pp. 147–178). New York: Plenum.

Bouchard, T. J., Jr. & Hur, Y. (1998). Genetic and environmental influences on the continuous scales of the Myers-Briggs Type Indicator: An analysis based on twins reared apart. *Journal of Personality, 66*(2), 135–149.

Bouchard, T. J., Jr., McGue, M., Hur, Y., & Horn, J. M. (1998). A genetic and environmental analysis of the California Psychological Inventory using adult twins reared apart and together. *European Journal of Personality 12*(5), 307–320.

Bradley, R. H., & Corwyn, R. F. (2008). Infant temperament, parenting, and externalizing behavior in first grade: A test of the differential susceptibility hypothesis. *Journal of Child Psychology and Psychiatry, 49*(2), 124–131.

Brawer, F. B., & Spigelman, J. M. (1964). Rorschach and Jung. *Journal of Analytical Psychology, 9*(2), 137–149.

Brazelton, T. B. (1973). *Neonatal Behavioral Assessment Scales.* London: Spastics International Medical Publications.

Brazelton, T. B., & Nugent, J. K. (1995). *Neotnatal Behavioral Assessment Scale* (3rd ed.). Cambridge, MA: Cambridge University Press.

Bronson, W. C. (1974). Mother-toddler interaction: A perspective on studying the development of competence. *Merrill-Palmer Quarterly, 20,* 275–301.

Buss, A. (1989). Temperaments as personality traits. In G. A. Kohnstamm, J. E. Bates, & M. K. Rothbart (Eds.), *Temperament in childhood* (pp. 49–58). New York: John Wiley & Sons Ltd.

Buss, A. H., & Plomin, R. (1975). *A temperament theory of personality development.* New York: John Wiley and Sons.

Buss, A. H., & Plomin, R. (1984). *Temperament: Early developing personality traits.* Hillsdale, New Jersey: Lawrence Erlbaum Associates, Publishers.

Butcher, J. N., (2002). *Clinical personality assessment: Practical approaches* (2nd ed.). New York: Oxford University Press.

Canli, T. (2006). *Biology of personality and individual differences.* New York: Guilford Press.

Carey, W. B. (1982). Clinical use of temperament data in pediatrics. *Developmental and Behavioral Pediatrics, 6*(3), 137–142.

Carey, W. B. (2000). *The Carey Temperament Scales Test Manual.* Scottsdale, AZ: Behavioral-Developmental Initiatives.

Carlson, R., & Levy, N. (1973). Studies in Jungian typology: I. Memory, social perception, and social action. *Journal of Personality, 41*(4), 559–576.

Caspi, A. (1998). Personality development across the life course. In W. Damon (Series Ed.) & N. Eisenberg (Volume Ed.), *Handbook of child psychology: Vol. 3. Social, emotional, and personality development* (pp. 135–160). New York: Wiley.

Caspi, A., Elder, G. H., & Bem, D. J. (1988). Moving away from the world. *Developmental Psychology, 24,* 824–831.

Caspi, A., & Silva, P. A. (1995). Temperamental qualities at age three predict personality traits in young adulthood. *Child Development, 66,* 486–498.

Cattell, H.E.P., & Schuerger, J. M. (2003). *Essentials of 16PF Assessment.* New York: John Wiley and Sons.

Cattell, R. B., Cattell, A. K., & Cattell, H.E.P. (1993). *Sixteen Personality Factor Fifth Edition Questionnaire.* Champaign, IL: Institute for Personality and Ability Testing.

Cattell, R. B., Cattell, A. K., Cattell, H.E.P., & Kelly, M. L. (1999). *16PF Select Personality Questionnaire.* Champaign, IL: Institute for Personality and Ability Testing.

Cattell, R. B., Cattell, M. D., & Johns, E. (1984). *High School Personality Questionnaire.* Champaign, IL: Institute for Personality and Ability Testing.

Cattell, R. B., & Coan, R. W. (1976). *Early School Personality Questionnaire* (Rev. ed.). Champaign, IL: Institute for Personality and Ability Testing.

Centers, K. L. (1999). *Educational affirmations for healthy self-esteem: An exploratory factor analysis.* Unpublished doctoral dissertation. Western Michigan University.

Chess, S., & Thomas, A. (1984). *Origins and Evolution of Behavior Disorders.* New York: Brunner/Mazel.

Chess, S., & Thomas, A. (1986). *Temperament in Clinical Practice.* New York: Guilford Press.

Christ, T. J. (2008). Best practices in problem analysis. In A. Thomas, & J. Grimes (Eds.), *Best Practices in School Psychology V* (pp. 159–176). Bethesda, MD: National Association of School Psychologists.

Coan, R. W., & Cattell, R. B. (1959). *Early School Personality Questionnaire.* Champaign, IL: Institute for Personality and Ability Testing.

Coffield, F., Moseley, D., Hall, E., & Ecclestone, K. (2004a). *Learning styles and pedagogy in post-16 learning: A systematic and critical review.* London: Learning and Skills Research Centre.

Coffield, F., Moseley, D., Hall, E., & Ecclestone, K. (2004b). *Should we be using learning styles? What research has to say to practice.* London: Learning and Skills Research Centre.

Cole, M., & Cole, S. R. (1996). *The development of children* (3rd ed.). New York: W. H. Freeman and Company.

Cornett, C. E. (1983). *What you should know about teaching and learning styles.* Bloomington, IN: Phi Delta Kappa Educational Foundation.

Costa, P. T., Jr., & McCrae, R. R. (1992). *Revised NEO Personality Inventory (NOE-PI-PR) and NEO Five Factor inventory (NEO-FFI) professional manual.* Odessa, FL: Psychological Assessment Resources.

Costa, P. T., Jr., & McCrae, R. R. (2001). A theoretical context for adult temperament. In T. D. Wachs, & G. A. Kohnstamm (Eds.), *Temperament in context* (pp. 1–21) Mahwah, NJ: Erlbaum.

Cote, S., Tremblay, R. E., Nagin, D., Zoccoliool, M., & Vitaro, F. (2002). The development of impulsivity, fearfulness, and helpfulness during childhood: Patterns of consistency and change in the trajectories of boys and girls. *Journal of Child Psychology and Psychiatry, 43,* 609–618.

Dawson, M., Cummings, J. A., Harrison, P. L., Short, R. J., Gorin, S., & Palomares, R. (2004). The 2002 multisite conference on the future of school psychology: Next steps. *School Psychology Review, 33*(1), 115–125.

DeAngelis, T. (2008). One treatment for emotional disorders? *Monitor on Psychology, 39*(9), 26.

Derryberry, D., & Reed, M. A. (1994). Temperament and attention: orienting towards and away from positive and negative signals. *Journal of Personality and Social Psychology, 66,* 128–1139.

Digman, J. M. (1989). Five robust trait dimensions: Development, stability, and utility. *Journal of Personality, 57,* 195–214.

DiTiberio, J. K. (1996). Education, learning styles and cognitive styles. In A. L. Hammer (Ed.) *MBTI applications: A decade of research on the Myers-Briggs Type Indicator.* Palo Alto, CA: Consulting Psychologists Press.

DuPauw, S.S.W., Mervielde, I., & Van Leeuwen, K. G. (2009). How are traits related to problem behavior in preschoolers? Similarities and contrasts between temperament and personality. *Journal of Abnormal Child Psychology, 37*(3), 309–325.

Ehrhardt-Padgett, G. N., Hatzichristou, C., Kitson, J., & Meyers, J. (2004). Awakening to a new dawn: Perspectives of the future of school psychology. *School Psychology Review, 33*(1), 105–114.

Elliot, S. N., Witt, J. C., Kratochwill, T. R., & Stoiber, K. C. (2002). Selecting and evaluating classroom interventions. In M. R. Shinn, H. M. Walker, & G. Stoner (Eds.). *Interventions for academic and behavioral problems II: Preventive and remedial approaches.* Bethesda, MD: National Association of School Psychologists.

Epstein, M. H., & Sharma, J. M. (1998). *Behavioural and Emotional Rating Scale: A strengths-based approach to assessment.* Austin, TX. Pro-Ed.

Evans, R. I., Leppman, P., & Bergene, A. (Producers). (1968). *Discussion with Carl Jung* [Film]. (Available from PennState Audio-Visual Services, University Division of Media and Learning Resources, University Park, PA, 16802)

Eysenck, H. J. (1986). Models and paradigms in personality research. In A. Angleitner, A. Furnham, & G. Van Heck (Eds.), *Personality psychology in Europe: Current trends and controversies* (Vol. 2, pp. 213–223). Lisse, The Netherlands: Swets & Zeitlinger.

Eysenck, H. J. (1995). *The Eysenck Personality Profiler (EPP) and Eysenck's theory of personality.* London: Corporate Assessment Network.

Eysenck, H. J., & Eysenck, M. W. (1958). *Personality and individual differences.* New York: Plenum Publishing.

Eysenck, H. J., & Eysenck, M. W. (1985). *Personality and individual differences: A natural science approach.* New York: Plenum.

Eysenck, H. J., & Eysenck, S.B.G. (1975a). *Junior Eysenck Personality Questionnaire.* San Diego, CA: Educational and Industrial Testing Service.

Eysenck, H. J., & Eysenck, S.B.G. (1975b). *Manual of the Eysenck Personality Questionnaire.* London: Hodder and Stoughton.

Eysenck, S.B.G., Eysenck, H. J., & Barrett, P. (1985). A revised version of the psychoticism scales. *Personality and Individual Differences, 6*(1), 21–29.

Fabricus, W. V., & Hagen, J. W. (1984). Use of casual attributions about recall performance to assess metamemory and predict strategic memory behavior in young children. *Developmental Psychology, 20,* 975–987.

Fahey, C. J. (2008). *Altogether governed by humors: The four ancient temperaments in Shakespeare.* Unpublished master's thesis, University of South Florida, Tampa.

Farris, D. (1991). *Type tales: Teaching type to children.* Palo Alto, CA: Consulting Psychologists Press.

Faulkner, M. (2002). Temperament in context: The Student Styles Questionnaire as a measure of temperament: An Australian study. *Australian Journal of Guidance and Counseling, 12*(1), 86–96.

Faulkner, M. (2009, July). *Teaching and learning applications of the SSQ.* Paper presented at the meeting of the International School Psychologist Association, Republic of Malta.

Fletcher, J. M., Shaywitz, S. E., Shankweiler, D. P., Katz, L., Liberman, I. Y., Stuebing, K. K., Francis, D. J., Fowler, A. E., & Shaywitz, B. A. (1994). Cognitive profiles of reading disability: Comparisons of discrepancy and low achievement definitions. *Journal of Educational Psychology, 86*(1), 6–23.

Fletcher, J. M., & Vaughn, S. (2009). Response to intervention: Preventing and remediating academic difficulties. *Child Development Perspectives, 3*(1), 30–37.

Floderus-Myrhed, B., Pedersen, N., & Rasmuson, I. (1980). Assessment of heritability for personality, based on a short-form of the Eysenck Personality Inventory: A study of 12,898 twin pairs. *Behavior Genetics, 10*(2), 153–162.

Francis, A., & Widiger, T. (1986). The classification of personality disorders: An overview of problems and solutions. In A. Frances & R. E. Hale (Eds.) *American Psychiatric Association Annual Review, 5,* (pp. 240–257). Washington, DC: American Psychiatric Association.

Freedman, D. (1974). *Human infancy: An evolutionary perspective.* Hillsdale, NJ: Erlbaum.

Fu, K. (1998). The healing hand in literature: Shakespeare and surgery. *Hong Kong Medical Journal, 4*(1), 77–88.

Fullard, W., McDevitt, S. C., & Carey, W. B. (1984). Assessing temperament in one-to-three-year-old children. *Journal of Pediatric Psychology, 9,* 205–216.

Galen (1916). *Galen on the natural forces.* (A. J. Brook, Trans.). Cambridge, MA: Harvard University Press. (Original work published date unknown.)

Galen (1992). *The art of cure-Extracts from Galen: Maimonides' medical writings.* (U.S. Barzel, Trans.). Haifa, Israel: Maimonides Research Institute. (Original work published date unknown.)

Garcia-Coll, C., Kagan, J., & Reznick, J. S. (1984). Behavioral inhibition in children. *Child Development, 55,* 1005–1009.

Goldberg, L. R. (1981). Language and individual differences: The search for universals in personality lexicons. In L. Wheeler (Ed.), *Review of personality and social psychology* (Vol. 2, pp.141–165). Beverly Hills, CA: Sage.

Goldberg, L. R. (1982). From ace to zombie: Some explorations in the language of personality. In C. G. Spielberger & J. N. Bucher (Eds.), *Advancements in personality assessment* (Vol. 1, pp. 203–234). Hillsdale, NJ: Erlbaum.

Goldsmith, H. H. (1989). Behavior-genetic approaches to temperament. In G. A. Kohnstamm, J. E. Bates, & M. K. Rothbart, *Temperament in childhood* (pp. 111–132). New York: John Wiley and Sons.

Goldsmith, H. H. (1996). Studying temperament via construction of the Toddler Behavior Assessment Questionnaire. *Child Development, 67,* 218–235.

Goldsmith, H. H., Buss, A. H., Plomin, R., Rothbart, M. K., Thomas, A., Chess, S., Hinder, R. A., & McCall, R. B. (1987). Roundtable: What is temperament? Four approaches. *Child Development, 58,* 505–529.

Goldsmith, H. H., & Campos, J. J. (1986). Fundamental issues in the study of early temperament: The Denver twin temperament study. In M. E. Lamb & A. L. Brown (Eds.), *Advances in developmental psychology* (pp. 231–283). Hillsdale, NJ: Erlbaum.

Goldsmith, H. H., & Gottesman, I. I. (1981). Origins of variation in behavioral style: A longitudinal study of temperament in young twins. *Child Development, 52,* 91–103.

Goldsmith, H. H., & Rieser-Danner, L. (1986). Variation among temperament theories and validation studies of temperament assessment. In G. A. Kohnstamm (Ed.), *Temperament discussed: Temperament and development in infancy and childhood* (pp. 1–9). Berwyn, PA: Swets North America.

Goldsmith, H. H., & Rieser-Danner, L. A. (1990). Assessing early temperament. In C. R. Reynolds & R. W. Kamphaus (Eds.), *Handbook of psychological and educational assessment of children: Personality, behavior, and context* (pp. 245–278). New York: Guilford Press.

Goldsmith, H. H., & Rieser-Danner, L. A. (1992). Assessing early temperament. In C. R. Reynolds, & R. W. Kamphaus (Eds.) *Handbook of psychological and educational assessment of children: Personality, behavior, and context*. (pp. 245–278). NY: Guilford Press.

Goldsmith, H. H., & Rothbart, M. K. (1988). *The Laboratory Temperament Assessment Battery (LAB-TAB): Locomotor Version, Edition 1.2* (Technical Report No. 88–01). Eugene, OR: Oregon Center for the Study of Emotion.

Gudbrandsen, B. H. (2006). *The effect of tutoring and metacognition on 5th- and 6th grade students' reading strategies, reading comprehension, and attitude toward reading*. Unpublished doctoral dissertation, Northwestern University.

Guerin, D. W., Gottfried, A. W., Oliver, P. H., & Thomas, C. W. (2003). *Temperament: Infancy through adolescence*. New York: Kluwer Academic/Plenum Publishers.

Hale, J. B., Kaufman, A., Naglieri, J. A., & Kavale, K. A. (2006). Implementation of IDEA: Integrating response to intervention and cognitive assessment methods. *Psychology in the Schools, 43*(7), 753–770.

Hart, D., Hofmann, V., Edelstein, W., & Keller, M. (1997). The relation of childhood personality types to adolescent behavior and development. *Developmental Psychology, 33,* 195–205.

Hartman, S. E., Hylton, J., & Sanders, R. F. (1997). The influence of hemispheric dominance on scores of the Myers-Briggs Type Indicator. *Educational and Psychological Measurement, 57*(2), 440–449.

Hegvik, R. L., McDevitt, S. C., & Carey, W. B. (1982). The Middle Childhood Temperament Questionnaire. *Developmental and Behavioral Pediatrics, 3,* 197–200.

Hergenhahn, B. R. (2001). *An introduction to the history of psychology* (4th ed.). Belmont, CA. Brooks/Cole.

Hippocrates. (1939). *Hippocrates, 1.* (W.H.S. Jones, Trans). Cambridge, MA: Harvard University Press. (Original work published date unknown).

Hippocrates (1988). *Hippocrates, 5.* (P. Potter, Trans.). Cambridge, MA: Harvard University Press. (Original work published date unknown).

Hippocrates (1994). *Hippocrates, 7.* (W. D. Smith, Trans.). Cambridge, MA: Harvard University Press. (Original work published date unknown).

Horsch, J. (2008, February). The way we are: Elizabeth Murphy teaches appreciation of differences through education of personality type (pp. 6–9). *The Carlow Journal.* Pittsburgh, PA: Carlow University.

Hubert, N. C., Wachs, T. D., Peters-Marten, P., & Gandour, M. J. (1982). The study of early temperament: Measurement and conceptual issues. *Child Development, 53,* 571–600.

Hwang, J., & Rothbart, M. K. (2003). Behavior genetics studies of infant temperament: Findings vary across parent-report instruments. *Infant Behavior and Development, 26,* 112–114.

Individuals with Disabilities Education Improvement Act of 2004. 20 U.S.C. § 1400 et seq.

International Test Commission. (2000). *International guidelines for test use.* Retrieved September 8, 2009, from www.intestcom.org/itc_projects.htm.

Jang, K. L., McCrae, R. R., Angleitner, A., Riemann, R., & Livesley, W. J. (1998). Heritability of facet-level traits in a cross-cultural twin study: Support for a hierarchical model of personality. *Journal of Personality and Social Psychology, 74,* 1556–1565.

Jimerson, S. R., Burns, M. K., & VanDerHeyden, A. M. (2007). *Handbook of response to intervention: The science and practice of assessment and intervention.* New York: Springer Science+Business Media.

John, O. P. (1990). The "Big Five" factor taxonomy: Dimensions of personality in the natural language and questionnaires. In L. A. Pervin (Ed.) *Handbook of personality: Theory and research* (pp. 66–100). New York: Guilford.

John, O. P., Angleitner, A., & Ostendorf, F. (1988). The lexical approach to personality: A historical review of trait taxonomic research. *European Journal of Personality, 2,* 171–203.

John, O. P., Caspi, A., Robins, R. W., Moffitt, T. E., & Stouthamer-Loeber, M. (1994). The "little five": Exploring the nomological network of the five-factor model of personality in adolescent boys. *Child Development, 65,* 160–178.

Joyce, D. (2005). Identified temperament-based learning styles: Implications for effective instruction. *Florida Journal of Teacher Education, 8,* 60–69.

Joyce, D. (2008). Cognitive interventions, enrichment strategies, and temperament-based learning styles. In O. Tan & A. S. Seng (Eds.), *Cognitive modifiability in learning and assessment: International perspectives* (pp. 39–57). New York: Cengage Learning.

Joyce, D., & Dempsey, A. (2009). The Diagnostic and Statistical Manual model of impairment. In S. Goldstein & J. Naglieri (Eds.), *Assessment of impairment: From theory to practice,* (pp. 77–92). New York: Springer Science+Business Media LLC.

Joyce, D., & Oakland, T. (2005). Temperament differences among children with conduct disorder and oppositional defiant disorder. *California Journal of School Psychology, 10,* 125–136.

Joyce, D., & Rossen, E. (2006). Transitioning high school students with learning disabilities into postsecondary education: Assessment and accommodations. *Communiqué, 35*(3), pp. 39–43.

Joyce, D., & Rossen, E. (2008). Personality. In E. Mpofu & T. Oakland (Eds.), *Assessment in rehabilitation and health* (pp. 790–836). Boston, MA: Allyn & Bacon.

Jung, C. G. (1926). *Psychological types* (H. G. Baynes, Trans.). New York: Harcourt, Brace, & Co. (Original work published 1920.)

Jung, C. G. (1933). *Modern man in search of a soul* (W. S. Dell & C. F. Baynes, Trans.). New York: Harcourt, Brace, & Co. (Original work published 1930–1932.)

Jung, C. G. (1945). *Contributions to analytical psychology* (H. G. Baynes & C. F. Baynes, Trans.). New York: Kegan Paul, Trench, Trubner, & Co. LTD. (Original work published 1928.)

Jung, C. G. (1953). *Two essays on analytical psychology* (R.F.C. Hull, Trans.). New York: Pantheon Books. (Original work published 1943.)

Jung, C. G. (1954). *The development of personality* (R.F.C. Hull, Trans.). New York: Pantheon Books. (Original work published 1915.)

Jung, C. G. (1967). *Psychological aspects of the mother archetype* (H. G. Baynes & C. F. Baynes, Trans.). New York: Pantheon Books. (Original work published 1954.)

Jung, C. G. (1971). *Psychological types* (R.F.C. Hull, Revision of Trans. by H. G. Baynes). Princeton, NJ: Princeton University Press. (Original work published 1921.)

Kagan, J. (1994). *The nature of the child: Tenth anniversary edition.* New York: Basic Books.

Kagan, J. (2009). *The three cultures: Natural sciences, social sciences, and the humanities in the 21st century.* New York: Cambridge University Press.

Kagan, J., Arcus, D., Snidman, N., Feng, W. Y., Hendler, J., & Greene, S. (1994). Reactivity in infants: A cross-national comparison. *Developmental Psychology, 30,* 342–345.

Kagan, J., Kearsley, R. B., & Zelazo, P. R. (1978). *Infancy: Its place in human development.* Cambridge, MA: Harvard University Press.

Kagan, J., & Moss, H. A. (1962). *Birth to maturity: A study in psychological development.* New York: Wiley (Reprinted by Yale University, 1982.)

Kagan, J., & Snidman, N. (1991). Infant predictors of inhibited and uninhibited profiles. *Psychological Science, 2*(1), 40–43.

Kagan, J., & Snidman, N. (2004). *The long shadow of temperament.* Cambridge, MA: The Belknap Press of Harvard University Press.

Kamphaus, R. W. (2001). *Clinical assessment of child and adolescent intelligence.* Needham Heights, MA: Allyn and Bacon.

Keirsey, D. (1998). *The Keirsey Temperament Sorter – II.* Del Mar, CA: Prometheus Nemesis.

Keirsey, D., & Bates, M. (1978). *Please understand me: Character and temperament types.* Del Mar, CA: Prometheus Nemesis Book Co.

Keogh, B. K., Pullis, M.E., & Cadwell, J. (1982). A short form of the Teachers Temperament Questionnaire. *Journal of Educational Measurement, 19,* 323–329.

Kirby, L. K., & Barger, N. J. (1996). Multicultural applications. In A. L. Hammer (Ed.), *MBTI applications: A decade of research on the Myers-Briggs Type indicator* (pp. 167–196). Palo Alto, CA: Consulting Psychologists Press.

Kise, J. A. (2007). *Differentiation through personality types: A framework for instruction, assessment and classroom management.* Thousand Oaks, CA: Corwin Press.

Kovaleski, J. F. (2003, December). *The three tier model for identifying learning disabilities: Critical program features and systems issues.* Paper presented at the National Research Center on Learning Disabilities Responsiveness-to-Intervention Symposium, Kansas City, MO.

Kretschmer, E. (1936). *Physique and character: An investigation of the nature of constitution and of the theory of temperament.* (W.J.H. Sprott Trans.). London: K. Paul, Trench, Trubner & Co. (Original work published 1921.)

Kucera, J. A. (2008). *The effect of implementation of a response to intervention model on student achievement, special education referrals, and special education eligibility.* Unpublished doctoral dissertation, Tarleton State University.

Lang, M.L.S. (2000). *A concurrent validity study of the MBTI, MMTIC-R, and SSQ with middle school students.* Unpublished doctoral dissertation, Texas Woman's University, Texas.

Lange, G., & Pierce, S. H. (1992). Memory-strategy learning and maintenance in preschool children. *Developmental Psychology, 28,* 453–462.

Lawrence, G. (1991). *People types and tiger stripes: A practical guide to learning styles.* Gainesville, FL: Center for Applications of Psychological Type.

Lawrence, G. (1997). *Looking at type and learning styles.* Gainesville, FL: Center for Applications of Psychological Type.

Lee, D. H., Oakland, T. & Ahn, C. (in press). Temperament styles of children in South Korea and the United States. *School Psychology International.*

Leon, C., Oakland, T., Wei, Y., & Berrios, M. (2009). Venezuelan children's temperament styles and comparison with their United States peers. Revista interamericana de Psicologia/Interamerican *Journal of Psychology, 43*(1), 407–415.

Lerner, R. M., Palermo, M., Spiro, A., & Nesselroade, J. R. (1982). Assessing the dimensions of temperament individuality across the life-span: The Dimensions of Temperament Survey (DOTS). *Child Development, 53,* 149–159.

Loehlin, J. C. (1982). Are personality traits differentially heritable? *Behavior Genetics, 12,* 417–428.

Levinson, E. M. (2008). Best practices in school-based career assessment and school-to-work transition for students with disabilities. In A. Thomas & J. Grimes (Eds.), *Best practices in school psychology* (5th ed., pp. 697–715). Bethesda, MD: National Association of School Psychologists.

Lichtenberger, E. O., Mather, N., Kaufman, N. L., & Kaufman, A. S. (2004). *Essentials of assessment report writing.* Hoboken, NJ: John Wiley and Sons.

Lowman, R. L. (1991). *The clinical practice of career assessment: Interests, abilities, and personality.* Washington, DC: American Psychological Association.

Magnusson, D. (1990). Personality development from an interactional perspective. In L. A. Pervin (Ed.), *Handbook of personality: Theory and research* (pp. 193–222). New York: Guilford.

Marneros, A. (2008). Psychiatry's 200th birthday. *British Journal of Psychiatry, 193,* (1), 1–3.

Martel, M. M., Pierce, L., Nigg, J. T., Adams, K., Buu, A., Zucker, R. A., Fitzgerald, H., Puttler, L. I., & Jester, J. M. (2009). Temperament pathways to childhood disruptive behavior and adolescent substance abuse: Testing a cascade model. *Journal of Abnormal Child Psychology, 37*(3), 363–373.

Martin, C. (1995). *Looking at type and careers.* Gainesville, FL: Center for Applications of Psychological Type.

Martin, R. P., & Bridger, R. (1999). *The Temperament Assessment Battery for Children–Revised.* Athens, Georgia: The University of Georgia.

Martin, R. P., Hooper, S., & Snow, J. (1986). Behavior rating scale approaches to personality assessment in children and adolescents. In H. Knoff (Ed.), *The assessment of child and adolescent personality* (pp. 309–351). New York: Guilford.

Marzano, R. J. (1998). *A theory-based meta-analysis of research on instruction.* Aurora, CO: Mid-Continent Regional Educational Laboratory.

Matheney, A. P., Jr., & Wilson, R. S. (1981). Developmental tasks and rating scales for the laboratory assessment of infant temperament. *Journal Supplement Abstract Service: Catalog of Selected Documents in Psychology, 11,* 81–82.

Mathiesen, K. S., & Tambs, K. (1999). The EAS Temperament Questionnaire: Factor structure, age trends, reliability, and stability in a Norwegian sample. *Journal of Psychology and Psychiatry and Applied Disciplines, 40*(3). 431–439.

McClowry, S. G. (1995). The development of the School-age Temperament Inventory. *Merrill-Palmer Quarterly, 41,* 271–285.

McClowry, S. G. (1998). The science and art of using temperament as the basis for intervention. *School Psychology Review, 27*(4), 551–563.

McClowry, S. G., Hegvik, R. L., & Teglasi, H. (1993). An examination of the construct validity of the Middle Childhood Temperament Questionnaire. *Merrill-Palmer Quarterly, 39,* 279–293.

McConaughy, S. H., & Ritter, D. R. (2008). Best practices in multi-method assessment of emotional and behavioral disorders. In A. Thomas, & J. Grimes (Eds.), *Best practices in school psychology* (5th ed., pp. 697–715). Bethesda, MD: National Association of School Psychologists.

McCrae, R. R., & Costa, P. T. (1985a). Updating Norman's adequate taxonomy: Intelligence and personality dimensions in natural language and in questionnaires. *Journal of Personality and Social Psychology, 49,* 710–721.

McCrae, R. R., & Costa, P. T., Jr. (1985b). Comparison of EPI and psychoticism scales with measures of the five-factor model of personality. *Personality and Individual Differences, 6,* 587–597.

McCrae, R. R., & Costa, P. T., Jr. (1989). Reinterpreting the Myers-Briggs Type Indicator from the perspective of the five-factor model of personality. *Journal of Personality, 57*(1), 17–40.

McCrae, R. R., Costa, P. T., Jr., del Pilar, G. H., Rolland, J. P., & Parker, W. D. (1998). Cross-cultural assessment of the five-factor model: The Revised NEO Personality Inventory. *Journal of Cross-Cultural Psychology, 29,* 171–188.

McCrae, R. R., Costa, P. T., Jr., Ostendorf, F., Angleitner, A., Hrebickova, M., Avia, M. D., Sanz, J., Sanchez-Bernardos, M., Kusdil, M. E., Woodfield, R., Saunders, P. T., & Smith, P. B. (2000). Nature over nurture: Temperament, personality, and lifespan development. *Journal of Personality and Social Psychology, 78,* 173–186.

McDevitt, S. C., & Carey, W. B. (1978). The measurement of temperament in 3–7 year old children. *Journal of Child Psychology and Psychiatry, 19,* 245–253.

McGhee, R. L., Ehrler, D. J., & Buckhalt, J. A. (2007). *Five Factor Personality Inventory–Children.* Austin, TX: Pro-Ed.

Meisgeier, C. H., & Murphy, E. (1987). *Murphy-Meisgeier Type Indicator for children manual.* Palo Alto, CA: Consulting Psychologists Press.

Merrill, K. W. (2008). *Behavioral, social, and emotional assessment of children and adolescents* (3rd ed.). New York: Lawrence Erlbaum Associates.

Merton, R. (1968). *Social theory and social structure.* Glencoe, IL: Free Press.

Millon, T. (1990). The disorders of personality. In L. A. Pervin (Ed.), *Handbook of personality: Theory and research* (pp. 339–370). New York: Guilford Press.

Miner, J. L., & Clark-Stewart, K. A. (2008). Trajectories of externalizing behavior from age 2 to age 9: Relations with gender, temperament, ethnicity, parenting, and rater. *Developmental Psychology, 44*(3), 771–786.

Mitchell, J. B. (1989). Current theories on expert and novice thinking: A full faculty considers the implications of legal education. *Journal of Legal Education, 39*(2), 275–297.

Montori, V. M., & Guyatt, G. H. (2008). Progress in evidence-based medicine. *Journal of the American Medical Association, 300*(15).

Murphy, E., & Meisgeier, C. H. (2008). *A guide to the development and use of the Murphy-Meisgeier Type Indicator for Children*. Gainesville, FL: Center for Applications of Psychological Type.

Myers, I. B. (1962). *Manual: The Myers-Briggs Type Indicator*. Princeton, NJ: Education Testing Service.

Myers, I. B. (1977). In M. H. McCaulley, *The Myers longitudinal medical study* (Monograph II). Gainesville, FL: Center for Applications of Psychological Type.

Myers, I. B., & McCaulley, M. (1985). *Manual: A guide to the development and use of the Myers-Briggs Type Indicator* (2nd ed.). Palo Alto, CA: Consulting Psychological Press.

Myers, I. B., McCaulley, M. H., Quenk, N. L., & Hammer, A. L. (1998). *MBTI Manual: A guide to the development and use of the Myers-Briggs Type Indicator* (3rd ed.). Palo Alto, CA: Consulting Psychologists Press.

Myers, I. B., & Myers, P. B. (1980). *Gifts differing: Understanding personality type*. Palo Alto, CA: Consulting Psychological Press.

National Association of State Directors of Special Education (2005). *Response to intervention*. Alexandria, VA: National Association of State Directors of Special Education.

Naughton, R. F. (2009). *Metacognition, writing samples, and learning styles in the ESL college writing classroom*. Unpublished doctoral dissertation, Biola University.

Neisworth, J. T., Bagnato, S. J., Salvia, J. J., & Hunt, F. M. (1999). *Temperament and Atypical Behavior Scale (TABS) manual: Early childhood indicators of developmental dysfunction*. Baltimore, MD: Brookes Publishing.

Newman, J. (1985). Hemisphere specialization and Jungian typology-evidence for a relationship. *Bulletin of Psychological Type, 10*(2), 13–27.

Newman, L. E. (1979). Personality types of therapist and client and their use in counseling. *Research in Psychological Type, 2*, 46–55.

Nichols, D. S. (2001). *Essentials of MMPI-2 assessment*. New York: John Wiley & Sons.

No Child Left Behind Act of 2002, 20 U.S.C. § 750 et seq.

Norquist, G., Lebowitz, B., & Hyman, S. (1999). Expanding the frontier of treatment research. *Prevention and Treatment, 2*(1), 1D.

Oakland, T., Alghorani, M. A., Lee, D. H. (2007). Temperament-based learning styles of Palestinian and U. S. children. *School Psychology International, 28*(1), 110–128.

Oakland, T., Banner, D., & Livingston, R. (2000). Temperament-based learning styles of visually impaired students. *Journal of Visual Impairments and Blindness, 91*(1), 26–33.

Oakland, T., & Callueng, C. M. (2009). Temperament styles of Filipino and U. S. children. Personal communication.

Oakland, T., Faulkner, M., & Bassett, K. (2005). Temperament styles of children from Australia and the United States. *Australian Educational and Developmental Psychologist, 19*, 35–51.

Oakland, T., Glutting, J. J., & Horton, C. B. (1996). *Student Styles Questionnaire: Star qualities in learning, relating, and working*. San Antonio, TX: The Psychological Corporation.

Oakland, T., & Hatzichristou, C. (in press). Temperament styles of Greek and U.S. children. *School Psychology International*.

Oakland, T., Illiescu, D., Dinca, M., & Dempsey, A. (2009). Temperament styles of Romanian children. *Psihologia Sociala, 22*, 70–84.

Oakland, T., & Joyce, D. (2006). Temperament-based learning styles and school-based applications. *Canadian Journal of School Psychology, 19*(1/2), 59–74.

Oakland, T., Joyce, D., Glutting, J., & Horton, C. (2000). Temperament-based learning styles of male and female students identified as gifted and students not identified as gifted. *Gifted Child Quarterly, 44*(3), 183–189.

Oakland, T., & Lu, L. (2006). Temperament styles of children from the People's Republic of China and the United States. *School Psychology International, 27*(2), 192–208.

Oakland, T., & Mata, A. L. (2007). Temperament styles of children from Costa Rica and the United States. *Journal of Psychological Type, 67*(10), 91–102.

Oakland, T., Mogaji, A., & Dempsey, J. (2006). Temperament styles of Nigerian and U.S. children. *Journal of Psychology in Africa, 16*(1), 27–34.

Oakland, T., Mpofu, E., & Sulkowski, M. (2006). Temperament styles of Zimbabwe and U.S. children. *Canadian Journal of School Psychology, 21*(1/2), 139–153.

Oakland, T., Pretorius, J. D., & Lee, D. H. (2008). Temperament styles of children from South Africa and the United States. *School Psychology International, 29*(5), 627–639.

Oakland, T., Stafford, M. E., Horton, C. B., & Glutting, J. J. (2001). Temperament and vocational preferences: Age, gender, and racial-ethnic comparisons using the Student Styles Questionnaire. *Journal of Career Assessment, 9*(3), 297–314.

O'Boyle, C. G., & Rothbart, M. K. (1996). Assessment of distress to sensory stimulation in early infancy through parent report. *Journal of Reproductive and Infant Psychology, 14,* 121–132.

Pastor, P. N., Rueben, C. A., & Faulkenstern, A. (2004). Parental reports of emotional or behavioral difficulties and mental health services use in U.S. school age children. In R. W. Manderscheid & J. T. Berry (Eds.), *Mental health, United States 2004.* Washington DC: U.S. Department of Health and Human Services.

Paunonen, S. V., & Ashton, M. C. (1998). The structural assessment of personality across cultures. *Journal of Cross-cultural Psychology, 29*(1), 150–170.

Pedrosa-Gil, F. P., Weber, M. M., & Burgmair, W. (2002). Images in psychiatry: Ernst Kretschmer (1888–1964). *American Journal of Psychiatry, 159*(7), 1111.

Pervin, L. A. (1990). *Handbook of personality: Theory and research.* New York: Guilford Press.

Peters, M. M., & Peters, D. (2007). *Juris types: Learning law through self-understanding.* Gainesville, FL: Center for Applications of Psychological Type.

Pintrich, P. R., Smith, D.A.F., Garcia, T., & McKeachie, W. J. (1991). *A manual for the use of the Strategies for Learning Questionnaire (MSLQ).* Ann Arbor, MI: National Center for Research to Improve Postsecondary Teaching and Learning, The University of Michigan.

Porter, R. B., & Cattell, R. B. (1968). *Handbook for the Children's Personality Questionnaire (CPG).* Champaign, IL: Institute for Personality and Ability Testing Inc.

Prior, M., Sanson, A., Smart, D., & Oberklaid, F. (2000). *Pathways from infancy to adolescence: Australian temperament project 1983–2000.* Melbourne, Australia: Australian Institute of Family Studies.

Provost, J. A. (1985). Type watching and college attrition. *Journal of Psychological Type, 9,* 16–23.

Quenk, N. L. (2009). *Essentials of Myers-Briggs Type Indicator Assessment, Second Edition.* New York: John Wiley & Sons.

Reynolds, C. R., & Kamphaus, R. W. (1990). *Handbook of psychological and educational assessment of children: Personality, behavior, and context.* New York: Guilford Press.

Reynolds, C. R., & Kamphaus, R. W. (2003). *Handbook of psychological and educational assessment of children: Personality, behavior, and context* (2nd ed.). New York: Guilford Press.

Reynolds, C. R., & Shaywitz, S. E. (2009). Ready or not: Or, from wait-to-fail to watch-them-fail. *School Psychology Quarterly, 24*(2), 130–145.

Rice, F. P. (1992). *Human development* (3rd ed.). Upper Saddle River, New Jersey: Prentice Hall.

Riemann, R., Angleitner, A., & Strelau, J. (1997). Genetic and environmental influences on personality: A study of twins reared together using the self- and peer-report NEO-FFI scales. *Journal of Personality, 65,* 449–475.

Rigley, D. A. (1993). *The relationship between personality type, academic major selection and persistence.* Unpublished doctoral dissertation. Illinois State University.

Rimm-Kaufman, S. E., Early, D. M., Cox, M. J., Saluja, G., Pianta, R. C., Bradley, R. H., & Payne, C. (2002). Early behavior attributes and teachers' sensitivity as predictors of competent behavior in the kindergarten classroom. *Applied Developmental Psychology, 23,* 451–470.

Rist, R. C. (2000). Student social class and teacher expectations: The self-fulfilling prophecy in ghetto education. *Harvard Educational Review, 70*(3), 266–301.

Rothbart, M. K. (1981). Measurement of temperament in infancy. *Child Development, 52,* 569–578.

Rothbart, M. K., Ahadi, S. A., & Hersey, K. L. (1994). Temperament and social behavior in childhood. *Merrill-Palmer Quarterly, 40,* 21–39.

Rothbart, M. K., & Bates, J. E. (1998). In W. Damon, & N. Eisenberg (Eds.), *Handbook of child psychology: Social, emotional, and personality development,* (Vol. 3, 5th ed., pp. 105–176).

Rothbart, M. K., Chew, K. H., & Gartstein, M. A. (2001). Assessment of temperament in early development. In L. T. Singer, & P. S. Zeskind (Eds.), *Biobehavioral Assessment of the Infant* (pp. 190–208). New York: Guilford Press.

Rothbart, M. K., & Derryberry, D. (1981). Development of individual differences in temperament. In M. E. Lamb & A. L. Brown (Eds.), *Advances in developmental psychology:* (Vol. 1, pp. 37–86). Hillsdale, NJ: Erlbaum.

Rowe, D. C., & Plomin, R. (1977). Temperament in early childhood. *Journal of Personality Assessment, 41,* 150–156.

Sanson, A., Prior, M., Garino, E., Oberklaid, F., & Sewell, J. (1987). The structure of infant temperament: Factor analysis of the Revised Infant Temperament Questionnaire. *Infant Behavior and Development, 10,* 97–104.

Sattler, J. M., & Hoge, R. D. (2006). *Assessment of children: Behavioral, social, and clinical foundations* (5th ed.). San Diego: Jerome M. Sattler Publisher Inc.

Saudino, K. J. (2003). Parent ratings of infant temperament. Lessons from twin studies. *Infant Behavior and Development, 26,* 100–107.

Scholte, R.H.J., van Lieshout, C.F.M., de Wit, C.A.M., & van Aken, M.A.G. (2005). Adolescent personality types and subtypes and their psychosocial adjustment. *Merrill-Palmer Quarterly, 51*(3), 258–287.

Schuerger, J. M. (2001). *16PF Adolescent Personality Questionnaire.* Champaign, IL: Institute for Personality and Ability Testing.

Schurr, K. T., Ruble, V. E., Palomba, C., Pickerill, B., & Moore, D. (1997). Relationships between MBTI and selected aspects of Tinto's model for college attrition. *Journal of Psychological Type, 40,* 31–42.

Schwartz, C. E., Snidman, N., & Kagan, J. (1999). Adolescent social anxiety and outcome of inhibited temperament in childhood. *Journal of the American Academy of Child and Adolescent Psychiatry, 38,* 1008–1015.

Shapiro, E. S., & Skinner, C. H. (1990). Principles of behavioral assessment. In C. R. Reynolds, & R. W. Kamphaus (Eds.), *Handbook of psychological and educational assessment of children: Personality, behavior, and context* (pp. 343–363). New York: Guilford Press.

Shaw, S. (2000a). Part I: School psychology and slow learners: The devolution of interest in slow learners: Can we continue to ignore? *Communiqué, 28*(3).

Shaw, S. (2000b). Part II: School psychology and slow learners: Academic interventions for slow learners. *Communiqué, 28*(5).

Sheldon, W. H. (1954). *Atlas of men: A guide for somatotyping the adult male at all ages.* New York: Harper.

Sheldon, W. H. (1940). *The varieties of human physique: An introduction to constitutional psychology.* New York: Hafner Publishing Co.

Shelton, J. (1996). Health, stress, and coping. In A. L. Hammer (Ed.), *MBTI applications: A decade of research on the Myers-Briggs Type Indicator* (pp. 197–215). Palo Alto, CA: Consulting Psychologists Press.

Shorter, E. (1997). *A history of psychiatry: From the era of the asylum to the age of Prozac.* New York: John Wiley & Sons.

Siegler, I. C., Zonderman, A. B., Barefoot, J. C., Williams, R. B., Jr., Costa, P.T., Jr., & McCrae, R. R. (1990). Predicting personality in adulthood from college MMPI scores: Implications for follow-up studies in psychosomatic medicine. *Psychosomatic Medicine, 52,* 644–652.

Singer, L. T., & Zeskind, P. S. (2001). *Biobehavioral assessment of the infant.* New York: Guilford Press.

Stafford, M., & Oakland, T. (1996). Validity of temperament constructs using the Student Styles Questionnaire: Comparisons for three racial-ethnic groups. *Journal of Psychoeducational Assessment, 14,* 109–120.

Stams, G.J.M., Juffer, F., & van Ijzendoorn, A. H. (2002). Maternal sensitivity, infant attachment, and temperament in early childhood predict adjustment in middle childhood. *Developmental Psychology, 28,* 806–821.

Sternberg, G. (1990). *Brain and personality: Extraversion/introversion in relation to EEG, evoked potentials and cerebral blood flow.* Unpublished doctoral dissertation, University of Lund, Sweden.

Stifter, C., & Fox, N. (1990). Infant reactivity: Physiological correlates of newborn and 5-month temperament. *Developmental Psychology, 26,* 582–588.

Stoebel, S. S., Krieg, F. J., & Christian, S. (2008). Best practices in planning for an effective transition from school to work. In A. Thomas, & J. Grimes (Eds.), *Best practices in school psychology* (5th ed., pp. 1581–1597). Bethesda, MD: National Association of School Psychologists.

Storr, A. (1991). *Jung.* New York: Routledge.

Strelau, J. (1983). *Temperament-personality-activity.* New York: Academic Press.

Strelau, J., & Angleitner, A. (1991). *Explorations in temperament: International perspectives on theory and measurement.* New York: Plenum Press.

Strelau, J., & Eysenck, H. J. (1987). *Personality dimensions and arousal.* New York: Plenum Press.

Strelau, J., & Zawadzki, B. (1997). Temperament and personality: Eysenck's three superfactors as related to temperamental dimensions. In H. Nyborg (Ed.), *The scientific study of human nature: Tribute to Hans J. Eysenck at eighty* (pp. 68–91). New York: Elsevier Science.

Sugai, G., Horner, R. H., & Gresham, F. (2002). Behaviorally effective school environments. In M. R. Shinn, H. M. Walker, & G. Stoner (Eds.), *Interventions for academic and behavior problems II: Preventative and remedial approaches.* Bethesda, MD: National Association of School Psychologists.

Syed, I. B. (2002). Islamic medicine: 1000 years ahead of its times. *Journal of the International Society for the History of Islamic Medicine, 2,* 2–9.

Teglasi, H. (1998). Introduction to the mini-series: Implications of temperament for the practice of school psychology. *School Psychology Review, 27,* 475–478.

Teglasi, H. (1998). Temperament constructs and measures. *School Psychology Review, 27,* 564–585.

Tellegen, A., Ben-Porath, Y. S., McNulty, J. L., Arbisi, P. A., Graham, J. R., & Kaemmer, B. (2003). *The MMPI-2 Restructured Clinical Scales: Development, validation, and interpretation.* Minneapolis, MN: University of Minnesota Press.

Tellegen, A., Lykken, D. T., Bouchard, T. J., Willcox, K. J., Segal, N. L., & Rich, S. (1988). Personality similarity in twins reared apart and together. *Journal of Personality and Social Psychology, 54*(6), 1021–1039.

Thomas, A., & Chess, S. (1977). *Temperament and development.* New York: Brunner/Mazel.

Thomas, A., & Chess, S. (1989). Temperament and personality. In G. A. Kohnstamm, J. E. Bates, & M. K. Rothbart (Eds.), *Temperament in childhood* (pp. 249–261). New York: Wiley.

Thomas, A., Chess, S., & Birch, H. G. (1968). *Temperament and behavior disorders in children.* New York: New York University Press.

Thomas, A., Chess, S., Sillen, J., & Mendez, O. (1974). Cross-cultural study of behavior in children with special vulnerabilities to stress. In D. Ricks, A. Thomas & M. Roff (Eds.), *Life history research in psychopathology 3,* 53–67. Minneapolis: University of Minnesota Press.

Tilly, W. D. (2002) Best practices in school psychology as a problem-solving enterprise. In A. Thomas & J. Grimes (Eds.), *Best practices in school psychology: Fifth edition* (pp. 21–36). Bethesda, MD: National Association of School Psychologists.

Torgesen, J. K. (2009). The response to intervention instructional model: Some outcomes from a large-scale implementation in reading first schools. *Child Development Perspectives, 3*(1), 38–40.

Trolley, B., Haas, H., & Patti, D. (2009). *The school counselor's guide to special education,* (pp. 1–193). Thousand Oaks, CA: Corwin Press Inc.

Upah, K. R., & Tilly, W. D. (2002). Best practices in designing, implementing, and evaluating quality interventions. In A. Thomas & J. Grimes (Eds.), *Best practices in school psychology: Fifth edition* (pp. 483–501). Bethesda, MD: National Association of School Psychologists.

U.S. Department of Education (2006). *Federal register: Part II, 34 CFR Parts 300 and 301 assistance to states for the education of children with disabilities and preschool grants for children with disabilities; Final Rule.* Jessup, MD: U.S. Department of Education.

U.S. Department of Education. (2008). *Twenty-eighth annual report to Congress on the implementation of the Individuals with Disabilities Education Act.* Jessup, MD: U.S. Department of Education.

US Department of Education (2009). *Profile of undergraduates in U.S. postsecondary educational institutions: 2003–2004: With a special analysis of community college students statistical analysis report.* Retrieved June 2, 2009, from http://nces.ed.gov/pubsearch/pubsinfo.asp?pubid=2006184.

U.S. Department of Health and Human Services. (1999). *Mental health: A report of the Surgeon General.* Rockville, MD: U.S. Department of Health and Human Services, National Institute of Health, National Institute of Mental Health.

U.S. Department of Health and Human Services. (2000). *Report of the Surgeon General's conference on children's mental health: A national action agenda.* Washington, DC: The National Institute of Mental Health, Office of Communications and Public Liaison.

US Department of Justice (2004). *A guide to disability rights laws.* Retrieved August 6, 2005, from http://www.usdoj.gov/crt/ada/cguide.htm.

Wangerin, P. T. (1988). Learning strategies for law students. *Albany Law Review, 52*(1), 471–528.

Waymire, C. H. (1995). *An analysis of first year dropouts from two church-related universities as profiled according to the Myers-Briggs Type Indicator.* Unpublished doctoral dissertation, University of Mississippi.

Wehr, G. (1971). *Portrait of Jung: An illustrated biography.* (W. A. Hargreaves, Trans.). New York: Herder and Herder. (Original work published 1969.)

Weinstein, C. E. (2002). *Learning and Study Strategies Inventory.* Clearwater, FL: H&H Publishing Co.

Wiggins, J. S. (2003). *Paradigms of personality assessment.* New York: Guilford Press.

Wills, T. A., Sandy, J. M., Yaeger, A., & Shinar, O. (2001). Family risk factors and adolescent substance use: Moderation effects for temperament dimensions. *Developmental Psychology, 37*(3), 283–297.

Wilson, M. A., & Languis, M. L. (1990). A topographic study of difference in the P300 between introverts and extraverts. *Brain Topography, 2*(4), 369–274.

Windle, M. (1988). Psychometric strategies of measures of temperament: A methodological critique. International *Journal of Behavioral Development, 11,* 171–201.

Windle, M., & Lerner, R. M. (1986). Reassessing the dimensions of temperamental individuality across the life span: The Revised Dimensions of Temperament Survey (DOTS-R). *Journal of Adolescent Research, 1,* 213–230.

Witte, R. (2008). Best practices in facilitating transition to postsecondary settings for students with learning disabilities. In A. Thomas, & J. Grimes (Eds.), *Best practices in school psychology* (5th ed., pp. 1599–1609). Bethesda, MD: National Association of School Psychologists.

Woodruff, R.G.V., & Clarke, F. M. (1993). *Understanding the academic needs of minority students at the University of Hawaii, Manoa.* Psychological Type and Culture –East and West: A Multicultural Symposium (pp. 199–205).

Ysseldyke, J., Burns, M., Dawson, P., Kelley, B., Morrison, D., Ortiz, S., Rosenfield, S., & Telzrow, C. (2006). *School Psychology: A blueprint for training and practice III.* Bethesda, MD: National Association of School Psychologists.

Zuckerman, M. (1997). Psychobiological basis of personality. In H. Nyborg (Ed.), *The scientific study of human nature: Tribute to Hans J. Eysenck at eighty* (pp. 3–16). New York: Elsevier Science.

Annotated Bibliography

Benson, N., Oakland, T., & Shermis, M. (2008). Cross-national invariance of children's temperament. *Journal of Psychoeducational Assessment, 20*(10), 1–14.

Temperament for children as measured by the Student Styles Questionnaire (SSQ) across eight countries were compared in this study. Strong four-factor support was found for Australian, Chinese, Costa Rican, Philippine, United States, and Zimbabwean students samples. Analyses of data from Gaza (Palestine) and Nigeria indicated a modest fit for the four bipolar factor model; extroversion-introversion, imaginative-practical, thinking-feeling, and organized-flexible. The authors recommend that if the instrument is utilized for Gaza or Nigerian samples items in two parcels of the measure should be revised as they may be interpreted differently in those cultures/languages. Use of the measure with samples from the other six countries is supported.

Berden, L. E., Keane, S. P., & Calkins, S. D. (2008). Temperament and externalizing behavior: Social preference and perceived acceptance as protective factors. *Developmental Psychology, 44*(4), 957–068.

The goal of this study was to determine if social preference and/or perceived acceptance were moderators of temperament and externalizing problems for kindergarteners. Students were assessed at both pre-kindergarten and kindergarten. Results were mixed indicating that high Surgency/Extroversion traits were positively associated with reports of hyperactivity and aggression in kindergarten. Social preference ratings and perceived acceptance moderated the predictability of pre-kindergarten Surgency/Extroversion scores for kindergarten hyperactivity ratings.

Bouchard, T. J., & Hur, Y. (1998). Genetic and environmental influences on the continuous scales of the Myers-Briggs Type Indicator®: An analysis based on twins reared apart. *Journal of Personality, 66*(2), 135–149.

Monozygotic and Dizygotic twins reared apart participated in this study and were administered the Myers-Briggs Type Indicator®. Analyses indicated the highest heritability on extroversion-introversion (.60) scales. Heritability for the sensing-intuition and judging-perceiving dimensions was approximately .40. In comparing the temperament profiles of spouses only one scale, sensing-intuition was significant.

Bradley, R. H., & Corwyn, R. F. (2008). Infant temperament, parenting, and externalizing behavior in first grade: A test of the differential susceptibility hypothesis. *Journal of Child Psychology and Psychiatry, 49*(2), 124–131.

Hierarchical regression analyses were utilized to test interactions between parenting and temperament qualities. Parent variables included harshness, sensitivity, and productive activity. Externalizing behaviors were reported by teachers in first grade. Results indicated the strongest relationships for children with difficult temperaments between maternal sensitivity and opportunities for productivity as compared to behavior problem reports.

Coffield, F., Moseley, D., Hall, E., & Ecclestone, K. (2004a). *Learning styles and pedagogy in post-16 learning: A systematic and critical review.* London: Learning and Skills Research Centre.

This compendium provides an overview of the major theories that constitute learning styles, some of which include temperament measures (e.g., MBTI) as they are related to recommendations regarding how persons may best learn. This study identified 71 models they categorize into 13 overarching models acknowledging the complexity and range of competing concepts in this field (e.g., Curry's, Vermunt's). Similarities and differences in the theoretical approaches are noted as well as strengths and weaknesses for all 13 models. In addition, a discussion of effects sizes for differing interventions is provided. The Should we be Using Learning Styles? What Research has to Say to Practice is a companion report.

Coffield, F., Moseley, D., Hall, E., & Ecclestone, K. (2004b). *Should we be using learning styles? What research has to say to practice.* London: Learning and Skills Research Centre.

This comprehensive report critiques decades of research on learning style theories including some temperament instruments that overlap with these concepts. Research needs, the appeal and objections to learning styles, as well as advice to practitioner's utilizing these constructs are noted. The Learning Styles and Pedagogy in Post-16 Learning: A Systematic and Critical Review is the companion report to this compendium.

DuPauw, S. S. W., Mervielde, I., & Van Leeuwen, K. G. (2009). How are traits related to problem behavior in preschoolers? Similarities and contrasts between temperament and personality. *Journal of Abnormal Child Psychology, 37*(3), 309–325.

An examination of 443 preschoolers' temperament and personality traits was conducted utilizing 28 temperament and 18 personality scales. The study was prompted by the authors premise that current temperament and personality models make significant contributions but lack an integrative conceptual basis upon which to inform child pathology. Utilizing joint principal component analysis a six-factor model was indicated: sociability, activity, conscientiousness, disagreeableness, emotionality, and sensitivity. Individual scales accounted for 23–37 percent of variances for problem behavior; however, combined the six factors accounted for 41–49 percent of the variance.

John, O. P., Caspi, A., Robins, R. W., Moffitt, T. E., & Stouthamer-Loeber, M. (1994). The "little five": Exploring the nomological network of the five-factor model of personality in adolescent boys. *Child Development, 65,* 160–178.

The work was funded by the National Institute of Mental Health through the Antisocial and Violent Behavior Branch to investigate correlations between Big Five theory factors and psychopathology for boys. Analyses variables included IQ, race, and social-economic status (SES). Results indicated four of the Big Five factors (Extroversion, Agreeableness, Conscientiousness, and Openness were significant in distinguishing four levels of delinquency (Neuroticism scale was not). A pattern of low agreeableness and conscientiousness with high extroversion was found in delinquent boys with externalizing disorders. High neuroticism and low conscientiousness were related to delinquent boys with internalizing disorders.

Goldsmith, H. H., Buss, A. H., Plomin, R., Rothbart, M. K., Thomas, A., Chess, S., Hinder, R. A., & McCall, R. B. (1987). Roundtable: What is temperament? Four approaches. *Child Development, 58,* 505–529.

This journal article reviews a national roundtable discussion by leading child temperament researchers delineating key components of their theoretical orientations. Each respondent details tenets of their concepts in response to six questions: how they define temperament, their core components of temperament, relationship between their constructs and data, how temperament is formed, the person-oriented or reciprocal nature of temperament, and explanations of temperamental difficulty. The commentators synthesize responses to emphasize convergent and divergent concepts and call for more heritability studies, as well as greater use of factor analytic methods across age groups.

Hubert, N. C., Wachs, T. D., Peters-Marten, P., & Gandour, M. J. (1982). The study of early temperament: Measurement and conceptual issues. *Child Development, 53,* 571–600.

This journal article provides an in-depth review of 26 early temperament instruments that laid the foundation for assessment. Measures include the work of Thomas and Chess, Carey, McDevitt, Rothbart, Bates, Buss, Plomin, and Bayley (e.g., PTQ, TCI, ATQ, RITZ, TTS, MCTQ, STQ, EASI-III, and DOTS). Validity and reliability data are summarized as well as scale content and standardization sample information. The authors conclude that most of the instruments had empirical support for high interrater agreement and adequate support for internal consistency, as well as test-retest reliability. Concern was indicated for a lack of research regarding convergent validity between instruments, and this was hypothesized to be directly related to the lack of consensus in temperament-definitions and constructs.

Joyce, D., & Oakland, T. (2005). Temperament differences among children with conduct disorder and oppositional defiant disorder. *California Journal of School Psychology, 10,* 125–136.

A comparison of temperament qualities for youth with a diagnosis of oppositional defiant disorder (ODD) or conduct disorder (CD) was implemented utilizing the Student Styles Questionnaire. MANOVA analyses indicated students with ODD expressed stronger preferences for the practical rather than imaginative style when compared to students with CD. The other three scales extroversion-introversion, thinking-feeling, and organized-flexible were not significant. When students with ODD were compared to a sample of those in the general population, they more frequently indicated a preference for practical and thinking qualities.

Lang, M. L. S. (2000). *A concurrent validity study of the MBTI, MMTIC-R, and SSQ with middle school students.* Unpublished doctoral dissertation, Texas Woman's University, Texas.

Concurrent validity between the Myers-Briggs Type Indicator® (MBTI), Murphy-Meisgeier Type Indicator for Children, and the Student Styles Questionnaire (SSQ) was investigated for a sample of 217 students (7th–8th graders). Two groups, gifted-talented and control were compared indicating significant correlations between all three instruments although the strength of correlation was variably by scale. Gender differences were significant with females preferring feeling and males preferring thinking. Gifted-talented students more often preferred imaginative as compared to practical styles.

Martel, M. M., Pierce, L., Nigg, J. T., Adams, K., Buu, A., Zucker, R. A., Fitzgerald, H., Puttler, L. I., & Jester, J. M. (2009). Temperament pathways to childhood disruptive behavior and adolescent substance abuse: Testing a cascade model. *Journal of Abnormal Child Psychology, 37*(3), 363–373.

This longitudinal study followed 674 children from the age of three to adolescence with parent, teacher, and self ratings of inattention/hyperactivity, disruptive behaviors, and substance abuse. The California Q-Sort temperament measure was also administered and indicated low reactive control was associated with risk for adolescent substance abuse and mediated by disruptive behaviors. Resiliency and negative emotionality traits were not significant.

Mathiesen, K. S., & Tambs, K. (1999). The EAS Temperament Questionnaire: Factor structure, age trends, reliability, and stability in a Norwegian sample. *Journal of Psychology and Psychiatry and Applied Disciplines, 40*(3), 431–439.

The EAS Temperament Survey was administered to 2,442 Norwegian children (3 groups, 18 months, 30 months, and 50 months). Cross-validation analyses indicated support for the three-factor constructs: Emotionality, Activity, and Shyness. Included items for the Sociability scales (which were still in development stage) supported Sociability as the fourth factor. Scales demonstrated good reliability, and there were no gender differences. Age trends were noted for increases in Emotionality and decreases in Activity and Sociability.

Miner, J. L., & Clark-Stewart, K. A. (2008). Trajectories of externalizing behavior from age 2 to age 9: Relations with gender, temperament, ethnicity, parenting, and rater. *Developmental Psychology, 44*(3), 771–786.

This study was funded by the National Institute of Child Health and Human Development and analyzed data from parent/caregiver/teacher ratings at ages 2, 3, 4, 7, and 9 years old. In general, mothers rated their children higher on externalizing problems than caregivers or teachers did. The predictive factors for high ratings of externalizing behavior at age 9 were gender (male), early difficult temperament (for harsh mothers), maternal depression, and low maternal sensitivity. Overall, caregivers and teachers rated African-American children as high in externalizing behaviors with increase over time, whereas African-American mothers had inverse ratings over time for externalizing.

Oakland, T., Faulkner, M., & Bassett, K. (2005). Temperament styles of children from Australia and the United States, *Australian Educational and Developmental Psychologist, 19,* 35–51.

Temperament qualities utilizing the Student Styles Questionnaire (SSQ) were compared for children in Australia and the United States. Consistent with prior international research gender differences were found for thinking-feeling with more males reporting a thinking orientation. Australian children as a whole more frequently endorsed a preference for thinking than feeling styles and imaginative than practical when compared to the United States. Balanced distributions of extroversion-introversion and organized-flexible preference were indicated for both samples.

Oakland, T., Stafford, M. E., Horton, C. B., & Glutting, J. J. (2001). Temperament and vocational preferences: Age, gender, and racial-ethnic comparisons using the Student Styles Questionnaire. *Journal of Career Assessment, 9*(3), 297–314.

This study reviews temperament data for 7,902 students utilizing the Student Styles Questionnaire (SSQ). Data are stratified by ethnicity, age (8–17), and gender. Results indicate reliable vocational interests demonstrated by ages 8–10 years old and distinctive career preferences for introversion-extroversion, imaginative-practical, thinking-feeling, and organized-flexible dimensions. Preferences for specific careers were also noted by gender and ethnicity.

Scholte, R. H. J., van Lieshout, C. F. M., de Wit, C. A. M., & van Aken, M. A. G. (2005). Adolescent personality types and subtypes and their psychosocial adjustment. *Merrill-Palmer Quarterly, 51*(3), 258–287.

In this study the researchers proposed two goals: to determine if the three temperament constructs—undercontrollers, overcontrollers, and resilients—were also distinctive in a large sample of adolescent Dutch boys and girls (N = 3,361) and to identify the existence of possible subtypes. In addition, the investigation measured factors of adjustment by group. Utilizing cluster analyses and Big Five personality factors the three types were substantiated with two subtypes in each category. Subtypes included communal or agentic resilients, vulnerable or achieving overcontrollers, and impulsive or oppositional undercontrollers. Differences by group were found in self-esteem, bullying behaviors, and delinquency. Prevalence of psychological well-being factors were distinctive by subtype suggesting the use of subtypes may assist in identifying at-risk students. Gender prevalence differences by subtype were indicated.

Stafford, M., & Oakland, T. (1996). Validity of temperament constructs using the Student Styles Questionnaire: Comparisons for three racial-ethnic groups. *Journal of Psychoeducational Assessment, 14,* 109–120.

The purpose of this investigation was to test construct and content validity for the Student Styles Questionnaire across three ethnic groups: African-American, Anglo-American, and Hispanic American. A similar four-factor bipolar model was supported across groups with relative independence of scales. Similar response patterns were supported when comparing Hispanic-American students to the other two samples. However, when comparing African-American and Anglo-American 25 percent of items had differences, especially on the organized-flexible scale suggesting a need for further study of cultural differences that may impact these results.

Wills, T. A., Sandy, J. M., Yaeger, A., & Shinar, O. (2001). Family risk factors and adolescent substance use: Moderation effects for temperament dimensions. *Developmental Psychology, 37*(3), 283–297.

This study investigated the relationship between parent/child conflict, family life events, and parent substance abuse to adolescent substance abuse. Temperament dimensions were measured with the Revised Dimensions of Temperament Survey utilizing multiple-group latent growth analyses. The impact of negative parental factors increased adolescent risk for substance abuse when activity level and negative emotionality were high. High resilience lowered the impact of parent factors (i.e., conflict, life events, substance abuse) on adolescent substance abuse.

Index

About the Author

Dr. Diana Joyce is an Associate Scholar in the School Psychology Program at the University of Florida with licensure as a psychologist and school psychologist. She has taught numerous assessment courses and supervises graduate student practica work across four county school districts and several clinic sites. Clinical sites include a child morbid obesity clinic, a hospital psychiatric unit, a university ADA office for college students with disabilities, and a child forensic law clinic. In addition, as a faculty-in-resident she consults with a K-12 research laboratory school on behavioral RtI implementation. Her research and publications have included studies of temperament qualities of gifted children, temperament characteristics of students with conduct disorder and oppositional defiant disorder as well as social-emotional issues.